MW01630399

ALSO BY VANCE TRIMBLE

THE UNCERTAIN MIRACLE
The History of Hyperbaric Medicine
(1974)

SCRIPPS-HOWARD HANDBOOK
Methods, Policies and People (Ed.)
(1981)

REAGAN, A Biography
Mosaic Press Classic Miniature Edition
(1982)

HEROES, PLAIN FOLKS, and SKUNKS
Autobiography of "Happy" Chandler
(1989)

FAITH IN MY STAR
Sayings of E.W. Scripps (Ed.)
(1989)

SAM WALTON
Biography of Founder of Wal-Mart
(1990)

THE ASTONISHING MR. SCRIPPS
Biography of America's Famous Penny Press Publisher
(1992)

OVERNIGHT SUCCESS
Biography of Fed Ex Founder Fred Smith
(1993)

AN EMPIRE UNDONE
Biography of "Whiz Kid" Chris Whittle
(1995)

ALICE & J. F. B.
Biography of Sister-and-Brother Seminole Chiefs
(2006)

Choctaw Kisses, Bullets & Blood

Choctaw Bullets

Vance H. Trimble

Kisses,
& Blood

Market Tech Books
Poets of America Press

Published by Market Tech Books/Poets of America Press,
a division of Market Tech Associates, Inc.
1304 Hilltop Avenue, Wilmington, DE 19809
First Edition, 2007

Manufactured in the United States of America
by Thomson-Shore, Inc., Dexter, Michigan

Library of Congress Cataloging-in-Publication Data

Trimble, Vance H.-1st ed.
Choctaw Kisses, Bullets & Blood
p cm.
1. Locke, Victor M. Sr.-biography 2. Locke, Victor M. Jr.-biography 3. Indians-Choctaw

ISBN 978-0-9705399-6-0 (alk. paper)
I. Title

Book electronically produced by Richard Ellwanger.

Title page sketch by Dolores Cary.

For my mother, Josie Crump Trimble, the poet,
and
my father, Guy Lee Trimble, the lawyer.

Both buried April 1940 in Oakwood Cemetery,
Wewoka, Oklahoma

CONTENTS

Foreword xi

1. The Renegade Soldier Boy 3
2. A Choctaw Love Story 15
3. Gunplay and a Passel of Babies 35
4. Antlers and The Iron Horse 55
5. Bullets, Ballots and Blood 73
6. 'The House is Shot to Pieces!' 90
7. Can't Cupid Shoot Straight? 105
8. 'I'm Mad—Mad as Hell!' 146
9. Little Roly-Poly Legs 169
10. 'Don't Worry One Minute...' 195
11. President Harding's Hatchet Job 213
12. Gobble Gobble Gobble! You Die! 246

13. 'Just Cut Your Dogs Loose!' 266

14. In The Shade of the Old Cedar 288

Afterword 299

Acknowledgements 301

Bibliography 303

Foreword

TO PORTRAY the sweeping panorama of the federal government's cruel herding of 60,000 Indians into the western wilderness that became Oklahoma, historians have churned out millions of words. This is a slender slice of that epoch, a "close-up," the extended biography of one white "intruder" more or less "accidentally" dropped into a crucial and dramatic role in the surging, dangerous frontier upheaval.

By shrewdness and guts, Confederate boy-soldier Victor Moreau Locke rose through romance and adventure to wealth and political power in the Choctaw Nation. His mixed blood son, Victor Jr., likewise flashed to prominence in these crucial eight decades that run from Abraham Lincoln to the last days of F.D.R.

Although Victor Jr. became principal chief of the Choctaw tribe, the Locke clan knew well the lethal whine of bullets—coming and going. Their violence helped spawn an Indian Territory "war" in 1893 that U.S. Army troops had to put down. As a Johnny Reb cavalryman, and otherwise, Locke Senior had blood on his hands. Two of his eight sons died of gunfire; and his namesake conceded his own hidden tendency toward malevolence, telling the *Tulsa World:* "I have the educated brain of a white man, and the heart of a savage." A few years later Victor Jr. sounded the tribe's dreaded turkey gobble warning to an enemy, and promptly shot him dead.

Steadily, relentlessly before statehood in 1907, the Oklahoma Indians were ripped off and crushed. Washington callously broke solemn treaties. And robbed the Indians of their open range, culture and tradition, their tribal government and laws—and almost their native tongue. Their Great Father forced them to become "white" citizens. He punished them for fighting with the Confederates. Washington ignored outlaws who hid out in the Choctaw "no man's land." Crooked lawyers came with free *fire water* to cheat their aboriginal intellect. The Choctaws were even sold out by bribe-taking officials of their own tribe.

In the heyday of the Locke involvement—from roughly 1866 into the 1940s—the spotlight on Choctaw Nation intrigue flitted erratically from the quiet wilderness of the Kiamichi Mountains and clear virgin streams to the marble corridors of Congress and the President's desk in the White House, from fatuous oratory in the United States Senate to the midnight scream of a *chito* panther on the melancholy shores of Push County's Dead Man's Lake.

Amid such uncertain factors, Locke clan exploits boldly play out against this kaleidoscopic backdrop of shameful times, and must be currently viewed in that perspective. History does not display an altogether enviable portrait of this pioneer white and mixed blood family; their achievements and their faults must stand today for judgment on their own merit.

This biography is authentic and fully documented, written to present a readable slice of the fascinating life in old Indian frontier times, a story of Choctaw kisses, bullets and blood.

VANCE H. TRIMBLE
January 9, 2007
at Wewoka

Choctaw Kisses, Bullets & Blood

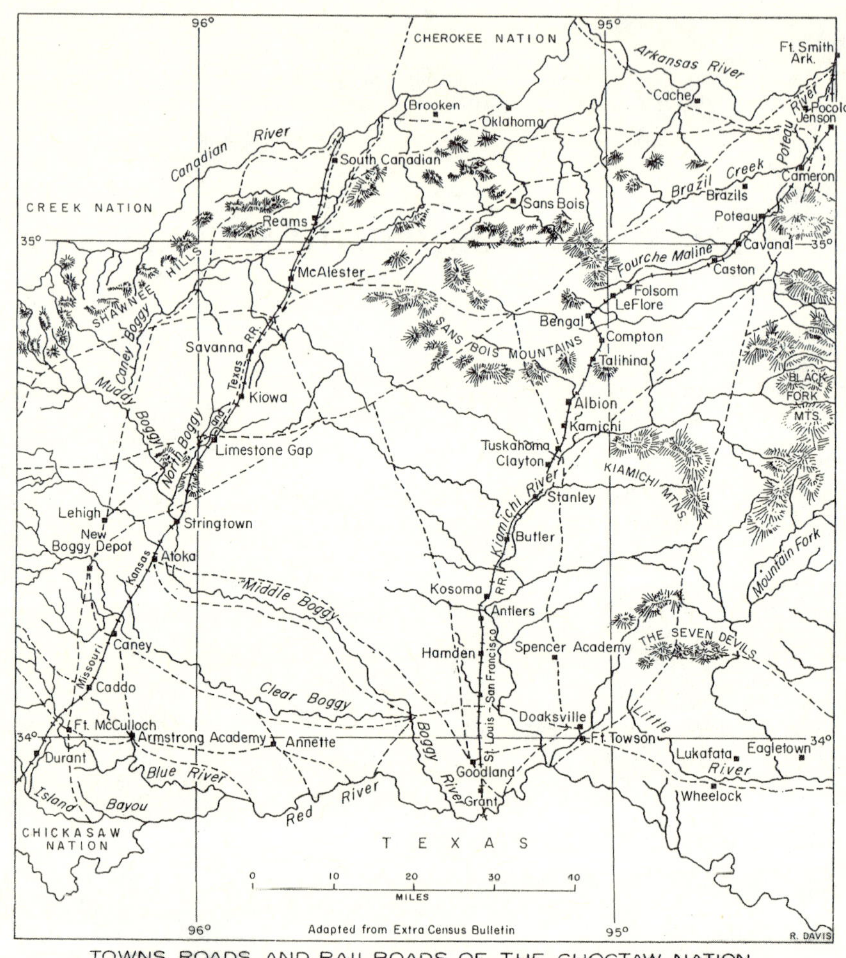

TOWNS, ROADS, AND RAILROADS OF THE CHOCTAW NATION
ABOUT 1887

1

The Renegade Soldier Boy

HIS WILD SCHEME to run away to Mexico was turning sour. On the windy hot Texas prairie, the haggard young man wearily slowed down, dragging his feet. By late afternoon he totally gave out and stopped. It was the first week of April in the year 1866. He turned and looked north, squinting against the last of the day's streaming sunlight. The Red River was in sight, and not many miles beyond the stream, under a drifting bluish haze, rose the raddled outlines of the Kiamichi Mountains.

In his grungy Johnny Reb cap and Confederate uniform, rumpled and missing half its brass buttons, he appeared wretched and hapless. His left coat sleeve was freshly ripped and a bloodstain blossomed where a bullet had struck his arm.[1]

Already he had walked seventy or eighty miles from the Louisiana border, a difficult and harried journey. Now he turned for a long look to the east back across the flat terrain he had crossed. Was the posse

---

[1] Betty J. Broyles, *Locke Family History,* (The College Press, Collegedale, Tenn., 1995), pp 202-209; Dorothy Arnote West, *Pushmahata County—The Early Years* (Privately printed, 2002) pp 249-254; O.L. Blanche, *Indian-Pioneer Papers,* (Vol. 61-358-361, May 21, 1937); *Antlers American,* Jan. 10, 1929, quoting Dr. E. Brantly's biographical interview with Victor M. Locke; author's interviews with Betty J. Broyles, March 20, April 6, May 10, July 13, 2004.

still after him? His emotions were atingle, fluttering. For a minute or two he held his breath and listened carefully and looked hard. Finally he gave a sigh of relief; there was no sign he was being followed.

His flight was so fraught with danger that he sneaked in the dark around a few towns and crossroads. Near Mount Pleasant, Texas he had a scare, but it was just his nerves. The noise was a jackrabbit skittering into the brush.

Again, he scanned the northern horizon, calculating and debating his predicament. His objective, Mexico, was a long, long way off. Yet he was standing barely a mile from the Red River, which was the northern boundary of Texas. On its far shore began the vast wilderness of the untamed Indian country. Perhaps in the very mountains his eyes now beheld he might find a safe hiding place.[2] That was something to think hard about.

His boots crunched the dry prairie grass, stirring a dusty haze that stung his reddening eyes. He was thirsty, hungry, grimy with sweat, and near exhaustion. Again he turned and stared glumly at the distant and unending western horizon. His weary mind tried to calculate how far he had to go to reach the Mexican border; it must be at least five hundred miles.

Pain twinges flickered in his wounded arm; the bullet was still embedded too deep to be visible.[3] He had learned to grit his teeth and stand it. Fortunately the bleeding had stopped.

In his scrape at the Louisiana border his horse had been shot out from under him—the faithful *Redbird*, his Tennessee family's last thoroughbred mount. Luckily, he managed to elude the posse, but in that wild encounter lost his Spencer rifle, his Colts pistol, and even his long knife and its bejeweled scabbard.

By his reckoning, he was at this moment about ten or twelve miles north of Clarksville, Texas, and standing beside a wagon road that led to a Red River ferry.

On *Redbird* he'd have literally *flown* to the Rio Grande, likely covering those five hundred miles in a week, but . . .

---

[2] *Loc., cit.*
[3] *Loc., cit.*

Hunched over, burdened by the heart-stab of losing such a fine steed plus the rigors of having to run for his life, the fugitive appeared small and apathetic. But when he stood upright, he was just short of six feet. The loose fit of his threadbare uniform gave him a shrunken look, yet he weighed a muscular one-eighty. In no wise did his face look old; his cheeks were weathered brown and dirt-streaked, but his quick eyes, deep-set, large and blue, flashed with the verve and impetuosity of true youth. He had short-cropped dark hair, a high forehead, close-set ears, a rather thin long nose slightly pinched where it joined his full, but not bushy, eyebrows. His hands were long and slender, with the roughness, calluses, and broken finger nails that came from four years of tending horses and campfires and keeping a Henry or Spencer and a steel blade fit for letting enemy blood.

His baritone voice was strong and commanding, and ordinarily he had about him an air of ease and confidence. This was not a young man willing to back away from insult or danger. He had been popular with his Johnny Reb companions; the learned ones were wont to characterize him with such words as: *sanguine, virile, valiant, dauntless,* or *indomitable.*

Just now, under the high prairie sky, he not only felt lonely and forlorn, but very much looked the part.

He could see the rope-tethered ferry rocking gently on the rusty-looking stream, and a rickety office shack with one man leaning against it. In the fading light the ferryman's face and arms appeared very dark. The boy's eyes widened in alarm. What if the ferryman was black? Negroes were the cause of his trouble in Louisiana. He regretted the Shreveport affair; it was unexpected and unnecessary, and totally senseless. But it had happened. He had been definitely minding his own business, just passing through, when confronted by newly freed slaves who were "mean and sassy." A fight broke out, and he killed one of them.[4]

That was by no means his first time to spill blood. As a soldier he could aim with deadly accuracy and splatter with no compunction a Union bluecoat's brains. The first lesson he learned riding with General "Fighting Joe" Wheeler's Tennessee cavalry was: *kill or be killed!*

---

[4] *Loc., cit.*

Living through the thunder and hell that stretched from Knoxville and Chickamauga to Atlanta's outskirts, he realized that God tossed the dice blindly and heedlessly. In a single day of battle, seeing soldiers fall all around him, he was astounded to later be told that by sundown at least eight thousand Confederates were killed or wounded, and the Yankees had three thousand or more casualties.

In one day! He was stunned. You grew reluctant to speak facetiously about cannon or muskets after you'd seen up close their crimson ruin and smelled their stink.

His emotions were entirely different, however, when it became personal—avenging his grandfather's murder after the war's end let him return to the home place in Tennessee. He was proud of possessing enough honor and courage to pull the trigger; but also sickened and a bit remorseful—until he reminded himself that Grandpa Sharp had been callously called to his own front door by a certain Union sympathizer and gunned down without mercy.

Feeling hair-trigger caution, Johnny Reb approached the ferry landing with slow step. The attendant, a middle-aged easy-going Negro, greeted him casually. They struck up a vague conversation. The ferryman's eyes shined with curiosity, but he asked no prying questions. The boy studied the river. It was too deep to wade, too wide to swim.

The posted sign said to ride across to Indian Territory cost five cents. The boy's pockets were empty, as was his belly. Though penniless, hungry, bedraggled, and exhausted, he was too proud to beg for help, certainly not from a black.

Just then on the opposite side, an Indian man came to the shore and began yelling across the Red River. He shouted strange words Johnny Reb did not understand.

The ferryman hollered back an acknowledgement, and turned to the boy. "Wants ah come get him," the ferryman said. He seemed to sense the boy's plight. "You welcome to ride over."[5]

When the ferry reached the landing on the Choctaw Nation side, the boy saw that the waiting Indian man was youngish, well built, and alert. His dark eyes glinted, dancing with intelligence and inspiration.

---

[5] *Loc., cit.*

The Indian stared boldly at the boy's sad face, and studied his garb. Then he blurted out something in the Choctaw tongue to the ferryman.

"He say," the ferryman again volunteered, "he wore uniform like yours. An' askin' what's wrong with your arm. An' is you hungry?"[6]

The Indian saw the boy's immediate look of gratitude. With a quick hand wave to the ferryman, he abandoned his intended river crossing, and led the young stranger a short distance up a hilly path to his little log cabin.

A comely Indian woman, presumably his wife, came out and promptly grasped the critical situation. Within minutes she produced strips of cloth and a slender probe that appeared to have been whittled from a cow's horn. She took charge and positioned his arm on a rough table in her kitchen. The boy submitted silently and gratefully. By lamplight, he watched her deftly dig deep, steeling himself. Out came the bullet. She applied a herb poultice and bandaged the wound, and fed him.[7]

Thus, in the Spring of 1866, Victor Moreau Locke, not quite twenty years old, arrived in the Choctaw Nation full of resentment, disappointment, and desperation. He had fought four hard years in the Confederate cavalry—having illegally joined underage at fifteen.

Toward the end he had been captured and held in prison, but set free after Appomattox to go home. Back in Tennessee he became involved in the Gothic nightmare of a revenge killing.

Now he was on the run, a fugitive from a Draconian past.

Victor Locke, acutely surprised, didn't know quite what to make of being taken in as a "guest" by this Indian couple. They were kind and friendly, and catered unstintingly to his obvious distress. Conversing was difficult. They undertook to speak slowly, did a lot of pointing, made many hand motions, and drew symbols in the dirt with sticks. By such means, they managed essential communication. The newcomer later began to comprehend a few everyday Choctaw words.

His bullet wound healed, and as the days passed, he relaxed. The Louisiana posse must have abandoned the chase. Nobody was after him. Back in Tennessee, he probably was under suspicion, but it would

---

[6] *Loc., cit.*

[7] *Loc., cit.*

be hard to openly accuse him. He felt a change coming over him. Never would he go back home. Even Mexico had somehow lost its allure. Looking around, he felt charmed by this Indian country. He liked the friendliness of the people and figured he ought to try to make his new life among them.

When he conceived such a thought, this runaway ex-Confederate soldier had not the slightest notion that destiny had marked him—a white man—to emerge within a decade or two as the head of one of the most prominent, wealthy and successful, and essential families in Choctaw Nation history.

And certainly among the most controversial.

The Indian looked closely at Victor Locke's C.S.A. jacket, and ran his fingers over it admiringly. He went to a cupboard and brought out his own Confederate Army tunic, neatly folded. Then he displayed his papers—he, too, had fought for the South. His military documents identified him as a cavalryman in the Choctaw Nation's First Mounted Regiment. His papers showed that his troop saw action in Arkansas and Missouri and in the dramatic Indian Territory battle at Honey Springs.

Even though his Indian hosts could not comprehend fully, Victor Locke tried to recount to them his own soldier story. He scribbled down a few important dates and places, and tried to explain them. Meigs County, Tennessee—his home. June 16, 1861—the day he ran away to enlist. January 19, 1862—when he saw his first action under Confederate General Felix Zollicoffer challenging Union forces at Fishing Springs, Kentucky. Zollicoffer was killed, the Southerners were repulsed, with 439 casualties.

Private Victor Locke got battle-hardened in the following months at places like Knoxville, Shiloh, Chattanooga, and at Murfreesboro—where a bullet made a furrow on his scalp, putting him in sick bay a couple of weeks.[8]

Victor Locke tried to tell how on July 21, 1864, cocky and eager, he rode into northern Georgia with Confederate cavalry to try to stop Union General Sherman's march on Atlanta. The fighting was ferocious. Private Locke told them he saw a Confederate sniper shoot U.S.A. Gen-

---

[8] *Loc., cit.*

eral James B. McPherson off his horse. Sherman's cannon repulsed the Confederates. Next day at Peachtree Creek, Private Locke's company was captured.

For several months he was held in Federal military prison near Richmond, Virginia. In the second week of April 1865, Private Victor Locke crawled out of his blankets on a chilly dawn to find the lockup awash with rumor. General Lee had surrendered to Grant! Who could believe that!

A short time later Private Locke lined up with hundreds of other men in gray in a great hallway, inching up to a desk to get release papers. A printed form was pushed out to him. It read: "The bearer [*and written on the blank space was his name*] Private Victor M. Locke, CSA, a paroled prisoner, now has the United States Army's permission to go to his home, and there remain undisturbed." It bore the chicken-scratched signature of a Yankee captain. He snapped: "Now pledge allegiance to the United States of America."[9]

The curt command did not immediately register on Victor Locke. His brain was already churning with a dozen disturbing rumors. The Yanks were going to rub the South's nose in it. Carpetbaggers would descend on helpless Dixie, and rob her. Every Secesh was to be harshly punished.

Victor Locke believed such gossip. Abe Lincoln's people couldn't be trusted. He'd already been outraged by a letter from home telling about Yankee soldiers capturing fifteen or twenty Rhea County girls, hauling them in filthy cattle cars to Chattanooga, where they were marched through deep mud to prison. *Girls! Good Lord Almighty. . . capturing girls!*[10]

He gave the parole officer a hard stare, but said nothing. The Yankee captain again began, "Now pledge . . ." Sensing defiance, he broke off, lifted his eyes and probably surveyed the long line of Rebs still waiting to reach his table. With a shrug, the officer snatched up a pen,

---

[9] *Locke Family History,* p 202

[10] Betty J. Broyles, interview with author, May 10, 2004

scrawled "deserter" on the sheet, thrust it into Private Locke's hands, and waved him away.[11]

The loss of the Southern Cause left a deep mark on Victor Locke's psyche. He was glad to see the end of bivouac, starvation marches, the murderous fire and chaos of battle—all that. But for the Confederacy to be so brutally crushed —that outrage left him nauseated and humiliated.

And bitterly defiant, angry enough to spurn the conquering enemy's demand that he swear allegiance. *Deserter*? Hardly—he was *unconquered!* Four years ago he had taken up soldier's arms as a jejune teenager, but now he was a full-grown man, strong, keen-minded, hard as steel, clever and quick, ambitious, and dangerously fearless.

Like his thousands of comrades, Victor Locke left Virginia afoot and began the long trek home. What changes, he wondered, had taken place on the Locke family plantation in Meigs County on the banks of the Tennessee River between Chattanooga and Knoxville? All up and down that section of middle Tennessee the opposing armies had clashed frequently and murderously. Bushwhackers too raced across the countryside, he had heard, pillaging storehouses, driving off livestock, stealing or destroying crops.

Before the war Victor Locke's parents had created a picture book Southern plantation. Near the river sat their two-story red brick mansion with sweeping verandahs and tall white columns, skirted by glistening green lawn, perfumed by stately magnolias. There were vast cotton fields and orchards, thoroughbred horses, and in large numbers cattle, swine, poultry. Slaves tended the household and tilled the fields.[12] The Locke clan, which was extensive in Tennessee, joyously lived in the top rung of the aristocracy of the genteel South.

They came from England. Victor Locke's grandfather was Thomas Locke who succumbed to the lure of adventure in the New World. About 1770, he is said to have abandoned his studies at a London university, and sailed to America. At age twenty-one or twenty-two, he established himself in Botetourt County, Virginia, and began to prosper. In

---

[11] *Locke Family History,* p 202

[12] *Ibid., pp 13-21*

1777, Thomas Locke married Susanna Henry, nineteen, a distant cousin of the American statesman Patrick Henry. They had eleven children, the last of which was Victor's father, Benjamin Franklin Locke.[13]

As early as 1806, the Thomas Lockes had gone west to acquire a six-hundred-acre farm near Little Pigeon River in the foothills of the Great Smoky Mountains, in a vast tract that the Cherokee Indians surrendered to settlers, and which became Sevier County, Tennessee. By the 1820s, most of Thomas Locke's eight sons had gone further west, acquiring rich bottom land in Rhea and Meigs Counties just east of the Tennessee River, and south of Knoxville.

The clan, as a whole, was intellectual, distinguished, prominent and prosperous, as agriculturalists and as professionals. The sixth son of Thomas and Susanna, Thomas K. Locke, born in July 1792, was not only a court clerk but also a plantation owner and breeder of thoroughbred horses. Their youngest son, Benjamin Franklin, born in 1803 probably in Sevier County, became a merchant, ferry operator, school trustee, road supervisor, and owner of a six-hundred-acre plantation with twenty slaves.

In 1840, Benjamin Franklin Locke at age thirty-seven married Mary Sharp, seventeen, daughter of a prominent neighbor. They had Victor and two other sons and three daughters.[14]

Victor Locke was only eight years old when his father at fifty-one died unexpectedly April 21, 1854 at his plantation, leaving Mary pregnant with their last child, Elisha, who would be born two months later when she was a comely widow only thirty-one years old.

Before leaving the Yankee prison to start his trek home, Victor heard news that greatly disturbed him—his mother was planning to remarry. Still too adolescent to completely comprehend the sexual dimensions of adult essentiality, he failed to comprehend his young mother's need to revitalize her romantic milieu, to share a man's laughter again, to be happy. The idea that in her early forties she could take a new husband

---

[13] *Ibid.,pp 5-11*

[14] *Ibid.,* pp 98-108

gave him pause; but what he was soon to learn would ignite him into furious explosion.[15]

The moment he walked through the mansion's front door, his mother rushed forward to smother him with kisses and hug him vigorously. Her smile and radiance lifted his spirits. Then her new husband came forward, a pleasant enough looking Tennesseean named William Foster.

They had married on March 30, 1865. The new Mary Sharp Locke Foster served cake and coffee to her Johnny Reb. The men sat and talked—and finally came to a discussion about Appomattox and General Lee's surrender, and the terrible consequences and new hardships the South could expect. Of course, Captain William Foster, too, had fought in the war. Only a few minutes into the conversation, Victor Locke sensed something that began to chill him and stiffen his face. Then his blood rose.

Captain Foster was a Yankee![16]

His mother's new husband had helped crush Dixie! Victor leaped to his feet and rushed out, fearing he would react with violence.

The situation left Victor almost suffocating with confusion. How could he ever accept a Yankee as stepfather? Perhaps he should just leave the plantation; his mother no longer would need his help—she had a man in the house!

His anger and depression lasted for days. He wandered about the countryside, considering his options. What would be his wisest course? He found himself in the family cemetery, kneeling at the grave of his mother's father, Elisha Sharp.

The tombstone legend was stark:

ELISHA SHARP
July 25, 1792
Dec. 6, 1863
Killed by J. P. Knight[17]

---

[15] Betty J. Broyles, interview with author, March 20, 2004
[16] *Loc., cit.*

Victor likely ran his fingers over the carved letters, bringing vivid again the story of his grandfather's assassination that had occurred while he was away at war. The Knights were close neighbors of the Elisha Sharp family but became enemies over the war—the Sharps Confederates, the Knights siding with the Union. They had a bitter feud over some horses stolen to resupply the rebel cavalry. On a dark night Elisha Sharp answered a knock at his front door. A rifle shot rang out and pierced his heart. The killer escaped unseen. Even without proof, the Sharp family carved on the gravestone as the killer a name—J.P. Knight. To his chagrin, Victor now discovered that J. P. Knight, in his thirties, still roamed free and unrepentant. That knowledge further infuriated his rebellious soul, and at the same time intensified his hatred for his mother's Yankee husband.

After days of indecision, Victor Locke sorted things out and made two decisions. He would strike out to find a new life south of the border. His imagination about Mexico had been piqued by army buddies. They regaled his naive mind with exotic tales of excitement and opportunity. He now decided to ride down to Laredo, Texas and there cross the Rio Grande River.

To execute his second decision he needed just one .44 calibre cartridge for his Spencer rifle.

At dawn Victor Locke went out to the stable and threw a saddle on the last of the Locke thoroughbreds, the spirited bay called *Redbird.* Mounting up, he headed south on a route that would take him across parts of Mississippi, Alabama and Louisiana before he reached Texas.

Pensively, he took a long look at the mansion he was leaving. For a moment he probably captured in his mind's eye a vision of the neighboring Knight plantation.

In his heart were conflicting emotions. First, the wrench of leaving home without a goodbye to his mother. Second, equally strong and vibrant, the great pride and enormous satisfaction that came from knowing that sure vengeance had been mightily delivered!

---

[17] Cemetery records of Meigs County, Tenn.

He could easily imagine the scene of somebody awakening in the Knight household this morning and venturing outside. Around behind the barn they would find a shocking surprise—J. P. Knight lying sprawled on the ground with a .44 calibre bullet hole in the middle of his forehead.

Victor Locke took a last look at the familiar Tennessee River, settled into the saddle, and noisily snapped the reins to start *Redbird* off at an easy pace. He was beginning a long journey, into a strange realm, and facing an unknown future.

Every sunrise was to bring him new adventure, much too much excitement and challenge for the lifetime of an average man. But, then, nobody ever said Victor M. Locke was average.

2

A Choctaw Love Story

COLONEL ROBERT M. JONES, the Choctaw Nation's first millionaire, emerged from his Rose Hill mansion one bright morning in Spring 1868, climbed into his handsome buggy with gleaming yellow wheels and matched grays, and set off to find Victor Locke for an afternoon's interrogation.

Until the Civil War intervened, Colonel Jones was considered one of the richest men in the American West. He operated twenty-eight general stores across Indian Territory, maintained six plantations along the Texas and Arkansas borders, owned two Red River steamboats. He had three hundred "head" of slaves and annually grew seven hundred bales of cotton. Two of his plantations were huge, one covering 10,000 acres, another 5,000.[1]

The colonel, now sixty, had become financially pinched because of the Confederacy's defeat. Secretly, he hid 7,000 bales of cotton in New Orleans, and counted on selling them to stake his post-Appomattox comeback; but the federals discovered his stash and were trying to "steal" it. He also was badly hurt, of course, when everybody's slaves were set free.

---

[1] Michael L. Bruce, "The Life and Times of Robert M. Jones," *Chronicles of Oklahoma,* (Vol 66—Fall 1988) p 295

Several lively suggestions being openly thrown around by Victor Locke filtered back to the colonel. This was a young man worth talking to, and he wouldn't be hard to locate. The Johnny Reb from Tennessee was clerking in the colonel's store a half-day's ride away in Shawnee Town near Horseshoe Bend on the Red River. In fact, he had been on the Jones empire payroll almost two years, having initially hired on as a cowboy herding cattle, and then driving ox-drawn freight wagons.

Jones found the twenty-two-year-old ex-cavalryman bustling around the Shawnee Town store with a confident, authoritative air. He was handsome. Locke stood about six feet, slightly taller than the stocky colonel, who was turning gray and wearing spectacles. They were equally thick-chested, and both radiated muscular strength. Locke presented a firm handshake; his slender strong hands were very brown from sun.

They talked at length about operating a general store, cotton gins and saw and grist mills, breeding horses and cattle, buying and selling timber, trading with the Indians for snakeroot and ginseng, as well as animal pelts. It was clear that Victor Locke did have an inquiring mind, and a sharp business sense. The colonel noticed Locke had deep-set blue eyes, what he considered quick eyes, surrounded by small seams of experience.

As they sat together, and smoked, Locke doubtless maintained a kind of watchfulness, along with his confident ease that bespoke unexpected maturity. He had a veiled smile and gave the impression of being able to shrug off the worries of the world, or do vigorous battle with them. His clothes were typical of the Territory, rough and casual, but neatly matched and clean. He had slightly wavy black hair and a neat mustache. His chin was round and slightly dimpled.

Jones was struck by one distinct similarity in their character. Victor Locke obviously had honed his innate ability to gauge human nature, and thus could easily instill confidence and launch strong friendships that enabled him to become a leader of men.

This realization gave the millionaire an inward chuckle. That was his own strong suit. One key to Colonel Jones' success was his ability to magically ferret out bright and ambitious men and employ their brainpower and energy to enhance and enlarge his enterprises. So he had perked up when he heard several times that Choctaws living around Shawnee Town were already bringing their financial and personal problems to Victor Locke, listening to his advice, and following it.

"The kid's got some bright ideas," the store manager told Jones. "About crops, cattle, horses—he really knows horseflesh. Says he could run about any general store. Nothin' gets by his eagle eye. Book-learned on readin' and writin'. Cyphers mighty fast, too. And he's fast picking up the Choctaw talk."[2]

Although strongly impressed by Victor Locke's confident handling of himself in this 1868 confab, the colonel could not just then spare the time to become his mentor. Jones was deeply involved in helping his tribe escape harsh penalties being imposed from Washington.

When the Choctaws signed the 1830 treaty surrendering their 10,000,000 acres in Mississippi to permit white settlement for about the same size Indian Territory tract, they were promised the "net proceeds" to compensate for buildings, livestock and crops left behind.[3] That amount later was set at $3,000,000.

But Washington now refused to pay, claiming the treaty was broken when Choctaw soldiers fought with the Confederate States against the Union. Jones accompanied tribal leaders on several trips to demand Congress pay the "net proceeds."

For his part, Victor Locke decided it would be wise to emulate this successful entrepreneur. He devoted free time to vigorously exploring the millionaire's life and techniques. He was told that Jones, a mixed blood who graduated from the highly regarded Choctaw Academy in Kentucky in 1830, had contracted to drive 500 horses in the tribe's removal to the new Choctaw Nation. Nearly half of them died. Despite that loss, Jones managed to start in business with $1,800 in tribal annuities his guardian had saved for him, and prospered steadily.

In Victor Locke's eyes, the colonel, despite wartime reverses, still was sitting on top of the world with "everything anyone could de-

---

[2] Dolly Locke Archer correspondence, Locke Family Papers, Garrard Ardeneum Manuscript Collection

[3] Angie Debo, *The Rise and Fall of the Choctaw Republic,* (Norman, 1934) pp 71, 81

sire," including his fifteen-room Rose Hill mansion, the biggest and most luxurious in Indian Territory.[4]

Victor Locke mused that he had changed course and for one purpose only fled into this frontier wilderness—to elude the Louisiana posse. But he now felt satisfied and at home in the Choctaw Nation. He believed he could spend the rest of his days with the Indians.

Day-dreaming of getting a business start for himself, Victor Locke set out to expose his young mind to the variety of existing opportunities. In the next two years he clerked in other Indian Territory trading posts and wound up in 1870 helping run the Abernathy general store at a crossroads called Lukfata near the Red River, thirty miles by wagon road north of Clarksville, Texas.[5]

He had no inkling that living in Lukfata would directly involve him with the family of the noted Choctaw merchant and politician Thomson McKinney, and thus set the stage for one of the most important changes in his life.

Thomson McKinney, had been educated at the Choctaw Academy in Kentucky and came to Indian Territory about 1836 as a teenager. He was first appointed secretary of the Indian agency in Scullyville, an important town not far southwest of Fort Smith, Arkansas. He rose rapidly in the Choctaw government, serving as National Secretary and making three trips to Washington on tribal business. Along with Colonel Jones, he was appointed a trustee of Armstrong Academy, the tribal school for boys which was opened in 1845 fifty-five miles west of Fort Towson.[6]

He married Letha Ann Amanda Malone and they had three children, two daughters, Susan Priscilla and Martha, and a son Thomson Junior. Both parents were mixedblood, he three-quarters Choctaw and she one-eighth, which meant their children were about five-eighths Choctaw and light-skinned for Indians. The McKinney family lived on a large plantation and owned one hundred slaves. He ran once for principal chief but was defeated. Even so, Scullyville acquaintances described him

---

[4] *Chronicles of Oklahoma* (Vol 66—Fall 1988) p 296
[5] Betty J. Broyles, *Locke Family History,* p 203
[6] *Ibid.,* pp 203, 292, 295

as "a pleasant, kind, generous, and important man—a good neighbor who frequently settled difficulties among his townsmen."[7]

At age fifty-eight, Thomson McKinney was struck down by bilious fever and died, leaving his widow in 1858 with the children aged four, two, and one, but "well-to-do." The Civil War outbreak set free her slaves and caused her additional financial loss.

For safety, she joined other war refugees in moving deeper into the Red River region close to Texas. She established herself in a small town called Wheelock, and put daughter Susan Priscilla under the care of the Reverend Charles C. Copeland, superintendent of the tribal seminary for girls, Wheelock Academy.

At war's end Mrs. McKinney met Joseph Hodges, a widower with two daughters, Lizzie and Martha, and four sons, including, John, a teen-ager. They were married and moved to nearby Lukfata, where her new husband opened a general store.[8] His eye fell on Victor Locke's trading post skills and he hired him away from the rival Abernathy establishment.[9] At once Victor Locke got acquainted with all the McKinney and Hodges children—except one. He didn't meet Susan Priscilla. She was living with a family in Scullyville, and teaching school nearby, having graduated from Wheelock Academy.

In early fall John Hodges entered the store with a girl Victor Locke had not seen before—a teenager with long black hair parted in the middle, a roundish broad face, small mouth and nose, wide-set dark eyes that glinted inquisitively.

"My stepsister Susan," John Hodges announced, with a slight bow.[10]

The girl acknowledged Victor Locke with only a quick nod, and moved so pertly toward a barrel of apples that the hem of her long linen dress flashed across her little black button shoes. He stared after her, feeling a sudden stir.

---

[7] Locke Family Papers, Garrard Ardeneum Manuscript Collection; Aleece Locke Garrard diary notes, p 3
[8] *Locke Family History,* p 203
[9] *Loc., cit.*
[10] Locke Family Papers

Over the next few weeks he would often encounter her in the store. He put on his best smile and tried to chat with her. She cut him off, but politely. She dazzled his mind, leaving him rapturously aware of the rich, racy current of vitality in her young body. He several times saw her on a pony riding with stepbrother John Hodges.

By inquiring, Victor Locke discovered that her birthday was approaching. On November 8, she would turn sixteen.

Victor Locke began having long talks with Susan McKinney, holding hands, taking her on romantic picnics, and pony rides—but only in his midnight dreaming.

Even though she continued to ignore or rebuff him, he wondered if he should buy her a birthday present, especially something that would cause her to think of him.[11] At times he felt dizzy with an unaccustomed emotion; the love bug had bit him!

Victor Locke was confused and uncertain how to develop a courtship. In picking up Indian lore, he had heard much about the intricacies and protocol of traditional Choctaw romance. Most of what he'd been told struck him as silly, and he felt gratified that old customs were now almost completely abandoned.

Boys, he was told, in the old days usually would visit a family, spot a fetching girl and flip a pebble or a bean at her. She might rebuff him by darting from the room. If she shyly flipped it back, she was interested. Then the boy would leave, formally saying "*eyali,*" meaning, "I go." The mother or father would assent in the formal term "*omig,*" meaning "very well."[12] Some swains believed they had to go into the woods at midnight and beg the moon for a favorable omen. At the wedding feast the bride tried to outrun her groom. Guests scrambled for trinkets and gifts tossed at the bride's head. Choctaws abandoned common law marriage and required a license and legal ceremony. An adulterous wife was beaten by her father, had her head shaved, or was killed.[13]

Of a sudden, Susan changed. She began to speak civilly to Victor. On occasion she would chuckle or laugh at his clever remarks. More

---

[11] Author interview with Francine Locke Bray, Oct. 27, 2003

[12] "Love and Marriage: Ancient Choctaw Style," *Bishinik,* December, 1980, p 10-ll

[13] *Loc., cit.*

often she stopped in the store just to talk to him. Within weeks his midnight dreams became real—picnics, pony rides, stolen kisses. Two things worried him: he was twenty-four and Susan was sixteen; further, he had mighty slim prospects to offer any bride.

Then came disaster. Shortly after Christmas, his employer called him into his office and warned Victor sternly to stay away from his step-daughter! On the heels of this blow, John Hodges, angry and red in the face, tried to pick a fight with him.[14] Susan came to Victor in tears and explained everything. Her mother wanted her to marry her stepbrother John Hodges, in fact issued an ultimatum. Victor told Susan to dry her tears, while he began scheming to outwit her mother.

On Thursday, February 2, 1871, Victor Locke rode over to their courthouse in Boktuklo County, Choctaw Nation. He looked up Court Clerk Alpheus Crosby and gave him a total of $12.50 to issue a license authorizing "any minister of the Gospel or anyone authorized to solemnize marriages" to marry him to Susan Priscilla McKinney.[15]

The lovers kept secret their plans to elope. On Monday night, February 6, they slipped away in the dark, mounted their ponies, carrying small valises. One held her skimpy trousseau.

They headed toward the Arkansas border, twenty miles to the east. By sunup they were nearing Hope, Arkansas. At midmorning they were there standing in the living room of a Judge Cartwright. He married them—and did more.

Noticing they were exhausted from the long ride, the kindly judge invited them to stay in his home a few days. Susan Priscilla McKinney Locke was sixteen years and three months old when they began their honeymoon.

In three or four days, Victor and his bride returned to Boktuklo *(Two Creeks)* County and recorded their marriage. They visited her mother and rode on to Scullyville, where Victor Locke easily found employment helping manage a general store. Nine months later, on October 27, 1971, their first child, a boy, arrived. Susan named him James

---

[14] Testimony of Victor M. Locke before Dawes Commission December 4, 1902. (*Oklahoma Historical Society, packets for citizenship, Choctaw #5746.*)
[15] *Locke Family History,* p 208

Shubetta Locke, but the wry father already had secretly selected for the infant an Indian nickname—*Epiachubbi,* which he would later shorten to "Shub."[16]

OUT OF CURIOSITY, Victor Locke turned off the old military road to take a quick look at the ruins of Fort Towson, on a high bluff a few miles north of the Red River. Nothing remained except vague outlines of the stockade's U shape, and a scattering of tall chimneys. He dismounted beside one of them to check out a tale he'd heard.

The mouth of the limestone fireplace was about nine feet high and seven feet wide; so it really was true you could roast a whole steer in it, with room left over for boiling and baking. It must have taken about twenty of these to heat barracks for 800 troops.[17] The rest of the fort was now gone.

To him this historic site held no special interest. He was passing by, and merely stopped for idle sightseeing. Fort Towson, built in the 1830s and the second military post in Indian Territory after Fort Gibson, had played critical roles on the frontier.

It began as an outpost against the wild plains Indians. From it later cavalry went into the war against Mexico. It became a pawn in the Civil War, alternately seized by both sides. The government abolished Fort Towson soon after Confederate General Stand Watie surrendered his beaten forces there on June 23, 1865.

Forget the war; forget its bullets and blood! Victor Locke had struggled three or four years to purge the dark memories haunting him. He hated nightmares that unreeled a panorama of ghastly landscapes strewn with bloody corpses that looked as though wolves had gnawed them. He awakened sweating, shuddering, regretting his soldier years.

But on this day in May 1872 he felt cheerful. He was on his way to the most prosperous and influential town in the Choctaw Nation—

---

[16] *Ibid.,* pp 291-292

[17] Frances Imon, *Smoke Signals from Indian Territory* (Wolfe City, Texas, 1976), p 64

Doaksville. His chaotic past was dead; he was only twenty-six, still young enough to work hard and make a bright future.

His old boss, Colonel Jones, had summoned him to run a general store in Doaksville. He was coming down from Scullyville to discuss the proposition. His ride took him about one hundred miles south over the old military road running from Fort Smith down to the Texas border at Red River and Fort Towson.

After three decades it was still a primitive wagon road. The route was scenic, crossing clay and sandy plains, boggy creeks, some of which had to be forded thrice within one valley, traversing steep mountain passes often only wide enough for one wagon, but scenically redeemed by the mysterious and liquid stillness of the wilderness and the odor of pine and cedar.

For travel, the Choctaws had only such roads and a few riverboats. Railroads had reached the northern edge of Indian Territory; but the iron horse would not cross the Choctaw Nation until about the 1880s. (Superstitious tribal rainmakers opposed train tracks, unsure that clouds could cross over the iron rails.)

Doaksville had sprung up in the 1830s around Josiah Doaks's trading post, located one mile west of Fort Towson. Within twenty-five years it had grown to the Choctaw Nation's largest trading center, was for a few years the Choctaw capital, published the Nation's first and second newspapers, had Indian Territory's first Masonic chapter, and got a U.S. post office as early as 1847.

Choctaw Agent William Armstrong reported to Washington in 1842 that Doaksville had five stores, all with large stocks, including sugar and coffee. He considered Doaksville "one of the most orderly and quiet towns" in the west, adding:

> There is a resident physician, a good tavern [hotel], blacksmith shop, wagon maker and wheelwright. A church has been erected . . .a temperance society is organized which numbers a large portion of the most respectable Choctaws and Chickasaws as well as our own population . . .
>
> The Choctaws have long since . . . acquired themselves . . . a name for honesty and fidelity . . . not surpassed by any of our Indian

> tribes. . . . They have by attention to their own business since they immigrated . . . greatly increased in wealth . . .[18]

Doaksville could be boisterous, too. It certainly had been when tribal members gathered there in November 1844 to receive cash annuities and rations provided by the federal government under the removal treaty. As the Reverend William H. Goode described the scene in his "Outposts of Zion":

> Some thousands of Indians are scattered over a tract of nearly if not quite a mile square around the payhouse. Here are cabins, tents, booths, stores, shanties; wagons, carts, campfires; ponies, mules, oxen and dogs; men, women and children; white, red, black and mixed in every imaginable shade and proportion and dressed in every conceivable style from the tasty American fop to the wild costume of the savage; buying, selling, swapping, betting, shooting, strutting, sauntering, talking, laughing. fiddling, eating, drinking, smoking, sleeping, seeing and being seen—and huddled together in one promiscuous and undistinguishable mass.[19]

Victor Locke found the deal with Colonel Jones, and the town of Doaksville, to his liking. He rented a comfortable house on a side street and moved in with Susan and one-year-old Shub. He needed a roomy residence; he and Susan wanted many children.

As their lives entwined, Colonel Jones took Victor Locke as a protégée and frequent companion. That included the Lockes visiting spectacular and expensive Rose Hill, near present day Hugo, Oklahoma. It was built for Jones's second wife, Susan Colbert.

To please her, he fenced in a deer park, planted thousands of roses, and a long hedge of cedar trees. His superstitious slaves shuddered at sight of the cedars. "Bad trouble begins," they muttered, "when a cedar tree gets tall enough to cast a shadow the size to cover a grave."[20]

---

[18] *Ibid.*, p 26-27
[19] *Ibid.*, p 27
[20] *Ibid.*, p 33

For whatever reason, the dark angel haunted the Jones family. All three children borne by his first wife, Judith Walker, had died in infancy. Soon his second wife Susan and two children were in graves covered by the shadows of Rose Hill cedars. And the curse of the cedars continued. His third wife was Elizabeth Earle, a missionary teacher. Three of their children, Henry, Jimmie and Frank, died in 1864, 1866, and 1867. At only sixty-five, the colonel was struck down by malaria and died February 22, 1873.

The cedar curse would continue to haunt his widow and two surviving children, Robert Jr., and Mary Jones. Widow Elizabeth married the family physician, Dr. Samuel W. Bailey. Eventually he was shot to death after a money quarrel with Robert Jr. The cedar shadows were waiting to cover at least one more family grave. Tom Paine, husband of the daughter by Colonel Jones's second marriage, strapped on two revolvers and attempted to countermand orders his wife Frances gave field hands to cut timber. The men stopped work, and then with their axes hacked Tom Paine to death.[21]

The untimely demise of his patron slowed down Victor Locke's burgeoning career only a trifle. He had gained a standing in Doaksville, and was talked of as a likely candidate for tribal office.

His family had grown again; his second son was born December 1, 1873, and named Charles Guffy.

Victor Locke's repute for wisdom in business, political, and moral matters caused Choctaw Nation officers to regularly seek his counsel. Such was the case when seventy-year-old William Bryant became principal chief. Confronted by an upsurge in violent crime, Chief Bryant took the problem to Victor Locke.

On this frontier, nearly every man went armed. Murders were frequent. Smuggled-in whiskey was one cause. Blame also fell on scores of desperadoes hiding out in the mountains to escape "Hanging Judge" Isaac Parker's federal court at Fort Smith. Indians, too, were killing each other in obscure feuds stemming from their ancient "blood for blood" code.

---

[21] *Ibid.*, p 35

Chief Bryant was most alarmed by an upsurge in horse and cattle stealing by organized gangs. He and Victor Locke agreed the solution lay in action—fast and severe. Chief Bryant ordered one of his district chiefs to destroy the gangs. An Oklahoma historian succinctly records what happened next: "About forty members of the gang were arrested, of whom fifteen were immediately tried and shot."[22]

BACK IN TENNESSEE Victor Locke's mother, Mary, had completely lost track of her runaway son. For ten years she heard absolutely nothing from him. She assumed he was still pouting because she had married a Yankee. But that husband had died and she was again a widow, living with Victor's two younger brothers.

Then in 1875 she heard in a roundabout way that Victor probably was in Indian Territory. Mary, now fifty-two, took it up with her two sons, Benjamin Franklin Jr., twenty-four, and Elisha, twenty-one.

The older son, just graduated from medical school in Nashville, was called Dr. Frank, but had not yet set up a practice. At his mother's behest, Dr. Frank agreed to go to Indian Territory and try to find his missing brother.[23] Elisha would stay in Tennessee with his mother.

Once inside the Choctaw Nation border, the searcher got instant word at every stopping place that pointed him straight to Doaksville. The brothers had a surprising and joyful reunion. Victor immediately rekindled his love for his kid brother, and talked him into staying in the Choctaw Nation. Spencer Academy, the tribal boarding school for boys, needed an attending physician. Victor introduced Dr. Frank to the superintendent, a friend, and got his brother the job.

Victor went even further and played matchmaker. His Choctaw friends John and Jane Wilson had a twenty-year-old daughter named Hattie. She was a beauty. Victor introduced her to Dr. Frank; and that's all it took. On June 1, 1875 they were married in the Wilson home.[24] Later on Dr. Frank would find the territory too thinly peopled to support

---

[22] *The Rise and Fall of the Choctaw Republic* (Norman, 1934), p 193
[23] *Locke Family History,* p 210
[24] *Ibid.,* p 211

a physician. He would open a pharmacy at Goodland, and finally turn to cattle ranching for his livelihood.

Letters from Dr. Frank excited and elated his mother. From Tennessee she quickly sent Victor a heartfelt message, but he was unable to answer it until July 20, 1875. He apologized, explaining he had "been out on the trail the last seven weeks." He said he was glad to hear from her.

"It appears," he wrote, "that your grandchildren is increasing quite rapidly. Frank has gone into the baby business. He was married some months ago to a Miss Hattie Wilson, a daughter of one of my best friends. I was highly pleased. Think he has got a splendid wife. I have known her the last eight or ten years, since I first came to this country."[25]

The newlyweds, he wrote, had "gone to housekeeping" on a farm given them by her father, along with fifty head of cattle and other live-stock. Dr. Frank, he said, had four or five hundred dollars in cash. Crops had been failing, Victor wrote, and "Times is hard—worse than I ever experienced. Some of the poor have actually starved to death. But we have prospects now for a moderate crop.

"We are having considerable sickness now, several deaths, etc. No news that is political concerning this country that would interest you. The probabilitys [sic] is that the next administration [meaning Washington] will bust this little government, or it is to be hoped it will. There are nothing going on among the tribes but steeling [sic] & killing up one another. It becomes unpleasant even for a man hardened to it to stay here. But they have it all among themselves. For they know well when a half-breed or a white man is missing the poor fellow will be made wolf bait of."

Victor Locke ended his letter on a more cheerful note.

"Susan is in fine health, also Shub and Top—two of the wildest little Chocs in the Nation. Shub thinks it would be a grand trip to visit you. I told him you weigh 230 and he said you must be a powerful squaw. He say that if you have plenty of back timber he will come out & stay a while with you. No more. Write soon. Affectionately, Dick Locke." (He had signed the name by which the Choctaws called him;

---

[25] *Ibid.,* p 205

eventually he would be universally known as “Uncle Dick.”) He also wrote his Indian name: *Glohoke.*[26]

Correspondence would continue between Mary Locke Foster and her wandering son. Their relationship would rapidly again become warm. Within a few years his mother, and also his kid brother Elisha, would join Victor “Dick” Locke out on the Indian frontier.

Dr. Frank was not the only Locke in “the baby business.” Susan and Victor, too, were pretty busy increasing their brood. On Thursday, March 23, 1876, at Doaksville, Susan gave birth to their third child, another lusty-lunged boy.[27]

The mother was a little over twenty-one and Victor still four months shy of thirty. The baby was named for his father, with a slight variation in spelling the middle name, Victor Murat Locke, Junior. There is no record of a reason for this change.

As with all their children, Victor Junior was one-quarter Choctaw blood—and thus qualified to occupy the highest office in the Choctaw Nation, which he would do by age thirty-four, and go on to pursue a political-military career that rivals the most sensational and spectacular in Indian Territory and Oklahoma history.

VICTOR LOCKE OPENED his front door in Doaksville to admit a wrinkled old Indian wearing a silk stovepipe hat and a hunting coat of many colors with a bushy strand of shoulder-length black and gray hair cocked over one ear. Principal Chief Coleman Cole had ridden into town astride a pot-bellied Choctaw pony fitted with only a wood saddle tree, some rawhide straps and stirrups as big as Star Navy Tobacco boxes to pick up his month’s mail.[28]

---

[26] Choctaw linguists consulted by author have been unable to recognize this word. The Choctaw alphabet does not include “G.” The last part of the word, *hoke*, is an emphasis, meaning “Indeed!”
[27] *Locke Family History,* p 292
[28] John Bartlett Meserve, “Chief Coleman Cole,”*Chronicles of Oklahoma,* (Vol 14 No. 1—March 1936), p 17, and V.M. Locke Jr., “Governor Cole,” *Chronicles of Oklahoma,* (Vol. 4—Sept. 1926) p 230.

He lived thirty miles north on Big Cedar in a one-room log cabin where he had no furniture and slept on the dirt floor. He ate outside, throwing bones to his dogs. His eccentricity was deceiving. Chief Cole was educated and came from noble Mississippi forebears, and adhered to early customs of the Choctaws. He spoke English clearly, in an Indian brogue. His eyes were indescribable—"they looked like fire at times." Coleman Cole was religious, a whiskey-hater, and led his tribe "with the highest probity and fidelity."[29]

His grandmother Shumaka survived a tribal massacre in Mississippi only because she was beautiful, lived to age 120, and from her bloodline came three other Choctaw chiefs.

At the post office, Chief Cole had filled an empty flour sack with his mail. He took it to Victor Locke's house to read. Because his pony-ride was hours long, the chief always spent the night. In the Locke stable, he belled and hobbled his pony.

His visits were much welcomed. They provided the opportunity to thoroughly hash over tribal problems. Susan Priscilla Locke joined these discussions, especially about politics. Her husband, she boasted to everyone, had qualities that eminently fitted him to serve the Choctaws as a judge or school executive. If not for being disqualified as a white man, she knew he could even perform splendidly as principal chief.

In his mail in early 1876, Chief Cole found a large envelope bearing a golden crest postmarked Philadelphia. Opening it with great care at the Locke house, he discovered it was an official invitation to attend the Centennial celebration.

Captain Nanamentubbee, another influential Choctaw, arrived just then at the Locke home. He had an identical Centennial invitation. The eyes of both Indians shone bright with importance. Writing years later, Victor Locke Jr. described the scene:

> A conference was held and it was concluded that such courtesy required an immediate reply. They called for pen, paper and ink. A small table was brought for their use and composition of a dignified reply was embarked upon. A detailed account of their many duties were

[29] *Loc., cit.*

set down, the distance to Philadelphia mentioned, and the absolute necessity of their presence with their people at all times were set forth in solemn words.

Finally, at the wind up of their reply, in order to soften the blow, to neutralize the disappointment (which must be theirs) of the officials of the Centennial at their inability to be present on the occasion of the celebration of the hundredth anniversary of the birth of the Union, they very gently penned the following sentence in closing: "I am sorry I cannot come this time; I will sure be there next time!"[30]

Other than committing such a transparent gaucherie, and dressing eccentrically, Chief Cole applied himself intelligently to tribal affairs, and with vigor and determination.

Emerging from a wilderness, the Choctaw Nation stumbled forward into a civilized world that posed a multitude of perilous challenges to the Indians. Two of the most explosive in 1875-76 were greedy demands by incoming railway promoters, and the accidental discovery of Choctaw coal deposits worth millions of dollars.

These episodes played out almost like the melodramatic scenario of an old "Perils of Pauline" silent movie cliffhanger. Chief Cole at one point arrested the leading coal men and ordered them shot by his Indian firing squad—but they escaped and hurried away in the dark on a railroad handcar.

There is no record that Victor Locke, who remained the chief's close consultant, gave him any specific advice on the coal crisis.

The principal personality in the coal mining controversy was a young former Confederate soldier from Arkansas named J. J. McAlester, often called by the honorific "Captain" or "Colonel" though he had been an enlisted man. Beyond doubt he was keenly intelligent, adventuresome, persistent—and extremely lucky.

After the Civil War, McAlester chanced to meet in Fort Smith a geologist named Weldon who earlier had helped the government survey the uncharted Choctaw Nation. Weldon had made a surprising find in the

---

[30] *Chronicles of Oklahoma,* (Vol. 4—Sept. 1926), p 231.

mountains—outcroppings of rich coal veins! He drew a map, gave it to the startled McAlester, and urged him to mine the coal and get rich.[31]

To travel into the Indian frontier, McAlester hired on to drive an ox-wagon carrying a sawmill to Fort Sill. With his map he then found the coal outcrops, and drove a claim stake into the ground. He believed Choctaw law entitled him to mine an area one-mile square.

The site was near where the Texas Trail crossed the California Trail, about the location of present day McAlester, Oklahoma. To acquire capital, young McAlester in 1869 talked a trading company into letting him open a store near the coal deposits at a village called Bucklucksy, and made a go of the store.

The Missouri, Kansas and Texas Railway Company, known as the "Katy," was poised at Parsons, Kansas to extend into Indian Territory and go on to Texas. Inspiration struck McAlester. He quietly mined a wagonload of coal, hitched up oxen, and in two weeks of hazardous travel reached Parsons. Katy men tested his coal, and cheered.

They called it "the best steam coal west of Pennsylvania." Because this coal was available, the Katy brought its line through Bucklucksy in 1872.

With a rail outlet, J. J. McAlester began mining coal. Trouble immediately exploded. Chief Cole ordered the mine shut down. McAlester felt he had legal rights, being intermarried to a Chickasaw woman. Boldly, he refused to comply. The Katy further inflamed Indian opposition by quickly building a switch track to the mine.

Cole's fury erupted. Tribal law provided that any Choctaw who "sold any part of the land" was subject to the death penalty. The chief considered the coal McAlester was mining "part of the land."

Cole dispatched his Lighthorse police to arrest McAlester and his three partners, and execute them. Next morning the Lighthorse captain found McAlester in his general store with partners Robert Reams, also an intermarried white, and an Indian named Pulsey. They were arrested, told they were to be executed, but were left at the store on their

---

[31] Paul Nesbitt, " J.J. McAlester,"*Chronicles of Oklahoma.,* (Vol 11, No. 2 — June 1933) p 758-763, and *The Rise and Fall of the Choctaw Republic,* pp 128-129

own recognizance while the Lighthorse went to arrest another Indian partner, Tandy Walker.

Colonel McAlester years later related what happened next:

> We didn't wait for the Lighthorse to return. I wasn't ready to get shot. We went out through the brush to the hill north of town and stayed there till night. When it was safe Dr. Hailey [another partner] brought us a roll of money and some guns. That night we walked north on the railroad till we came to the first section house.
>
> We waked up the section boss, and I said, "We want a handcar and two of the best men you've got; don't ask any questions and you won't know anything." It stumped the boss and he hesitated, but we let him know we meant business. So he rousted out two big Irishmen who were as stout as a team of mules. They got out the handcar and we all piled on, and all of us began to pump . . . We were anxious and went too fast and jumped the track. We managed to get the handcar back on the rails . . . By midnight we were in Eufaula—in the Creek Nation—and out of jurisdiction of the Choctaws.
>
> I stayed in Eufaula making plans to combat Governor Cole. As I was the largest owner of coal rights, it was me he was after. Pulsey and Walker got together secretly and raised fifty men. They went to Governor Cole and laid down the law to him. At the same time I sent some of my friends to Cole . . . They told him if a hair of my head was harmed they would hang his hide on the fence, and he believed them . . .[32]

After "things settled down," McAlester called on Governor Cole in Atoka, where he had moved his office. "I pulled the paper out of my pocket," McAlester recalled, "and showed him that I had a right to the lands occupied by me and my partners; that right had been given me by the government agent and sanctioned by his own Choctaw government.

"He claimed he never knew this and if he had known he would never have moved against me. I never had trouble with Cole after that. I proposed to divide the coal royalty with the Choctaw Nation and this

---

[32] *Chronicles of Oklahoma,* (Vol ll, No. 2—June 1933), p 763

settled the question until the Dawes Commission came down here and made a lot of trouble."[33]

Playful raccoons, it turns out, helped save McAlester from the firing squad. "I was told later," he said, "Governor Cole cleared off a place at the mouth of Bushy Creek and said we would be shot there next day, but if coons came out and played that night on the cleared place it would be a bad omen. Lucky for us—that night coons came out and wallowed all over the clearing!"[34]

The Choctaw, Oklahoma and Gulf Railway came into the Territory but its greed kept Bucklucksy from being renamed "McAlester" and resulted in creating two towns—North McAlester and South McAlester. As Colonel McAlester explained: "I wanted the railroad to come to my town, but the promoters wanted me to give then ten thousand dollars and all interests in my townsite. I refused. They moved the tracks a mile south and started a town of their own called 'South McAlester.' I told them they could not get title to that land . . . In the courts they learned their titles were no good . . .I bought up the judgments and in that way became a large property holder in their townsite."[35]

A few years later, as both grew, the two McAlesters were joined into one town.

Indians hated the railroad invasion. They were powerless to stop it. The federal government had browbeaten the Five Civilized Tribes in an 1866 treaty into authorizing two railway lines in Indian Territory. One would cross north to south, the other east to west. They were needed, Washington argued, to permit efficient troop movements —"so as to help us better protect our red brothers."

Eastern capitalists sent in agents to badger and bribe tribal leaders for greater right-of-way land grabs, tax abatement, other extra privileges. It got worse when the trains started running. Fares were doubled in the Territory for passengers and shippers. Trains ran over cattle and hogs roaming loose on the range, and damage payment was denied. Engineers

---

[33] *Loc., cit.*
[34] *Loc., cit.*
[35] *Ibid.,* p 764

willfully blocked road crossings. Whiskey was sneaked in. Railroads connived to gain control of Indian coalmines.

Chief Cole in 1876 dispatched to the Secretary of the Interior a list of seven suggested changes to create a new government railroad policy that was fairer to Indian tribes. There was no immediate change; the Indians were accustomed to Congressional foot-dragging. Yet over the next few years the situation was somewhat bettered.

Victor Locke, closely watching these maneuvers over Chief Cole's shoulder, profited personally. He picked up quite a few pointers on how to finagle and influence Indian Territory railroaders. A few years down the road he would put that knowledge to good use for his own purposes.

3

Gunplay and a Passel of Babies

AT THE AGE of only fifteen, Victor Locke closed his left eye, squinted with his right down the sights of his rifle, squeezed the trigger—and killed his first man. Seeing his .58 calibre bullet pierce the Yankee's blue jacket jolted this Confederate boy-soldier's nerves. But over time he grew accustomed to the battlefield routine. He killed the next, and the next, and the next . . . In four years as a cavalryman, he lost count.

As a civilian, too, he had blood on his hands. At least two deaths he readily admitted—assassinating his grandpa's murderer, and the fatal fight with the "sassy" freed slave in Louisiana.[1] For the rest of his turbulent life, Victor Locke's right hand would never be far from a loaded six-shooter or a Winchester. He was destined to be involved in too many shooting scrapes to count. One would go down in government records as "the Locke-Jones War."

He was a crack shot; with a .22 at seventy yards he unfailingly could hit a chicken in the head or neck.[2] Locke never ran from a gunfight, and grew gray without losing much sleep over where his bullets found their mark.

---

[1] *Locke Family History*, p 202

[2] *Pushmataha County—The Early Years*, p 239

In this rough wilderness frontier the plain facts of life were that the scales of justice quite frequently were tipped by the fastest draw of a six-shooter. When cattle rustlers and desperadoes became brazen, vigilantes saddled up and went out with a rope and firearms to personally mete out lethal punishment.

There existed an established apparatus for Choctaw and Chickasaw lawbreakers to be haled before judges and juries in tribal courts. The guilty suffered inhumane lashings or the firing squad. It was no rarity, however, for Choctaws in their blood-for-blood feuds to personally settle scores with gunplay, often in stand-up duels.

The Indians' deep fear of sorcery also could turn Choctaws into a killer mob. An Indian even falsely accused of being a witch, usually an old woman, most often was executed on the spot without trial.

White people in Indian Territory were then under the jurisdiction of federal court for the Western District of Arkansas, located at Fort Smith. That always meant a long trip—by horseback or wagon—to appear before "Hanging Judge" Isaac Parker. From the lower part of the Choctaw Nation that required traveling about one hundred miles each way; the trip was burdensome for defendants, attorneys, and especially witnesses. Even though Judge Parker held court virtually daylight to dark six days a week, trial of Indian Territory crimes was anything but rapid.

Serving arrest warrants and delivering witness summons from Judge Parker's court in Indian Territory was a tiring, saddle-sore burden for the two hundred or so deputy U.S. Marshals from Fort Smith and at times deadly. Over the thirty- or forty-year span of frontier lawlessness, between one hundred and two hundred marshals were killed on duty.

In June 1878 one such United States deputy rode horseback from Fort Smith into Doaksville carrying in his saddlebags a warrant to arrest Victor Locke for murder.

Little is known today about that accusation against him—except that it turned out to be an unsolved murder mystery!

Lengthy research seeking facts about this 125-year-old murder turned up no details except a half-dozen pages of records from the files of the U.S. Commissioner attached to Judge Parker's court. They don't tell much. There are three main documents—an "information," the arrest warrant and a summons for witnesses. These papers are stored away in the National Archives and Records Administration at Fort Worth, Texas.

The confrontation between the U.S. Marshal and Victor Locke was apparently without incident. The accused man was handed the deputy's warrant, called a capias, which reads:

> United State of America
> Western District of Arkansas
>
> The President of the United States, to the Marshal for the Western District of Arkansas—Greeting:
>
> WHEREAS, complaint on oath hath been made before me, charging that William Spring, V. M. Locke, one Jones, one Durham, and Walter McDonald did, on or about the 1st day of April A.D., 1878, in the Indian country, Western District of Arkansas, commit the crime of murder contrary to the form of the statute in such cases made and provided, against the peace and dignity of the United States.
>
> Now, therefore, you are hereby commanded, in the name of the President of the United States, to apprehend the said Wm. Spring, V. M. Locke, one Jones, one Durham and Walter McDonald and bring their bodies forthwith before me, James Banzzolana, Commissioner appointed for the United States District Court for said District, wherever they may be found, that they may be then and there dealt with according to law for such offence.
>
> Given under my hand, this 15th day of June 1878 in the 102 year of our independence.
>
> JAMES BANZZOLANA
> Commissioner, U.S. District Court,
> West. Dist. Ark.[3]

The witness document summoned the following: "two brothers Reid, one Mock, Dr. McDonald, and two witnesses, names unknown."

Only in the formal "information" is it revealed that there were two victims—William Holsten and William Jacks, and that the dastardly

---

[3] District Court of U.S.,Western District of Arkansas, Criminal Defendant Records Group 21, National Records and Archives Administration, Southwest Division, Fort Worth

deed took place April 1, 1878. The place is not mentioned. For jurisdiction purposes, the document identifies the dead as "white men, not Indians." There is nothing in hundreds of pages of Locke family correspondence and records and Choctaw history examined for this book that sheds any more light on this intriguing misadventure.

Normal procedure would have been followed. Victor Locke doubtless was taken into custody and his "body" transported to Fort Smith. What happened after that is too murky to clearly understand; except that Victor Locke somehow went free!

The reason for his release can be deduced from hand-written notations that appear on the cover of the arrest warrant:

---

not much evidence

---

investigate further

Can not find any evidence
to connect these parties
No corpus delicté shown

[4]

Nothing seemed to change for him in Doaksville. There is no evidence that being embroiled—in fact, arrested—in a mysterious double-murder investigation in the least diminished "Dick" Locke's standing as a prominent consultant and activist in Choctaw Nation governmental and successful business affairs.

He was expanding further into the cattle and horse business. He was much taken with the runty "wild" Choctaw ponies. They had markedly odd characteristics including potbellies plus frizzy long manes and tails. Victor Locke concluded they were a truncated breed

---

[4] *Loc., cit.*

ignobly evolved from mares that Spanish explorers brought to the American West.

He also made money by creating a gathering and marketing strategy for snakeroot, which Indians dug up and traded for food and necessities. Found in the forests, it was any of various plants, such as black cohosh, rattlesnake master, sanicle, or wild ginger, whose roots were reputed to cure snakebite, and be otherwise useful medicine.

Perhaps his most rewarding success in the early Doaksville years required the 100 percent co-operation of Susan Priscilla, who seemed breathlessly happy. She was not only energetic and active in housekeeping, but was understudying her husband so as to pick up business technique and acumen. None of that kept them from being in the baby business in a big way!

After three boys, the oldest then eight, Susan gave birth February 5, 1879 to her first daughter. She was a Wednesday child, small and fragile. She was named Mary A., but was known in the family as "Dolly" on account of her size. [As an adult, she became a Francophile and was sometimes called *Tantè.*]

On Monday, December 5, 1881, came another boy, named Japhet Sharp (both family names from Tennessee). His nickname was simply "Japhie." Born frail and sickly, he was doomed to a short life—one year and eight months. Japhie died August 10, 1883.

One of the most talented children, Benjamin Davis, was born Wednesday, October 17, 1883. He was to become an Indian writer, storyteller, and poet. He would have a distinguished military career before meeting tragic illness.

Five days before her thirty-first birthday, Susan Locke delivered her seventh child—all within a span of fourteen years. This was another boy, born Tuesday, November 3, 1885. He was named Jesse Nelson, but grew up not fond of the name, and was elated that his father called him "Babe." As an adult he was happy-go-lucky, and probably had as many friends as any contemporary in the Choctaw Nation; but at age twenty-seven he was to die of a mysterious gunshot.

Basically that was the Locke brood during their years in Doaksville. As the family resided elsewhere in the Choctaw Nation, Susan bore three more children, two of whom were star-crossed and one who by sheer luck escaped a sensational death in the Atlantic Ocean.

On Sunday, February 12, 1888, a boy was born, who was named Edwin Snow. For some unknown whim, his father labeled him "Alexander Hamilton," and the new moniker stuck. Alex would leave home to become a Catholic priest, traveling further from the nest than any of his siblings. Alex, on honeymoon in London, in 1912 was scheduled to sail home on the maiden voyage of the *Titanic.* He and his bride failed to get aboard because money to buy their tickets didn't reach him in time. The ocean liner never made it to America, striking an iceberg the night of April 14-15, 1912 and sinking with the loss of 1,500 passengers.

The final Locke children were Thomson McKinney, born Tuesday, July 22, 1890, and Hugh White, born Monday, March 21, 1892. The last baby arrived about seven months before Susan's thirty-eighth birthday; she had delivered ten children in twenty-one years.

Father Dick chose a perky nickname for Thomson McKinney—"Dude." This was their only child with blue eyes. The boy lived only eight years. He was killed February 23, 1898 by a supposedly accidental blow to the head by a baseball bat. Details of the tragedy are sketchy, cloaked in an aura of mystery.

Hugh White was another of their frail, sickly infants. Victor dubbed him "Little Boss." The boy failed to develop any strength or stamina and died at age two years three months on August 21, 1893.

THE AGE OF INNOCENCE was not denied the Locke children in the 1880s despite growing up in a raw and rambunctious frontier town like Doaksville. Their eyes were opened to the good as well as the brutal. At an early age they learned to swim, ride ponies, to appreciate parental love and the beauty of scintillating sunsets, and enjoy the magic of primeval forest and spring-fed crystal stream.

They were likewise steeled by observing the darker side of mankind—the flash of a six-gun and the bullet-riddled man falling in the street.

Victor Junior as an adventuresome eight-year-old often had Dolly, five, as his exploring partner. They boldly went to play inside the dim-lit small rock building that had been abandoned as Doaksville's jail. They ran out, swatting their legs and arms, screaming. The place swarmed with fleas.

An ancient hand-drawn map shows Doaksville to be a collection of thirty or so buildings, primarily on a north-south street intersecting the old military road. Nearby is spring-fed Gates Creek that runs into a large swamp separating the town from old Fort Towson. The creek also runs southeast of Doaksville through a cancerous-looking area shown in black on the map, and labeled "hills and gullies."

Little numbered squares represent building locations. Names on the identification list include: Church, school, Byrd Hotel, John Kingsbury, Forbis Leflorė, Dr. Pugh, Dr.'s office, first tin shop, very nice white residence, Davis drugs and notions, Berthletts general store, one room stone jail, old log building used as a school, blacksmith shop, and Dr. Davis residence. On the western edge of town was "the graveyard." Pine Ridge Mission School was shown about two miles to the northwest.

The young people had nothing to fear because "our community was safe," Dolly reminisced years later, writing about strolling with two "nice and refined" older neighbor girls:

> Often we walked miles. They took a little bucket with them once, to gather strawberries for their papa. I was sorry I never thought to bring one. We walked across an abandoned field and along an old rail fence and found so many luscious strawberries. After we had gathered and eaten strawberries, we went on and came to a pretty branch with sandy banks and water like crystal.
>
> We thought how nice to go swimming and we did. After quite a while we knew it was time to get on our clothes and start back. On our way we would stop, climb young saplings, bend them over and pretend we were riding our ponies. We would not just walk along, but look around to see something new.
>
> We had such happy years. They were like fairyland. When we would get home, our parents never asked where we had been—they knew we were safe.[5]

---

[5] Mary E. Archer to Susan Locke Charlesworth, June 1949, from "To Susan and Her Sisters," collection of letters and stories written by Dolly Archer to the daughters of her nephew Nelson A. Locke and his wife Arlene in the 1940s and

Dolly loved clouds "very much" and one afternoon found herself watching them sail overhead. With one foot on an old iron kettle and holding a low branch of a tree, she began singing, *Oh, my little brother up in the clouds. Oh, my little brother!*

"That was after my baby brother Japhet had passed away," she recalled. "I heard someone say he had gone to Heaven and knowing Heaven was up in the clouds I was singing to him because I missed him very much."[6]

After a heavy rain, she discovered a partially buried new boulder. The older neighbor girls told her it fell from Heaven. "We were just little children, but I thought it was true." In the spring Dolly would gather resin and sweet gum, cook it with grapes or berries, and make a durable chewing gum. A platter of venison often graced the Locke breakfast table, she recalled:

> Another large bowl of grits, and one of gravy. A standard dish of wild honey and at the other end was a dish of ham or bacon and fresh eggs. Venison is very strengthening, and we all had perfect constitutions.[7]
>
> * * *
>
> When snow comes, I always think of blackbird pie. Blackbirds were flying all around with snow on the ground. Our teacher's husband killed enough to make a pie for all the pupils. It was delicious, in a large pan, very highly seasoned in true Southern style, with a brown crust and good sauce. My first treat of this celebrated dish, and I never had it so good again.[8]

Victor Junior saw more of the grittier side of life in Doaksville, and seemed to take it all in stride. He observed and admired Judge E. W. Timms, who ran a general store and the post office out of a large warehouse kept heavily stocked because occasional floods blocked the trails

---

1950s, owned by Francine Locke Bray and filed in Garrard Ardeneum Manuscript Collection

[6] "To Susan and Her Sisters," July 14, 1949

[7] *Ibid.,* January 12, 1955

[8] *Ibid.,* undated

traveled by freight wagons. The judge acted "as sort of banker" for the community and "kept a lot of money on hand." In later years, Victor told an interviewer:

> One night the store was broken into and robbed. Only money was taken, several thousand dollars in gold, money Judge Timms had hoarded up for banking. An eighteen-year-old boy was prowling around that night and saw the robbers and recognized them.
>
> They found out this boy knew . . . and a few days later that boy was 'piddling around' in a boat on the Kiamichi River, and he was shot and killed. Shot from the bank of the river. It was never investigated. Then one man supposed to have taken part in the robbery killed the other one.
>
> That's the way things went those days.
>
> Three young men met on the streets of Doaksville one evening. They really were sworn enemies, but each one, being afraid the other 'would get the drop' on him, pretended friendship. They went to the home of a beautiful Choctaw woman with whom all were infatuated. They sat around and talked, watching each other like tigers.
>
> The woman sent one out to feed his horse, which had been hard-ridden. Pretty soon one followed him outside. A shot was heard. One man came back in. About ten o'clock the two men went outside and "discovered" the third man's body. They pretended they thought that instead of feeding his horse, he had ridden off.
>
> Nothing was done about it. His folks just came and buried him.
>
> Two brothers, Cub and Sam Stanley, were at the table eating at the home of Jack Crittendon when they began a violent quarrel over a woman. They decided to 'settle' the feud, so they fought a duel and killed each other.
>
> I wonder that so many killings did not depopulate the country. It was clearly a time of the 'survival of the fittest' or perhaps it would be best to say it was the survival of the one who could draw a gun the quickest.[9]

On the family pony named "Sewell," Dolly would ride "double" sitting behind her mother who was in the saddle. Sometimes they went

---

[9] *Locke Family History*, p 294

on trips of ten or fifteen miles. "Sewell" had a very easy pace but could run fast. Dolly yearned to ride like a "grown-up, holding the reins and quirt." One afternoon when Susan was busy with household chores, the little girl seized her chance. She remembered it thus:

> I knew to go somewhere one had to be fixed up. So I got my new hat. I climbed up into the saddle—a man's saddle. I reached and reached and finally got the bridle reins. Then I took the riding quirt and gave Sewell a big whack. He bounded off in a flying run, me holding the saddle horn and crying and yelling.
>
> I do recall losing my precious new hat and mother coming with it in her hands, and how all the boys in the swimming hole stood up and looked in such wonder as Sewell and I flew by. At the store about two blocks away, Sewell stopped as suddenly as he had started.
>
> The clerk was outside and lifted me off. I ceased to weep, and even so young had a somewhat victorious feeling. I had taught myself how to ride! I tried to everything the men and boys did.[10]

Dolly was still a small child when the carefree days in Doaksville came to an end.

For some time Victor Locke had felt hemmed in, feeling his desire for business expansion stifled. He rode out to carefully explore the open and verdant plains closer to the Kiamichi Mountains. In the foothills he found an attractive location. It was twenty miles northwest of Doaksville, on the banks of White Creek, and close to the Kiamichi River.

On moving day, cowhands rounded up his horses and livestock and hit the trail. Into a string of freight wagons Victor Locke loaded their furniture and household effects, his essential general store stocks, and most everything else moveable. He cracked his bullwhip and the caravan rolled out.

Reaching the prairie banks of White Creek, Locke unloaded, set up temporary shelter—and founded his own town. He called it White Church (in Choctaw *Itissa-Busha*). Under his hard drive, it soon flourished into a village. Since it was one of the precincts for Choctaw elec-

---

[10] "To Susan and Her Sisters," Aug. 6, 1949

tions, the tribal government changed the name to "Lockstown," in honor of the founder.[11] (In present day Oklahoma it is Dela, on State Highway 3, in Pushmahata County.)

In a burst of activity, Victor Locke opened a general store, and set up a sawmill, a gristmill, and a cotton gin, all located on White Creek. He also expanded his herds of cattle and horses as there was plenty of good open range free for Indians, and the Choctaw blood of his wife and children qualified the family enterprise.[12]

His son, Victor Junior, recalled that his father "had a foreman named Bill Flinchum who ran these mills for him. The gristmill took a toll of one-fourth of the corn after it was ground. The saw mill sold lumber green for 50 and 75 cents per hundred feet and the cotton gin took cotton seed as pay for ginning."

Another profitable Locke venture was a ferry across the nearby Kiamichi River. Though small, it was the only crossing of the Kiamichi within miles, and was kept busy. Running the ferry was turned over to a Negro handyman named Mack Hill, who became Victor Locke's lifelong aide-de-camp and "bodyguard."

Lockstown drew customers from a wide area, and its monarch rapidly grew rich. But within a few short years he would get itchy feet—and again pull up stakes and move.

AS HE ENTERED HIS FORTIES, Victor Locke frequently stoked up his pipe, drew on it, and spewed angry smoke into the night sky with a frown that was half perplexity and half determination. The state of tribal affairs in the 1880s had turned increasingly perilous. He was not at all certain that every Choctaw Nation leader was up to riding the tiger. That made him stew and mutter that perhaps the time had come for him to get involved.

Of course he couldn't be chief, even though wife Susan boasted he would be an excellent head man. Indian blood was required; he had

---

11 *Locke Family History,* p 203

12 *Loc., cit.*

not a drop. Yet, if he went at it cleverly, he might wedge himself in behind the scenes to become a mover and shaker. So he set out to do that.

To achieve influence, Victor realized, would mean going around or through the celebrated McCurtain family, and either charming or head-butting them. He felt up to that challenge. Victor Locke had no particular quarrel with the McCurtains. Their concerns for the future of the Choctaw, in general, were his. But the tribe was precariously split; it would take a lot of work to corral and meld the variant opinions for forward movement.

Being an "outsider," a renegade from the Civil War who had luckily gained refuge in Indian Territory and married a Choctaw girl, he realized he came close to being one of the hated white settler intruders who were resented by the Choctaws. On the other hand, he had become almost one of the tribe; they had taken him as a friend and counselor. He was regarded as a "white" Choctaw.

Over the years, Victor Locke had learned much about the fantastic history of the McCurtains, and the events that had propelled them into prominence from Mississippi days into leadership in the new country. Their roots were deep, reaching back to Shomaka, the maiden spared in a tribal massacre because of her beauty, and who lived to be 120. Her granddaughter, Mahayia, affectionately called "Amy," married Cornelius McCurtain in Mississippi. Three of their seven children were to become Choctaw principal chiefs in Indian Territory. [13]

The McCurtains were proud and fearless. It was widely known that any harm done the family would bring certain retaliation. They lived by the ancient blood-for-blood creed, and did not hesitate to use it. Two McCurtain men were murdered in 1874 and their brothers boldly carried out revenge assassinations. Hearing these dramatic stories brought back Victor's own dark memories of avenging his Tennessee grandfather's murder. In the McCurtain tragedies he saw distinct similarities.

In April 1874 David McCurtain was killed by a Negro named Charles Brown. A day or two later Brown was slain by David's brother, Green McCurtain, then twenty-six years old, and destined to become in

---

[13] John Bartlett Meserve, "The McCurtains," *Chronicles of Oklahoma,* (Vol 13, No. 3): pp. 298-300

about two decades principal chief. Five months later, in August, another brother, Robert McCurtain, was murdered in Scullyville at the home of former Governor Tandy Walker. The killer, Tandy Walker's son Henderson, leaped on his horse and fled the territory. Motive for the unprovoked shooting was never explained. Henderson Walker ventured back to the Choctaw Nation three years later. That was a mistake. Jackson Frazier McCurtain, Robert's forty-seven-year-old brother, found and shot him.[14] Three years later Jackson was the first of the McCurtain brothers to become principal chief.

Like many Choctaws, the McCurtains were mixed blood, white men having married into their family as early as the 1700s. Few of them had more than brief primary education, but their three chiefs were men of culture, purpose, and intelligence. Each served their red brothers exceptionally well in the turbulent and turgid transformation from tribal government to American citizenship and finally Oklahoma statehood.

Victor Locke was impressed with the sheer size of Jackson Frazier McCurtain, six-two and weighing two hundred twenty pounds. He came with his family to Indian Territory at age three. At fourteen he spent two years in Spencer Academy. He was a member of the National Council when the Civil War erupted, and joined the First Regiment of Choctaw and Chickasaw Mounted Rifles as captain of Company G. During the war, a hard-boiled Confederate inspector wrote about him: "Zealous, diligent and attentive to duties. Sober."[15]

At war's end Jackson McCurtain came back to his home, "The Narrows," at Red Oak in Sugar Loaf County. He won election to the Choctaw senate, a seat he held steadily. Principal Chief Isaac Garvin, died in 1880 and Jackson McCurtain, as president pro tem of the senate, was automatically elevated to serve the unexpired seven months of Garvin's term. In the next two elections for principal chief, Jackson McCurtain won easily, and served the maximum four years until 1884.

It was then Edmund McCurtain's time. He was elected at forty-two to succeed his celebrated brother, but felt overshadowed by Jackson's achievements, and declined re-election. Described as "modest and

---

[14] *Ibid.*, p 301
[15] *Ibid.*, p 302

retiring but inflexibly honest," his term as chief in no way blemished the splendid McCurtain tradition.[16]

In Jackson McCurtain's four years (1880-1884) as principal chief, the tribal government was encountering crossroads that stumped and confused the typical Choctaw. Most of these still largely primitive natives faced perplexities and decisions that were too daunting for their limited knowledge of the onrush of civilization and change.

Their world was a remote and isolated cocoon—the wilderness that stretched one hundred miles north of the Texas' Red River boundary and extended one hundred miles west of the Arkansas border, a vast chunk of bluestem prairie and forested mountains which is the present day southeastern quarter of Oklahoma. In his then fifteen years of living among these people Victor Locke observed they evolved into two sharply divided economic classes—*haves* and *have-nots.*

Up in the hills or valleys, usually near a spring or stream, he would regularly find the typical Choctaw family on a one- or two-acre farm, in a rude log cabin, raising minimal crops of corn, beans, pumpkins, and melons. At most they would have a small cattle herd, four or five ponies, a dozen hogs, and chickens. To augment their 100 annual bushels of corn, they hunted rabbits, squirrels, turkeys and deer, and caught fish.

These were the poor.

Largely content with their lot, lacking ambition, most were just living day by routine day, peaceful (except when stirred to violence by whiskey or feuds). Since all tribal land was commonly owned, any citizen was entitled to have as large a farm as he could handle, and to graze big herds on the free open range. For two main reasons, the poor opted to stay small. First, they rarely received actual money because government annuities or interest payments to the tribe were slow and niggardly. Even the Choctaw Nation's treasury was modest; the year 1884 ended with a balance of $38,958.62.[17]

Secondly, they suffered all too frequent crop failures, due to flood or bad weather. Each loss of their mainstay corn threatened the

---

[16] *Ibid.*, p 306

[17] *The Rise and Fall of the Choctaw Republic*, p 194

poor with famine. Such a disaster caused great distress, perhaps some starvation, in 1874. The Choctaw Nation asked Congress to release $200,000 in tribal funds for relief, which it did. But Interior Secretary Delano refused to send the money.[18] When crops failed in 1881, without waiting for National Council approval, Chief Jackson McCurtain used $6,000 of tribal funds for destitute families.[19] His quick action was praised and promptly approved at the next Council meeting.

Of the 20,000 Choctaws, Victor Locke estimated only two hundred or three hundred constituted the affluent and influential class. From their ranks almost exclusively came the elected officials who guided the destiny of the Choctaw Nation.

They were the *haves,* the rich.

Ambitious, bold, risk-takers, they were inclined to seize what they wanted, often by heavy-booted action. On arrival from Mississippi in the 1830s, owning slaves, affluent Choctaws jumped in and established plantations that stretched across miles of Indian Territory bottomland. Several grazed cattle by the thousands on the enormous open free range. Later laws were enacted limiting individual holdings to one square mile. Generally these restrictions were not retroactive; as a result some wealthy Choctaws were able to retain their huge ranches. One such spread covered ten square miles, and another six square miles.[20] Even Chief Edmund McCurtain had 300 acres under cultivation, and grazed 500 head of livestock.[21]

"The labor on these farms," says historian Angie Debo, "was usually performed by several white or Negro tenants, who lived in small cabins and cultivated the land for a share of the produce."
She adds:

> If a Choctaw wished to extend his holdings he would employ a "laborer" for a period of five to ten years and locate him on some unimproved portion of the public domain. In this case the white man paid no rent, but he was expected to break the land, fence it, and erect a

[18] *Ibid.*, p 112
[19] *Loc., cit.*
[20] *Ibid.*, p 110
[21] *Ibid.*, p 111

> house. At the end of the time the improvements became the property of the Indian. This custom also enabled thrifty Choctaws to provide improved farms for their children when they should come of age. The leasing of the public domain to non-citizens was made illegal in 1877, but the law was generally evaded by the simple fiction of classing the lessees as laborers.[22]

What did Victor Locke hope to accomplish by slipping in through the back door of the Choctaw government apparatus? In his mind the *have nots*—the little people—needed a champion in the councils where the fate of the tribe was being decided. Victor Locke would be their champion.

There was clear irony here. He was not poor; in fact, his extensive business interests flourished. He grew richer by the day. If not one of the *haves,* he was in spitting distance of being.

Still his eagle eye discerned all kinds of injustices that demeaned, denied, and subdued the tribe's weak and impoverished. That wasn't right. Especially when many advantages enjoyed by the affluent came from crooked practices—bribery, peculation, nepotism, and so forth. A lot of winking went on in high places. A law was enacted in 1880 to punish embezzlers with 100 lashes; but no Choctaw official ever had a bloody back.[23] Bribery was outlawed in 1890, and that law, too, was ignored.

Steadily Victor Locke developed effective contacts in the tribal hierarchy. His easy smile won friends, as did his wit, his incisive grasp of the perplexing pressures designed to rob the Choctaws of their tribal independence, and his cogent ideas for workable solutions. He was gaining ground on his goal of becoming a behind-the-scenes power.

Then he hit a roadblock.

The sensible McCurtains listened to Victor Locke's opinion. They went along with his helpful suggestions. But he got the definite fish-eye from the "Indian cattle king" of the Choctaws, one of the richest men in the Territory, a mixed blood named Wilson Nathaniel Jones.

---

[22] *Loc., cit.*.

[23] *The Rise and Fall of the Choctaw Republic,* p 149

Their rivalry and vocal jousts would gradually turn bitter and louder. Ratcheting up into bloody violence was the next looming threat. Within a decade their political opposition would explode into the most infamous "war" in Choctaw Nation annals.

Victor Locke hardly could have made a worse enemy. Wilson Jones clearly had his wolfish eye fixed on becoming principal chief; he'd stomp anything in his way.

The "cattle king" was lucky. But some of his luck was bad, personally tragic. With only $500, Wilson Jones had started a small farm in the late 1840s. He avoided military service in the Civil War. With a partner, he opened a general store in Caddo. Since little money was circulated, he traded merchandise for livestock. Quickly he was on his way up.

At his peak, Wilson Jones had 5,000 cattle grazing on 17,000 acres between Caddo and the Boggy River.[24] His mansion near Caddo rivaled the finest in the Territory. He had a 550-acre farm, mainly planted in cotton. His Caddo store hummed; he operated a cotton gin, and had lucrative shares in coal mining.

On his way to getting rich, the cattle king took a hard blow. In 1871 he and a partner, James Myers, had accumulated one thousand cattle. Myers drove the herd overland to market in Fort Scott, Kansas. He sold the cattle, pocketed the money—and disappeared. That left Wilson Jones stuck with big debts. He managed to liquidate them, and again get rich. But personal tragedy lay ahead.

The cattle king sent his only son, William "Willie" Jones, to "the states" for a good education, and on his return in 1883 at age twenty-three made him foreman of the ranch. "Willie" was "loveable" but "addicted" to whiskey. [25]

And drunk or sober, Willie was quick with his six-gun.

On the Caddo main street on September 18, 1885, Willie was walking and talking with Madison Brouton, a friend and neighboring rancher. Without warning, Willie drew his pistol and fatally shot Brou-

---

[24] John Bartlett Meserve, "Chief Wilson Nathaniel Jones," *Chronicles of Oklahoma,* (Vol 14, No.3) p 423
[25] *Ibid.*, p 425

ton. Then he calmly mounted up and rode back to his father's ranch. Nothing was done about the murder; gossipers said Brouton was complaining to Willie that the Jones brand had been put on some of his calves.[26]

In this lawless age of range wars and the law of the six-gun in the Choctaw Nation, rivals of Wilson Jones were wise to stay wary of his son Willie. An intermarried Choctaw named Alex Powell did not. Powell opened a small store and cattle ranch, which began growing, slightly competing with Jones. Powell answered the night bell at his store and two shots rang out. He lived long enough to identify Willie and the latter's ranch sidekick, Steve Belvin, as his attackers.

Belvin also took shots at a Caddo store clerk named L. A. Morris, who was blamed in 1882 by Wilson Jones for getting him in a financial jam. Belvin's bullets seem to have missed their mark. (Later Steve Belvin was elected sheriff of Jackson County, Choctaw Nation.)

"No effort seems to have been made by the Choctaw Nation authorities to apprehend and punish either young Jones or Steve Belvin for these outrages," wrote historian John Bartlett Meserve. "There were no Ten Commandments around Caddo in those days—mostly rules of the jungle."[27] At that time Wilson Jones was climbing higher in the tribal government. He had just finished a two-year stint as school trustee, and was the current Choctaw National Treasurer.

Then Willie's luck ran out.

In happened the night of January 26, 1888 near Garrett's Bluff on the Red River. Willie was hosting a drunken carousal for three pals, brothers Tuck and Chris Bench and Josh Crowder, who was sheriff of Jackson County. As they downed a lot of booze, Willie turned belligerent. Tuck Bench, sober enough to be afraid, pulled his revolver and killed Willie.

"Sheriff Crowder, half-crazed with drink, witnessed the tragedy and is reputed to have offered no interference," writes Meserve.[28]

Willie was twenty-eight.

---

[26] *Ibid.*, p 424
[27] *Ibid.*, p 425
[28] *Loc., cit.*

When Wilson Jones found his only son's corpse on a Red River sandbar next morning, he went wild. Tuck Bench had fled to Arkansas. Sheriff Crowder and Chris Bench were in hiding. The furious Wilson Jones got all three indicted in the Choctaw district court. He wanted vengeance—but in public and legally.

The indictments got snarled in court. Tuck Jones was never apprehended. Robbers killed Sheriff Crowder while he was trapping. The case against Chris Bench finally was dropped.

Wilson Jones remained an angry father. About to turn sixty, he realized time was growing short to seize the prize he now wanted most desperately— principal chief.

The angry cattle king launched a wild-swinging political campaign that would be relentless and ruthless. Trying to block his path stood a man equally fierce and resolute, Victor M. Locke.

The bullets would soon be flying.

4

Antlers and the Iron Horse

UP TO HIS CHIN in the spring-fed pool, Victor Locke felt the mineral water soothing the ache in his crippled joints. He tilted back his head on a mossy limestone ledge and aimed his blank stare on gauzy cloud ships sailing the high Choctaw sky. He looked quiet and dreamy; but his brain was on fire. His inner eye was picturing a new town. He was ready and anxious to build it here in this virgin forest of tall pine and oak.

The thud of an axe was reassurance son Shub had started chopping down trees to clear the town's first road. He craned his neck and listened. From the north came faintly the clamor of teams struggling to pull over-loaded wagons, of sweaty men shouting at work. And the clang of hammers driving spikes to hold heavy iron rails onto cedar ties.

The railroad was coming!

Major John Gist Farr, scouting the route of the St. Louis and San Francisco Railway's new line from Fort Smith to Paris, Texas, had ridden to Lockstown to consult Victor Locke.

"You know this territory," said Major Farr. "You can help me find locations for stations."[1]

---

[1] *Pushmahata County—The Early Years,* p 34

Their meeting occurred last year, 1885. The Frisco had been struggling to build its roadbed and tracks through this rugged country since 1881 when it got Choctaw Nation approval. Laying the rails all the way from Arkansas across the border into Texas would take another year, maybe two.

On horseback, they had begun their station site search at the Texas boundary. Fifteen miles to the north they found the first location on a grassy plain, and drove a Frisco stake. Major Farr consulted his list. "This station is called Hamden," he said. They rode on.

Another seven miles up the right-of-way brought them to Beaver Creek. Half a mile further north this beautiful mineral spring gushed from a rocky spot. Locke knew this area well. It was only seven miles northeast of his home, his store, his grist and sawmills, and his cotton gin.

This bubbly spring was a watering hole for deer. For Victor Locke it was a health spa. He told Major Farr how rheumatism had last year crippled him, forcing him to walk with crutches. But, he crowed, drinking and bathing in the mineral water "cured me."

Major Farr, who had just resigned as one of "Hanging Judge" Parker's deputy U.S. Marshals, was impressed. With the spring, with the spa story, and with the location as a station site.

"This is it," said Major Farr.[2]

Victor Locke was busily pointing out the dim wild animal trails and telling the history of the Kuniotubbe spring, and how hunters regularly killed deer here, and often nailed the antlers on the tree trunks. He directed the railroad scout's eyes to a tall pine where hung a magnificent nine-prong rack. For a long moment Major Farr looked pensive.

"Antlers," he said. "That makes sense. We'll call this station Antlers."[3]

Thus Victor Locke became the "father" of Antlers, Choctaw Nation, Indian Territory. Fifteen-year-old Shub Locke had the honor of felling the first tree that cleared the town site.

---

[2] *Ibid.*
[3] *Ibid.*

Having this advance knowledge of the Frisco station location was a prize not lost on Victor Locke. Antlers would become the transportation hub for miles and miles of this wilderness. Freight now moved only by wagon, usually with slow ox teams; it took a week for a round trip across the Red River to Paris. Any journey meant saddling a horse or hitching up a buggy. The railroad would change all that!

The railroad tracks would pass near the Antlers spring. Major Farr had staked the location of the railway station close to this spa. Victor Locke and Shub felled trees and created a street connecting the proposed depot to a site fifty yards away where he intended to erect a general store. He would get the jump on everybody, and be the first merchant in Antlers.

Everything worked out. In addition to a two-story trading post, he also opened a livery stable and blacksmith shop, and built a ten-room house. By freight wagon, he moved "lock, stock and barrel" from Lockstown to the new place before the track-laying crews arrived.

As the rails came near, track workers pitched their tents in Antlers in the vicinity of the bubbly spring. Business hummed in the Locke store.

On Friday, July 1, 1887, by horseback, buggy, wagon and on foot, hundreds of Indians and white settlers flocked to Antlers for the arrival of the first "iron horse."

Shortly before noon the waiting crowd at the depot heard the lonesome whistle reverberating from the hills. The train, No. 5, was coming in from Fort Smith. Ten minutes later it thundered to a stop at the Antlers station, belching sooty smoke and cinders.

First passenger off was Major Farr, waving his hat joyfully. He was accompanied by wife Anna Eliza and son Arthur. The major, forty years old, had decided like Victor Locke to go into business in Antlers. He had a sawmill running to turn out railroad ties and bridge timbers.

A South Carolina officer in the Civil War and disenchanted after the South's defeat, Farr had gone to Mexico. He came back to Texas, helped break up the Red River log "raft," and then spent ten years as a deputy U.S. marshal. He studied law by mail, and later would sell his sawmill and practice law in Antlers before becoming its highly praised postmaster for many years.[4]

When Shub Locke chopped down the first tree, no more than three families, all Indians, lived within a mile of the spring. By two or three months after Frisco No. 5 arrived, a dozen or so wooden business buildings and houses were going up. Martha Ann Milligan Miller, a widow, was an early arrival from Dexter with sons John and William to set up a boarding house for the Frisco track workers.[5]

Antlers boomed from the start. Expectations were that coming of the railroad would create a badly needed major shipping point, especially for timber, livestock, and cotton. Choctaws and white settlers alike flocked to the new town. They were ranchers and farmers along with business and professional people.

George Washington Colbert, a prominent Indian stock raiser, left his home at Hickory Grove and brought his wife, daughter and grandson to Antlers. He established a meat market, livery stable, and merchandise business. He built a splendid two-story house called "The Oaks."

A Methodist preacher, Colonel Coleman E. Nelson, arrived and erected a log church one-half mile west of the spring, and a house two miles west of town. Annie Taaffe, whose parents were dead, came with six younger siblings and a lively work ethic. She built a house and opened a successful subscription school.

To clerk in the Locke store, came several young men, including Paul C. Harris, Will Everidge, and Thomas Lowe. Nic Nash came, saw the need for a physician; he promptly went off to study medicine in Louisville and New Orleans. He came back to practice with Antler's "mainstay" doctor, his brother Dr. H. C. Nash.

By Christmas 1887, almost two hundred people lived in Antlers where beef and pork sold for 10 cents a pound at the butcher shop, a cup of coffee was 5 cents, a ham sandwich a dime, and a man could get a shave for 10 cents and a haircut for a quarter. And about every day

---

[4] *Ibid*, p 202
[5] *Ibid.*, p 36

somebody was stepping off the Frisco's two daily passenger trains to stay.[6]

Advent of the railroad gave the Choctaw Nation vastly easier access to "the states," but did not immediately help much in taming the lawless territory. Gunplay, robbery and illegal whiskey running challenged the best efforts of tribal and U.S. lawmen.

Historian Angie Debo estimated that one hundred people were murdered in a single year in the Choctaw Nation, perhaps more. "In one cemetery," she wrote, "there were thirty-one Indians and whites that 'had died with their boots on.'"[7]

Renegades and white "intruders" provoked a "vile and vicious condition" throughout Indian Territory in the mid 1880s that "made crime rampant and human life unsafe," says historian John Bartlett Meserve.[8] During his time as Principal Chief, Jackson McCurtain fought back aggressively. "No one ever bought, bulldozed or bluffed Jackson Frazier McCurtain."[9] The lawbreakers were not easily crushed. And they did manage to frighten the chief.

Teaming up with "Hanging Judge" Parker, McCurtain and his Indian militia managed to run off a great many of the criminal element. Gradually evil "intruders" filtered back into the Choctaw wilderness. They threatened retaliation against McCurtain, and he took the warnings seriously. For safety sake he abandoned his home at "The Narrows," which was isolated and hazardous in the wildest of the Kiamichi range, and moved to a farm south of Antlers. He believed this made his family safer.[10]

Robbers killed a member of the Victor Locke family. Susan's brother, Thomson McKinney Jr., twenty-seven, ran a store in Whitefield, Indian Territory on the Canadian River. Returning from a buying trip to

---

[6] Judge C. E. Dudley, *Days Gone By,* (Pushmahata County Historical Society, reprint 1988) pp 18, 21

[7] *The Rise and Fall of the Choctaw Republic* , p 192

[8] John Bartlett Meserve, "The McCurtains," *Chronicles of Oklahoma,* (Vol 13, No. 2), p 305

[9] *Ibid.*

[10] *Ibid.*, p 304

Fort Smith, he was waylaid by armed men near present day Stigler, Oklahoma, on December 17, 1881 and murdered.[11]

A mixed blood named Reuben Lucas was caught, tried, convicted and sentenced to be shot. Walking to his execution, Lucas put his hand on the shoulder of Camby McKinney, his victim's cousin, and said, "*Camby, aiaulthtubba chi hoke.*" In English that is "you shall be paid."[12]

Camby McKinney could not understand the meaning, unless it was an inapplicable threat of commonly accepted lextalionis. The Indians still held sacred the aboriginal code of blood-for-blood vengeance. Judge Miashintvbbi of Wade County, for one, felt not only justified, but also honor-bound, to go after his brother's killer, a man named Stephens at Mt. Zion.[13] "I am going to Mt. Zion," the judge announced, "and get revenge, or I shall never return."

A bullet dispatched Stephens to an early grave, and Judge Miashintvbbi came proudly home.

At least one prominent Choctaw was innocently caught up in the frontier crime splurge, and dishonored. He was a minister named William McKinney, brother of Principal Chief Thompson McKinney (no relation to Victor Locke's brother-in-law).

The episode involved the celebrated Indian Territory "bandit queen" Belle Starr (1848-1889)—and fortunately for the preacher, and the chief, it turned out well in the end.

In the summer of 1887, Chief McKinney handed his brother a bag containing several thousand dollars to carry to Paris, Texas where the Choctaw Council would distribute the money to tribal schools. What happened next—and the denouement—are told in the Choctaw Nation's official biography of Chief McKinney:

> Placing the money in his saddlebags, William McKinney began his long journey. He was waylaid at a lonely spot by two persons he thought were men. McKinney, unhurt, hurried on to Paris and told the council members what had happened.

---

[11] Locke Family Papers, untitled ms, Garrard Ardeneum Manuscript Collection
[12] *Ibid.*
[13] "The Reminiscences of Peter J. Hudson," *Chronicles of Oklahoma* (Vol. 12, No. 3) p 299

They did not believe his story and he was accused of being an accomplice to the thieves. Thompson McKinney was also under suspicion because he selected his brother to carry out the important mission.

Because of the rumors and accusations, William McKinney was forced to withdraw from active work in the church.

Later, after Belle Starr's death on February 1, 1889, an account of the robbery of William McKinney was found in her handwriting. She told that she dressed as a man and with one of her henchmen had staged the daring holdup.

After this escapade was brought to light William McKinney was immediately exonerated and restored to the full confidence of the tribe. (Coincidentally, Chief McKinney also died in 1889, at his home in Wilburton, only forty-two.)[14]

The coming of the railroads made it easier to smuggle whiskey into the Choctaw Nation, at least for a while. Certain wholesale merchants in St. Louis disguised shipment of liquor in almost every package.[15] Indian Lighthorse tried to inspect freight, but the railroads stopped them. When liquor was discovered, the Lighthorse poured it on the ground. But booze was not easy for the law to find.

Indians, known for their weakness for drink, were encouraged to imbibe. Victor Locke knew personally that in Paris, Texas, a wholesale house kept a bucket of whiskey in a back room where freighters from the Territory could tank up with a handy dipper. In the Choctaw Nation, greedy white speculators would slip booze to Indians, hoping to get them drunk enough to make a foolhardy trade. Fake doctors toured the crossroads selling patent medicine "tonics" that were heavily laced with alcohol.

Then came "Choctaw beer." In its wake, arose extremely complicated enforcement snags.

Choc beer was a distillation of tobacco, fishberries, barley, hops and a small amount of alcohol. It originated in the mining towns around McAlester. The Indian agent banned its sale. But a federal judge approved shipping malt into Indian country. Saloons opened. Indian Agent

---

[14] "Chiefs, Thompson McKinney," Choctaw Nation of Oklahoma

[15] *The Rise and Fall of the Choctaw Republic,* p 189

Leo Bennett tried to close them under his authority to "regulate trade," but nobody went to jail. It was not safe, Bennett said, for a woman to walk the streets.[16]

Congress prohibited the "introduction" of liquor into Indian Territory. That law closed the saloons and breweries. Until a clever lawyer discovered that the one critical word did not extend to "manufacture" or "sale" of booze.

Using this newfound legal dodge, the saloons reopened and flourished.

But not for long. Congress closed all loopholes by passing a law forbidding anyone to "manufacture, sell, give away, or in any manner, or by any means furnish to anyone, either for himself or another, any vinous, malt, or fermented drinks of any kind whatsoever, whether medicated or not, or who shall carry, or in any manner have carried, into said Territory any such liquors or drinks."[17]

That returned whiskey to the realm of sly bootlegging.

Yet immediately after Oklahoma statehood a decade later, the prohibition law would again be stood on its head. Fatuously, the Oklahoma legislature opened state liquor stores, with inadequate safeguards. Fortunately, that unwise law was to be quickly repealed, and these liquor stores closed.

As the railroad boomtown of Antlers grew steadily, the Victor Lockes entered the most pleasant and prosperous period of their lives.

In 1888, the one-time Johnny Reb turned intermarried Choctaw husband was forty-two, healthy and active. Susan, now thirty-four, was nursing her latest and eighth baby, Alex; and was happily eager for more children. (There would be two others, Dude in 1890, and Hugh in 1892.)

Shub, their first, had turned a strapping eighteen, and with a headstrong will of his own. Victor Junior was twelve, and a dedicated and serious student, with a flair for writing. Ben D. and Babe, five and four respectively, were underfoot about the house, or store, or livery stable.

---

[16] *Ibid.*, p 190

[17] *Ibid.*, p 191

Their only daughter Dolly was a bright nine-year-old schoolgirl unleashing her insatiable curiosity about everything on the frontier, and learning to be dauntless as the only feminine foil in a gaggle of boys. Two sons were dead, Charles Guffy, nicknamed "Captain Jenks," in 1879 at almost six, and Japhie in 1883, the frail one who was doomed at seven months.

Even when all of his skies were sunny, Victor Locke was becoming a bit fidgety, and at times looked almost unhappy. His political itch was a rapidly growing torment.

Hopping on the Frisco, going north or south, he ventured out frequently to consult and gossip with Choctaws he counted on as knowledgeable and influential. Those living off in the hills he visited on horseback.

Twice-a-day passenger trains were now bringing him what he found to be a real treasure—newspapers from "the states" that were up-to-date. He pored fairly regularly over the dailies from St. Louis, Kansas City, and Fort Smith. In late March he came across a copy of the *New York Herald* reporting a terrible East Coast blizzard. New York's temperature fell to 10.7 degrees, with snowdrifts 15 to 20 feet high, pedestrians and horses freezing in the streets. Four hundred died, and the storm wrecked 200 coastal ships.

His chief interest was in Washington news; the future of the Choctaws, he was convinced, hung on the whims of Congress and government administrators. All that lay ahead for Indian Territory, he muttered, was probably to get kicked around some more.

Victor Locke smiled when he recalled tales he had been told of the old chiefs being invited to Washington demanding the government outfit them in elaborate $150 coats and $40 pantaloons. Now in the Choctaw Nation, Indian men dressed "American," wearing pants, shirts, coats and shoes; women wore long dresses. He had never seen a Choctaw in leather leggings and war paint. They had for so many years intermarried with whites few had the appearance of savages. Victor Locke laughed when told about two men from "the states" who stepped off the Frisco at the Antlers depot, skeptical and wide-eyed.

One pulled out a $5 bill. "I'd give this," he said, "to see a *real* Indian!"

A black-haired young man dressed about as they were stepped up and grabbed the bill. "You have," he said.[18]

Victor Locke puzzled over news stories about the 1888 election of Benjamin Harrison as the ninth president. What he read was a jumble of information too undecipherable to command attention in Indian Territory. President Cleveland actually had a 100,000-vote plurality, said the *St. Louis Post-Dispatch,* but lost because he captured only 168 electoral votes to Harrison's 233. Reporters went on, too, about the decisive influence of the New York "Irish vote," and British ire over Cleveland's tariff policies.

That was *so what* information to Victor Locke. What he, and in fact the whole Indian Territory, wanted desperately to know was whether President Harrison would do anything to rectify the abuses long heaped on the Five Civilized Tribes.

Would his administration continue to push legislation that inexorably was bent on extinguishing tribal governments, allotting individual tracts of land to Indians, creating the state of Oklahoma, and taking "excess land" from the Indians for white settlement?

Most Choctaws told Victor Locke they saw no sign the tide would change. [Their pessimism would be confirmed in less than a year when President Harrison opened Oklahoma Territory lands formerly reserved for Indians to white homesteaders at high noon, April 22, 1889.]

The Choctaw Nation continually sent tribal delegates to plead their causes in Washington. The trips were expensive, and largely fruitless. With fire in their eyes when they departed Indian Territory, the delegates usually would be cozened in Congress, at the Interior Department, and the White House. The dazzle of the nation's capital city could wreck their focus. They rarely came home with good news. But they were rapt by sight of the Potomoc river greensward, and the height of the just completed Washington Monument stunned them. *"Laksha chito!"* exclaimed some, craning necks to see its five hundred fifty-foot peak.

The key to protecting the Choctaw "little people," Victor Locke concluded, lay in having an intelligent, powerful and aggressive principal

[18] *Days Gone By,* p 33

chief. He kept working with his behind-the-scenes influence to make that happen. Some of his best efforts were getting derailed.

The powerful McCurtains seemed to be drifting away. And more distressing, his "enemy," Wilson Jones, the rich cattle king, decided to run in 1888 for principal chief to succeed Thompson McKinney, who was not seeking reelection.

Victor Locke immediately set out to defeat Jones, urging his followers—perhaps about a thousand—to support the rival candidate, Benjamin Franklin Smallwood, fifty-nine, a wealthy merchant and cattleman, who for a decade had filled several tribal legislative positions, including Speaker of the House.

And the campaign battle was on. The approximately 2,000 to 2,500 Choctaws eligible to vote usually were well divided. That meant a few hundred "swing" ballots could tip the chief's race either way. Victor Locke set out to get them.

In looking for chinks in the armor of Smallwood's rival, Victor Locke discovered a bit of startling tribal history. Wilson Jones had run for principal chief back in 1866. The tally was recorded in the *Journal* of the Choctaw House of Representatives. It showed:

Allen Wright...........552 votes
Jerry Wade............. 367 votes
Coleman Nelson.....265 votes
Peter Folsom.......... 199 votes
Samuel Garland....... 80 votes
Wilson Jones .... 1 vote [19]

"One vote?" Victor Locke couldn't believe his eyes. "One vote!" There would be no such anomaly, he knew, in the 1888 race. The cattle king now had twenty-two years of political experience, and was widely known. He had been elected school trustee and national treasurer.

---

[19] Peter James Hudson, "A Story of Choctaw Chiefs," *Chronicles of Oklahoma,* (Vol.17, No. 2) p 199

For the first time, Choctaws had organized competing political parties—the Progressives, dominated by the McCurtains and Wilson Jones; the Nationals, under the Smallwood-Locke banner.

The campaign was bitterly fought, with vituperative charges and counter slander, and name-calling. To their opponents, the Nationals became the "Buzzards." Locke and his forces taunted the Progressives as "bald eagles" and "pole cats."[20] There was no profanity in the Choctaw language; to "cuss" they had to use white man's words. Their worst epithet is "*Chim ofilusa okpullo*" which means "you are a mean, black, dirty dog."[21]

When the ballots were counted, Victor Locke threw his hat in the air, and was tempted to fire celebratory shots from his six-gun. The cattle king had been beaten; Smallwood was elected principal chief.

It was a squeaky victory—and far from complete. Wilson Jones's Progressives had won control of both houses of the Council. That gave them the power to cut off Smallwood's legislative programs at the knees; and they did.

Animosity remained so high, in fact, Smallwood refused to go to the capitol to be sworn in; instead, he took the oath at the Roebuck Hotel in Tuskahoma.

The paramount reason there had been such a furious battle to win the chief's office was a tempting prize—money. The United States government was poised to send the tribe a large payment of cash. Choctaw officials—many of whom were known to possess sticky fingers—would be responsible for its distribution.

The money, a partial payment on the 1853 sale by the tribe to the government of excess land known as the Leased District, came soon after Smallwood's election.

The money's arrival gave Smallwood a black eye.

As related by historian John Bartlett Meserve:

---

[20] *Report Commissioner of Indian Affairs,* 1892, p 260.

[21] John James, "My Experience With Indians," *The Kiamichi Journal,* October 2002, p 8

> The Chief called a special session of the Council to authorize a distribution of the monies to be made without an audit by the Net Proceeds Commission.
>
> For this rather unseemly action, it appears that the Chief was paid the sum of $5,500 from the monies so received.
>
> The collection and disbursement of this old claim constitutes one of the dark pages in Choctaw history and bears heavily upon the integrity and efficiency of the political life of the Choctaw Nation.[22]

With his legislative program stalemated, Principal Chief Smallwood made a poor showing. Towns were springing up but he was too stiff-necked to let them have self-government for water, sewer and fire protection. He also vetoed vesting the coalmines in the Nation.

Two miserable years as chief disenchanted Benjamin Smallwood. However, he let Victor Locke and the Nationals talk him into running for re-election in 1890. It was a re-play of 1888. The Progressives again put up Wilson N. Jones. Once more it was a mean fight.

John Bartlett Meserve says:

> Jones waged a spectacular campaign . . . The biennial elections in the Choctaw Nation were bitterly contested. There were no dividing issues to provoke a discussion and so the controversy became one of personal vilification of the opposing candidates.
>
> Each campaign became an arena of fierce controversy in which many sordid and illogical were said and done. Appeals were made to passion and prejudice by the use of buncombe and whispered slander.
>
> Politics in the Choctaw Nation were rotten to the core. With the election of Jones, the McCurtains resumed their leadership.[23]

Though trounced politically by the cattle king and the Progressives, Victor Locke could take pride and comfort in the growth of *his* town. Business continued to boom in Antlers. Sawmills and planing mills were humming, powered by dammed streams or by steam boilers.

---

[22] John Bartlett Meserve, "Chief Benjamin Smallwood," *Chronicles of Oklahoma,* (Vol 19, No. 3) p 215
[23] *Ibid.*, pp 215-216

Giant trees whose trunks were two to three feet thick were being felled. They were dumped in the rivers and creeks and floated to saw mills, or hoisted onto ten-wheeled wagon rigs and transported by teams of four to eight oxen.

To do banking, the Choctaw residents had to travel across state lines to either Texas or Arkansas. But there was talk Antlers would soon get its own bank. The coming of the railroad had quickened the arrival of supplies, and helped reduce prices. One hundred pounds of flour now was available for only two dollars.

Cotton growers were increasing the size of their fields. And the snakeroot business had picked up; diggers were now earning $1.50 to $4 a day. Considering the progress of Antlers helped take Victor Locke's mind off the fact that his archenemy Wilson Jones and the Progressives were charting the future of the Choctaw Nation.

Though he had virtually lived by the sword since his boy-soldier days, Victor Locke was at times shocked by the degree of lawlessness on the Indian frontier.

Even children of the Locke clan witnessed the flash of gunfire and bloodletting of the Eighties. The violence was distinctly recalled by Susan Hampton Locke, who married Wilson Locke, a son of Dr. Benjamin Frank Locke. [Susan's relationships were complicated. Her mother Jane Yahombie divorced Julius Hampton and in 1893 married Elisha Locke, brother of Victor and Dr. Frank Locke. That made Elisha Locke her stepfather, and Dr. Frank her father-in-law.]

In an interview in her adult years for the Oklahoma Historical Society, Susan Hampton Locke vividly remembered the wild drama of the frontier days:

> When I was about eight years old my stepfather and my uncles had a shooting scrape; they all shot into our house. It was peppered with bullets. I was in a rocking chair holding the baby when the shooting began.
>
> I crawled under the chair and a bullet entered the wall just behind the place where my head had been. At the first opportunity I slipped out of the kitchen and hid.
>
> My stepfather and Momma's people could not get along. When they had that shooting scrape, a horse was shot out from under

my uncle George Davenport, and he suffered injuries from which he died months later.

I kept wishing we could move to Texas because they said they didn't have such shooting scrapes over in Texas.

x x x

I saw man killed at a camp meeting. He was a full blood Indian, perhaps Choctaw, named Camp Battiest, and he was an officer, too. He was standing in the door of one of the camp cabins when Isaac Ruebens, another full blood Indian, maybe Choctaw, rode up and started shooting him.

He fell. Reubens's horse reared up on his hind legs and Reubens kept shooting down at the man on the ground, whose clothing was in flames from the bullets. Everybody else but poor, silly me was hiding, scared to death.

I didn't have enough sense to be afraid. I wanted to see it. Reubens rode off. Folks came out and poured water on Battiest's burning clothing, but he was already dead. Reubens was sent to the penitentiary, and died there.

Now that was at church. They would let me go to church, but no parties; they were afraid somebody might get rough.[24]

Shub Locke was in love. He would leap on his horse in Antlers and dash northeast up the forest trail four or five miles to the home of the Sherrod family of Choctaws. He was courting their pretty daughter Sinai. Shub tingled to her kisses and vigorously proclaimed his passionate love.

Fully aware of their first-born's romantic quest, Victor and Susan offered no restrictive counsel or caution. After all, Shub was within months of twenty years of age, and he was in all ways, to their minds, a grown man.

Victor had taught him manliness, honor, and how to use firearms in defense of his life and of those he loved. Shub became quick and deadeye with the reliable and popular Winchester rifle, and he could draw and fire the Colts revolver in what the frontiersmen called "a split second."

Still, Victor Locke secretly worried about his first-born son.

---

[24] *Locke Family History*, p 213

Shub Locke was undoubtedly high-strung and headstrong. That was a chancy combination, in his father's view. Still, it would be awkward and perhaps counter productive for him to give too much advice to a still maturing son. So, Victor Locke stood aside and watched and waited.

It was a mistake to not rein in the rambunctious boy.

In his giddy independence, Shub began drinking. He turned—on rare occasions—unruly and offensive. On Tuesday, September 20, 1891, Shub, obviously intoxicated and belligerent, wandered into a religious meeting in Antlers and created a disturbance.

Some one called Antler's deputy U. S. Marshal, James Ashford. The deputy knew and readily recognized Victor Locke's son. Ashford encouraged him to leave and go home and sober up. Shub's resentment and anger flared. There were harsh words. Deputy Ashford finally prevailed, and Shub left the church meeting

That should have ended the encounter. But it did not.

Anger swirled all night in Shub Locke's mind. Next morning, he got up, strapped on his Colts revolver, and went looking for Deputy Jim Ashford.

Shub found him, drew his Colts, and left the deputy marshal lying in the Antlers street with blood pouring from a bullet hole.

Jim Ashford was mortally wounded but lingered for a week. He died Tuesday, September 27, 1891.

A tribal Lighthorse was sent to the Locke home to arrest Shub. At the front door, Victor Locke met the officer with a Winchester in hand. His son, he asserted, would not be surrendered.

When the Lighthorse left to get reinforcements, Victor Locke took Shub high up into the Kiamichi wilderness and hid him in a mountain cave.

Exactly what transpired after that is unclear. Family historical papers suggest that Victor Locke gathered loyal henchmen to keep Shub out of the toils of Choctaw law. There is no indication any confrontation erupted.

Since both the deputy and his slayer were mixed blood Choctaws neither was within the jurisdiction of the federal court in Fort Smith.

A search of "Hanging Judge" Parker's dockets available in the government historical archives at Fort Worth, Texas, comes up blank.

Likewise it is puzzling that apparently no blood-for-blood vengeance was attempted, although the deputy had a father, King Ashford, and a brother, Tom, at the town of Soper, within a half-day's ride.

Within a week or two—again no date is available—Victor Locke agreed to surrender Shub to the custody of the Lighthorse on "condition nothing happens to him."[25]

As near as can be determined, Shub paid no penalty. It is puzzling also that Victor Locke was successful in extricating his son from an outright murder when the Choctaw Nation was under the control of his foremost enemy, Principal Chief Wilson Jones.

Their long and bitter rivalry was by no means a closed chapter.

Simmering hatred and anger on each side was nearing the boiling point. Victor Locke's National henchmen were oiling their Winchesters and plotting gunplay. The "pole cats" in the Wilson Jones Progressive camp were in a similar murderous mood.

By the time the oak leaves fell on the political rivals in September 1892, guns would begin spitting hot lead. Blood would spill, by the gallons. The shooting violence would go down in the record books as the worst war in Choctaw Nation history!

---

[25] Locke Family Papers, Garrard Ardeneum Manuscript Collection

5

Ballots, Bullets and Blood

SUSAN PRISCILLA LOCKE, with sickly four-month-old Hugh in her arms and worry lines deep around her eyes, watched her husband come in their front door carrying three Winchesters glinting the oil of newness. Shub was a step behind, lugging a wooden box of ammunition.

For a moment, Victor Locke paused. He held up the rifles. "In case trouble comes!" he said. She noticed he wore his pearl-handled Colts with a full cartridge belt. Shub stowed the ammo box in a corner of the parlor.

This was mid-July 1892, a torrid afternoon. She hated the relentless summer sun that already had savaged her lilacs, the cuttings for which had been sent by Arkansas kinfolk. Not all landscaping was lost. From the kitchen window her eyes were gladdened by mock orange, hydrangeas, and purple iris abloom. Some wild honeysuckle remained, attracting sparrows, redbirds, blue jays, thrushes, chickadees, hummingbirds, and woodpecker. And her pear trees drew a hated flock of destroying crows.

The fragility of her ninth baby, "Little Boss," filled her heart with constant dread. The little towhead was constantly listless. The doctor could rouse him but little. Her prayers availed nothing.

But by far her greatest worry was her husband's peril. He might be an assassin's target. Nightmares had lately terrorized her. In cloudy dreams she saw men being gunned down. But the images were too vague to tell if Victor was slain. Awake, she admired his courage, but at times considered him "too reckless."

Her passion for Choctaw Nation political life was now flagging. Not so for Victor. He was leading a vigorous effort to unseat Principal Chief Wilson N. Jones, the cattle king he so despised.

The National Party under the Locke banner had nominated a strong, well-educated candidate, Jacob Battiest Jackson, a full blood who had attended college in "the States." A handsome, popular lawyer, and seasoned in public life, Jackson was presently Secretary of the Choctaw national government.

The campaign for principal chief had become hotter than the weather, mean and bitter—and perhaps crooked as well, judging from the tenor of talks she overheard Victor having in the parlor with a steady stream of politician visitors.

Fortunately, the house could accommodate many guests. It was an imposing two-story mansion in a grove of tall trees, with a high attic roof, encircled by verandahs with steamship filigreed railings, forty six-foot windows, stately front steps, and a gazebo just behind the rear entrance. It contained ten large rooms and was easily the largest residence in Antlers.

The race for chief looked like a toss-up right down to election day which fell in the first week in August 1892. The Choctaw Nation had never experienced a political contest so nasty and dangerous. The newspapers stirred up partisan agitation with inflamatory articles. The *Choctaw Herald* supported the in-power Progressives, and the *Indian Citizen* backed the National Party candidate.

At conventions in all seventeen counties of the Choctaw Nation, Jackson men hurled charges of corruption against the Chief Jones administration. These centered on the tribe's "National Agent," Dr. Eliphalet Nott Wright, and Green McCurtain, the nation's Treasurer and brother of former chiefs Jack and Edmund McCurtain.

Dr. Wright had ignited a storm of protest by awarding a contract to Green McCurtain to exclusively sell the timber off the tribal land, refusing to accept competing bids from other Choctaws. That raised fears that McCurtain, in his post as Treasurer, might stoop to chicanery in making per capita payments from the upcoming $3,000,000 Leased District payment.

The campaign rancor became personal and widespread. Peter James Hudson, tribal educator and historian, recounted one hair-trigger episode in Nashoba County a few days before the election. On horseback, he encountered three Choctaws, William Garland and Watson Leflore, both sober, and John Wilkin, who had been drinking.

"John Wilkin walked up to the left side of my horse," Hudson wrote, "and began to talk to me about politics . . . bantering me for a fight. The more he talked the worse he got, finally grabbing my Winchester which I had in a scabbard on the left side of my horse, pulling it out with his left hand and throwing it into his right as if to shoot.

"His two companions came to my rescue, one grabbing the point of the gun and the other the trigger, and held him. They persuaded him to give my gun to me, which he finally did, putting it in the scabbard himself."[1]

Behind the scenes of such public wrangling two political kingpins were pulling the strings—Green McCurtain for the Progressive Party and "Uncle Dick" Locke for Jackson and the Nationals.

This was a deadly game. As early at May, the *Indian Citizen* reported there were "constant accusations on the part of the Nationals to kill Green McCurtain and other opponents."[2] These rumors were heard everywhere every day. They said Dr. Wright was marked for assassination, along with seventeen others.

The election was believed extremely close. The campaigning was hotly disputed, each side claiming poll books were stolen, noncitizens allowed to vote, and returns manipulated. The Nationals gathered unofficial precinct tallies showing that Jackson had defeated Jones, 1833 votes to 1799. They announced their "victory" on both August 5 and August 11 in the *Indian Citizen.*[3] That claim of victory by 39 votes

---

[1] "Reminiscences by Peter J. Hudson," *Chronicles of Oklahoma* (Vol 12, No. 3) p 302

[2] *Indian Citizen,* May 5, 1892

[3] Angie Debo papers, OSU, Box 36, 88-031, and *Indian Citizen,* Sept. 1, 1892

was promptly disputed. The Progressives in the first week of September obtained their own unofficial returns showing Chief Wilson Jones had been re-elected by 47 votes.[4]

With both sides vigorously proclaiming their candidate elected, something had to give.

"The leaders of both factions," states the official U.S. Government report, "called secret meetings of their followers at which meetings it was resolved that certain of their respective opponents must be removed."[5]

The stage was thus set for a shooting war.

The Nationals started it.

Late in the afternoon of Saturday, September 10, 1892, a band of twenty-four mounted Jackson men rode into Gaines County, in upper Choctaw Nation, about eighty miles north of Antlers. They surrounded the home of Joe Hecklechubbie, called him out, and shot him dead. By dark they had assassinated three additional Gaines County Progressives—Frank Frazier, Elias Colbert, and Robison Nelson; all four were officials in the Jones administration.[6] The murderers then rode toward McAlester, eighteen miles to the west, to do some more killing.

By first light on Sunday, September 11, the band of assassins rode through McAlester and set up camp two miles west of town. They hunted up a local National Party member, told him they had killed four Gaines County men, and asked him to lead them to their next intended victim. Their grisly story stunned him.

"You have done a grievous wrong," protested the "terribly shocked" man. "You must stop!"[7]

Rebuffed angrily by the hostiles, he straightway sent a telegram to the U.S. Indian Agent at Muskogee, Dr. Leo E. Bennett, requesting immediate intervention. The wire was delivered about 10 o'clock that

---

[4] *Indian Citizen,* Sept. 8, 1892

[5] *Report Commissioner of Indian Affairs,* 1892, p 260.

[6] Peter James Hudson, "A Story of Choctaw Chiefs," *Chronicles of Oklahoma* (Vol. 17, No. 2) p 207, *Report Commissioner of Indian Affairs,* 1892, p 260, and *Report Commissioner of Indian Affairs,* 1893, p 83.

[7] *Report Commissioner of Indian Affairs,* 1892, p 261

Sunday morning to the thirty-five-year-old man who was to become the key mediator and "hero" of the infamous Choctaw War.

Keen-witted and frank, with piercing dark eyes that reflected courage, tall and slender, Dr. Bennett was one of the most singular men on the Indian frontier in the 1890s. Son of a Union military surgeon, Dr. Bennett became a newspaper reporter in 1869 at Fort Smith, where his father had been appointed the "carpetbagger" postmaster by President Grant. He then studied at Rugby and the University of Michigan before switching to the University of Tennessee where he earned his medical degree in 1883.

He began his private practice in Eufaula, I. T., and married an Indian girl, Louie Stidham, youngest daughter of the Chief Justice of the Creek Nation. Dr. Bennett established two newspapers, the *Indian Journal* at Eufaula and the *Phoenix* in Muskogee (February, 1888). He sold the Muskogee paper in 1889 when he was appointed U. S. Indian Agent for the Five Civilized Tribes.

Dr. Bennett was a man of wealth. He owned 1,000 acres of improved farmlands in the Creek Nation, two eighty-acre farms in Arkansas, town property in Muskogee, Eufaula, and Wagoner, one hundred cattle and twenty horses. He was a director and shareholder in Muskogee's First National Bank and Adams Hotel Company. A prominent Mason, he served three terms as grand master of the Indian and Oklahoma Territories.[8]

His two children, Gertie Ethel and Louis Albie, were seven and five, respectively, when the Choctaw war broke out. "Few men have risen so rapidly or attained so much in a brief period as Agent Bennett," said O'Beirne's *Leaders and Leading Men in Indian Territory.* "Not only does he stand high with the present government, but with the people of all races and denominations. He is a gentleman of high moral rectitude and a good Christian."

All that praise of the Indian Agent was about to be put to the acid test by the bloodthirsty rivals fighting for Choctaw Principal Chief, usually referred to as Governor.

---

[8] Harry O'Beirne, *Leaders and Leading Men in the Indian Territory,* (Chicago, 1891), p 122-124

The desperate telegram from McAlester came on a day that Dr. Bennett felt unable to immediately leave Muskogee. He at once telegraphed his captain of Indian police to take a force of men to McAlester.

About noon that same day Chief Jones wired from his home at Caddo asking Bennett to meet him in South McAlester (which is two miles south of the rival McAlester) "as there was trouble among the Choctaw people."[9]

The Indian police captain reached the scene Sunday afternoon and found chaos. He immediately telegraphed that Bennett must come and confront the crisis at once.

While these rampaging events unfolded, Victor Locke remained eighty miles away in Antlers, but was kept posted by messengers on horseback and by the telegraph wire. Sooner than he imagined the shooting war would arrive furiously at the front door of his shining mansion.

That Sunday night Dr. Bennett took the train to McAlester, about sixty miles from Muskogee, found "an excited condition of affairs," and got the facts on the murders.[10]

Early next morning, Monday, September 12, a dapper gentleman astride a white stallion and waving an American flag rode up to the United States courthouse in South McAlester. That man was Dr. Bennett.[11] Fifty heavily armed Indians had taken over the courthouse the night before, despite officials' protests. Chief Jones was not there. He wired that he was afraid to leave his home, and asked Dr. Bennett to come to Caddo.[12]

On a Katy freight train, the Indian Agent by mid-afternoon Monday reached Caddo and conferred with Jones. Angry and defiant, as well as fearful for his own life, the Choctaw chief demanded U.S. troops be sent to quell the rebellion. Dr. Bennett relayed the request by wire to Indian Commissioner D. M. Browning in Washington, which seemed to calm down Jones a bit.

---

[9] *Report Commissioner of Indian Affairs,* 1892, p 261

[10] *Loc. cit.*

[11] Peter James Hudson, "A Story of Choctaw Chiefs," *Chronicles of Oklahoma* (Vol. 17, No. 2) p 207

[12] *Report Commissioner of Indian Affairs,* 1892, p 261

At 2 o'clock next morning, Tuesday, September 13, the Indian Agent took the train back to South McAlester, accompanied by Chief Jones and thirty of his men toting pistols and Winchesters. The situation was still perilous. The Jones party joined his other men at the federal courthouse and Dr. Bennett went on to the Nationals' camp to parley.

He succeeded. The Nationals were willing to end the bloodshed. They sent three men with Dr. Bennett to meet Jones and two of his men. The Jackson men feared treachery and demanded Bennett's Indian police go along to protect them. The parley went well. The Nationals agreed the men who committed the murders would surrender within twenty-four hours for trial in the tribal courts. Both sides signed a pledge to abide by law, to disperse, and not re-arm.

Abruptly next day, Wednesday September 14, the "peace treaty" began falling apart, making the crisis again explosive. First a telegram came telling Bennett that thirty men had surrounded Sheriff Perry's home at Hartshorne, threatening to kill him. The Indian Agent immediately dispatched a runner on horseback to race twelve miles to the scene to tell the mob that agreement had been reached to let the law settle the trouble.

"If he reaches there in time," Dr. Bennett said in a telegram to the Indian Commissioner in Washington, "Perry's life will be saved."[13]

At the same time, Chief Jones had second thoughts, and peremptorily decided to not keep the deal he had made. He went to Hartshorne to look into the report Sheriff Perry was besieged. He found one hundred of his armed followers there, and started to order them to disband. They protested, arguing that the Nationals were pulling a clever trick, surrendering some innocent men to shield the guilty killers.

Convinced this was true, Jones became furious and led these Indians back to his "fort" in the South McAlester courthouse, creating an army of two hundred excited Progressives itching to start shooting.[14]

As his tribesmen milled around ranting, the chief took an adamant stance. He dispatched Green McCurtain on horseback to Dr. Bennett demanding possession of the seventeen Nationals who had surren-

[13] *Report Commissioner of Indian Affairs,* 1893, p 83
[14] *Report Commissioner of Indian Affairs,* 1892, p 262

dered for trial in the killings. They were then held prisoner by Bennett's Indian police at their camp west of McAlester.

The Indian Agent flatly refused; he was willing only to turn the men over to a sheriff with proper arrest warrants, not to "a mob." The beleaguered Bennett attempted to arrange a new conference between the rivals. But he found the National leaders already had departed to return home. Bennett sent runners to summon them back to McAlester.

The crisis exploded next day, Thursday, September 15. Forty-two of the restless Progressives mounted up and rode within hailing distance of the prisoners' camp. The Indian police captain halted them, but the angry riders milled around on the hillside trail, brandishing weapons. Anticipating an attack on the camp, the Indian policemen took cover behind rocks and trees and cocked their rifles.

Dr. Bennett, alerted, rushed to the scene before shots were exchanged. He summoned Jones and McCurtain, who grudgingly called off the attack, and sent their riders back to South McAlester. Then the Chief, McCurtain and a few others joined Bennett in another urgent conference in McAlester. His report to the Indian Commissioner says:

> This conference was more or less stormy and it seemed that all efforts to prevent further trouble would be unavailing and I would be forced to call for military aid.
>
> As I had pledged my honor to the prisoners that if they would surrender they should not be taken in charge by any mob, but should be turned over to the proper officer of the nation when he came with proper warrants, I became, as it appeared to me, personally responsible for carrying on that part of the agreement.
>
> I knew that I had but twenty men upon whom to depend as against over two hundred of the opposing faction, yet I told my policemen that the prisoners could only be taken from us over our dead bodies, and we prepared for what seemed an inevitable conflict.[15]

---

[15] *Loc. cit.*

In the back of his mind, Dr. Bennett considered sneaking the prisoners away in the night aboard a freight train. He had secretly made that tentative arrangement with the railway officials. But he kept trying to talk sense into Jones and McCurtain. He read them the Act of Congress of June 1888 that prohibits any Indian interference with an agent or policeman discharging his duty.

"Your men might forcibly take my prisoners," he warned them, "but it would only be at the loss of many lives on both sides.

"Even then all of you would have to answer for the deed before the United States court, which I have no doubt would take great pleasure in breaking your necks!"[16]

Wisdom overtook the anger and anxiety of Jones and McCurtain. The conference became friendly, and it was once again mutually agreed to follow the law, and bring the accused Nationals to trial for murder.

Although the political rivals had resolved this catastrophe, Chief Jones feared a fresh outbreak of violence was imminent. At the Choctaw Council House at Tuskahoma on Monday, October 3, trouble was almost certain to break out, he told Bennett. That was the day the National Council would convene to make the official canvas of election returns.

Jones formally requested Dr. Bennett bring his Indian police and a troop of U. S. soldiers to Tuskahoma to protect the Council. That would be the only way to avoid another flare-up. The Indian Agent agreed to do so.

On Friday, September 16, Sheriff Perry came to take the prisoners to jail in Gaines County, which was the jurisdiction in which the murders had taken place. His arrival almost triggered a gun battle. Seeing the sheriff, one hundred fifty Progressives, afoot and on horseback, again converged on the dusty road leading to the prisoner camp. With blood-curdling war cries, they charged west out of McAlester at full speed.

"They stopped, however, about a half mile from the camp," Dr. Bennett informed Washington, "which was very fortunate for them as well as others."[17]

---

[16] *Loc. cit.*
[17] *Loc. cit.*

While this feverish drama unfolded at Hartshorne and McAlester, Victor Locke remained in Antlers. Reports reached him steadily and quickly of all back-and-forth developments.

In his parlor, "Uncle Dick" discussed strategy with Jacob Jackson. Locke hunched forward in his rocking chair, animated, pondering; the candidate Jackson clenched his fists while he watched the clock. His mien was grim; he advocated maintaining the threatening stance that seemed to be engulfing Governor Jones's camp in a cloud of fear.

Victor Locke, on the other hand, considered the fact that Dr. Bennett had been catapulted into the fight an unexpected and significant "victory" for the Nationals.

"The Indian Agent is wise and honest," Victor Locke told Jackson. "He'll play it right down the middle. And . . ." Abruptly "Uncle Dick" was struck by inspiration. "We ought to make him the referee!"[18] Victor Locke seated Jackson at his desk, brought out ink, paper and pen, and coached him on writing a proposal to dispatch to Chief Jones. It was intended to add a significant new requirement to the October 3 official canvas of votes at Tuskahoma.

For several more days, the situation remained a powder keg. In Antlers the streets were thronged by about one hundred fifty Nationals, mounted, armed, angry, and excited. They were waiting a signal from Locke or Jackson.

Both the candidate and Locke were anxious to calm them down; there already had been too much violence. They summoned a prominent Progressive respected by the Indians, Judge C. S. Vinson. With him at their side, they gathered the mob inside the schoolhouse and explained the peace agreement, persuading them to disperse and disarm. "We should let the law take its course," urged Jackson.[19]

Fear of secret assassins persisted, however. All across the Choctaw Nation, Indians were skittish. In Scullyville, Tom Ainsworth heard he was the target of unknown enemies. With two friends he undertook to escape in a hack to safety in Fort Smith, fifteen miles away.

---

[18] Author interview with Dorothy Arnote West, Antlers, June 20, 2004

[19] *Report Indian Commissioner of Affairs,* 1892, p 263; 1983, p 83; *Indian Citizen,* September 22, 1892.

At a narrow in the road, they saw three mounted men approaching.

"Huh-uh, boys, we're done for now," said Ainsworth. "Yonder comes those fellows after us!"

"Wait a minute," said one companion. "Don't be in too big a hurry."

But Ainsworth got out of the buggy, prepared to flee into the woods, but keeping a sharp eye on the approaching riders.

"Huh-uh!" Tom Ainsworth suddenly shouted, cheerfully. "One of those fellows is riding a mule. I saw its old long ear flop. Shucks, they're white men and ain't thinking about us. No Injun' would be riding a mule. Especially, if he was starting out to kill somebody!"

Tom Ainsworth got back in the hack and went on to Fort Smith.[20]

The proposition that Jacob Jackson submitted, at Victor Locke's urging, to Chief Jones on September 22 was that any disputes arising in the canvas of election returns be referred to Dr. Bennett for settlement.

Jones, ever wary, refused to respond with an immediate answer. First he wanted to make certain such an arrangement would not violate the Choctaw constitution. He would reply when the Council met October 3.

Resentment and suspicion continued to rise in both camps. Expectations were that the next scene of action would be Tuskahoma (*tuska*—red / *homma*—warrior), the national capital, located almost in the center of the Choctaw Nation. Hardly more than a village, Tuskahoma lay in scenic grandeur on a broad natural valley of the Kiamichi River ringed by the dark pine-clad peaks of the serrated Potato Hills and southwest of the forbidding Winding Stair Mountains.

Jones received reports that armed Nationals were marching on Tuskahoma on the eve of the crucial tally of the vote. On the night of October 2 he sent out Lighthorse scouts who encountered a band of forty-eight Indians, arrested them, and locked them in the third floor garret of the Capitol.

---

[20] "Notes on E.N.W.," Muriel Wright papers, April 22, 1926, Oklahoma Historical Society

Despite the strain, nothing else untoward happened. The climax, as reported by historian Angie Debo:

> On the morning of October 3, hundreds of Indians from all parts of the Nation were assembled in Tuskahoma. An observer reported that not a drunken man was in the crowd, and that all were strongly impressed with the gravity of the situation.
>
> Bennett, in response to the request of both parties, was present with United States cavalry—a circumstance new in Choctaw history. The members of the Council were sworn in and both houses were seen to be overwhelmingly Progressive. C.S. Vinson was chosen as President of the Senate and Wesley Anderson was unanimously elected Speaker of the House.
>
> In the afternoon there was a conference of the two leaders and their advisers, at which Bennett was present, and Jones definitely rejected Jackson's offer to refer disputed points to Bennett for arbitration.[21]

It took three days of wrangling to resolve the question of whether Jacob Jackson had won the office of principal chief or Wilson Jones had been re-elected. First the Council voted to bar everyone except themselves and their officials from the chamber where election returns were canvassed. Lighthorse guarded the doors, backed up by Bennett's soldiers.

A joint session of the Council on the third day declared Chicf Jones the winner by a mere eight votes! The official tally was: Jones 1705, and Jackson 1697.

That was a bitter pill for the Nationals. Victor Locke and Jacob B. Jackson swallowed it quietly. Such a razor-thin margin might have merited a recount, but they accepted the tally without further protest.

Even so, Jones remained furiously angry. In his inaugural message, the chief castigated the opposition party, flatly accusing the Nationals of trying to assassinate him and other officials, and to destroy the

---

[21] *The Rise and Fall of the Choctaw Republic*, p 171

tribal government. He did not trust the Jackson-Locke faction; be on guard for another outbreak, he warned.[22]

Quiet was restored, however, and Dr. Bennett left Tuskahoma on October 12. He had other Indian Territory problems, since his office supervised all Five Civilized Tribes. The U. S. soldiers under command of Captain R. M. Hayes remained two weeks longer and then marched back to Fort Reno.[23]

But trouble was by no means at an end. Storm clouds still hovered in the air. They could be seen, and felt.

Judge Temaye Cornells of Muskogee was warned by his clerk, W.L. Austin, in South McAlester: "The Indians got mad and now things are bad. I do not expect the war to end soon. The Jackson party would not have started killing if they hadn't meant to keep on."[24]

It deeply disturbed Indian Agent Bennett that the Choctaws were "well armed with Winchester rifles and Colts revolvers, and have an abundance of ammunition . . . . Unless the people can be reconciled . . . there are likely to be many secret assassinations. In fact, this is the greatest dread which now possesses the Choctaws themselves, and of itself is a moving cause to arouse them to other or further acts of violence."[25]

If the Choctaw people could not be restrained "from these acts of outlawry," Dr. Bennett saw no course for officials in Washington except the "placing the superintendence of their affairs in the hands of the War Department," meaning imposing martial law.

"There is yet a *possibility* of trouble," he wrote the Commissioner of Indian Affairs. "I do not believe that there is a *probability* of trouble of such a character as to necessitate action on my part . . ."[26]

In this lull, Victor Locke turned his attention to business and family affairs. His storekeeping was prospering steadily. The cattle business alone brought him great new wealth. Now he was expanding his timber operations—and heading for unexpected trouble on that score at an awkward time.

---

[22] *Indian Citizen,* October 18, 1892

[23] *Report Commissioner of Indian Affairs,* 1893, p 85

[24] Angie Debo Papers, OSU, Box 36, 88-031

[25] *Report Commissioner of Indian Affairs,* 1892, p 263

[26] *Report Commissioner of Indian Affairs,* 1893, p 86

America's westward expansion in the 1800s demanded enormous amounts of lumber for building. It was becoming scarce. Logging had severely depleted the forests of the northeast and north-central United States. Now new timberland was needed to feed the construction spree's voracious appetite. The sawmill people descended on the Choctaw Nation where three or four million acres of hills were covered with virgin cedar, pine and oak. Victor Locke found himself a profitable niche in the timber harvest.

His Antlers mansion gave him a great feeling of pride, which he expressed in pseudo-deprecating jocularity to visitors: "My place is where the roosters crow the loudest, the babies cry the longest, and the dogs always bark at strangers at night."[27]

Susan Priscilla was a busy wife, mother, part-time storekeeper and ever-ready hostess. Business and political associates flocked to the mansion for conversations with her husband, often at mealtime. Relatives dropped in, at times in such a multitude that the men had to be bedded down in the barn. It was up to Susan, now thirty-eight, and eight years her husband's junior, to see to multitudinous chores. From seeing that the milk lowered in a pail down the well to cool to supervising the children's education. She especially wanted them exposed to culture, to learn art and music.

Benjamin Davis, nine, and Babe, seven, were attending Jones Academy in Paris, Texas. Both Victor, sixteen, and Dolly, thirteen, were in boarding schools in Sherman, Texas, she in Kidd-Key College and he in Austin College, getting involved in the student military corps.

Underfoot at home were four-year-old Alex and two-year-old Dude. The frail "Little Boss" Hugh was now eight months old and not healthy at all.

Coming of age was proving a difficult journey for their first-born, twenty-one-year-old Shub. He sawed off his schooling, turned stubborn, and became romantically adventurous. Shub "very flatly declined an education," his sister Dolly wrote in adult memoirs, "saying he

---

[27] Locke Family Papers, *Aleece Locke Garrard notes,* June 16, 1954, p 15, Garrard Ardeneum Manuscript Collection

knew enough. Being indulged to a ruinous degree, he conducted himself as to be imagined."[28]

His ardor for the Indian girl Sinai Sherrod had cooled and he was "playing the field." A pretty, studious eighteen-year-old caught his eye. She was Anabel Fleming, who lived just across the Red River in Clarksville, Texas. They quickly became serious, but had differences.

Anabel Fleming had her eyes on the stars. Her goal was to become a lawyer. Since age ten she had amused herself reading her father's legal reference books. Shub wanted a wife to join him in farming, timber operations, and cattle ranching. Anabel would not let love shortchange her ambition.

Dolly vividly recalled the rupture of the Shub-Anabel romance:

> His fiancée at one time & likely his first was the most accomplished of all my brothers' friends. It was Anabel who was the first woman in Oklahoma [Indian Territory] to be admitted to the bar. A woman lawyer, and unusual any time. She was musical, could sew, could teach, and socially held her own with my mother's parlor full of beaux and belles.
>
> And odd to say, we all liked & loved her, especially our parents. She visited us on Christmas before my father's political troubles and Shub visited her home, and returning said all was over with—which is regrettable.
>
> Anabel was just right for our family of boys & her suggestions as to their education would have been such aid to my parents. I frequently wondered about their dissolution. We never knew—but knowing of course it was his fault.[29]

(At age twenty-five, Anabel was to become on November 14, 1899 one of the first women admitted to the Indian Territory bar.)[30]

---

[28] "To Susan and Her Sisters," August 18, 1949

[29] *Loc. cit.*

[30] *Leading The Way*, Oklahoma Bar Assn. (Oklahoma City, 2003) pp 88-89. Because she made such a high score on her bar examination and was identified as the first woman lawyer licensed west of the Mississippi River, Anabel Fleming received national recognition in Munsey's Magazine and Harper's Bazaar. On Nov. 4, 1901, Anabel married Charles Harold Thomason, a lawyer.

Though handsome, entertaining, and aggressive, Shub seemed a bit unlucky in love. His mother wrote her half-sister, Alice Hodges Hilseweck, about another of "Shub's old girls":

> Well, our town has taken a marriage fever. Dr. Nash married Lizzie Griggs. Nanni Edmonds got her a deputy marshal; she is one of Shub's old girls. Henry Almond got him an Arkansas girl. They was married today at ten. So Miss Byrd's marriage was postponed. Wonder if her fellow was not drunk. Your Pelin is all right in his tight pants and flowing mustache, trying to marry well.[31]

Shub Locke resumed his courtship of Sinai Sherrod; they would be married in 1893 when she was twenty and Shub twenty-two, and have three children in the next six years.

The first snow flurries of the fall in November 1892 brought what Dr. Bennett took to be a return of quiet and calm to the Choctaw Nation. At his office in Muskogee, he got encouraging reports that tension between the political rivals was evaporating.

Embroiled in the maze of problems besetting others of the Five Tribes, Dr. Bennett had been unable to go back to McAlester or Antlers for personal observation.

If he had done so, he surely could have become aware that the appearance of a placid atmosphere was deceiving. The "buzzards" and the "pole cats" still seethed in anger, but mainly kept it hidden.

Into December, until almost Christmas, Antlers seems to remain tranquil—on the surface. Behind the scenes, tempers were flaring. The National-Progressive feud had not died. Wild threats flew in both camps. Chief Jones had a snit of his own. The Government imposing martial law on his tribe was an "insult" he could not forgive.

Everyone, or so it seemed, had their nerves on hair-trigger.

With so much hostility festering, the least new sinister incident could ignite another explosion.

What did set it off was a notorious old black magic curse, emerging from the melancholy depths of Dead Man's Lake.

---

[31] Susan Priscilla Locke to Alice Hodges Hilseweck, November 10, 1894, Locke Family papers, Garrard Ardeneum Manuscript Collection

6

'The House is Shot to Pieces!'

DEAD MAN'S LAKE, in the feeble rays of the winter sun, looked murky, mysterious, and malevolent. Jason Bullis rode up onto the south bank to check its water level.[1] He was afraid his nearby home would be washed away should the lake, two miles north of Antlers, overflow.

Already the Kiamichi River was beyond flood stage, inundating much of the lowland around Antlers, causing damage and suffering.

Despite wearing a thick leather coat, Bullis, a Choctaw, shivered in the December 1892 chill. Hunching forward in his saddle, he took a hard look at the lake's huge flotilla of green water lilies. Ordinarily they floated on the surface. The lilies, he saw, now were nearly a foot under water, a bad sign.

All of a sudden Jason Bullis yelped and jerked upright. Floating into view among the lily pads was the face of an Indian man, with staring eyes and stringy black hair.[2]

Jason Bullis wheeled his bay and clattered away to get help.

This gruesome discovery should not have surprised the Indian, according to Francine Locke Bray, whose decades of tracing the lives of

---

[1] Mary Ann West, "The Locke-Jones War," *Real West*, October 1986, p 44
[2] *Loc., cit.*

her ancestors in the Victor Locke clan gives her a keen grasp of Choctaw history.

"When Indians killed someone," she says, "they were apt to dump them in Dead Man's Lake. They say in Antlers that's how the lake got its name."[3]

When the corpse was pulled out, it was found he had been shot to death. He was Abner Maytubby, a prominent member of the Progressive party, and a close friend of Chief Jones.

There seemed only a thin veil of mystery over the murder. Maytubby had disappeared three days earlier, and was last seen with a Choctaw named Willis Jones (no relation to the chief), who was a member of the National Party.

Willis Jones promptly became a suspect. He already was under indictment for participating in the Gaines County assassinations, but had not yet been arrested. News of this new murder threw Chief Jones into frenzy, eager for vengeance.

The chief sent his Lighthorse to Antlers to arrest Willis Jones. They had trouble finding him. It was not until Sunday, February 12, 1893, that the fugitive was captured near the Kiamichi River east of Antlers.

Albert Jackson, a Choctaw friend, witnessed Willis Jones's arrest. He was fearful the Indian police would just shoot Willis Jones and throw him in the river. He summoned two other armed National friends and rode to the rescue. The Lighthorse ran off, leaving their handcuffed prisoner standing in the middle of the Rock Chimney Crossing Road.[4]

Albert Jackson and his companions hurried Willis Jones to "Uncle Dick" Locke's home for sanctuary.

The rescuers' fear that the lawmen might kill their prisoner was historically valid. That happened not infrequently. As far back as 1883, Chief Jack McCurtain was alerted by an anonymous letter that since a

---

[3] Author interviews with Francine Locke Bray

[4] O.L. Blanche, *Indian-Pioneer Papers,* OHS, Vol. 61-5873, p 360-361. [A previously published version of this escape has Willis Jones held in an Antlers house, and Victor Locke disguising a boy in a dress as a girl to smuggle in a basket of whiskey which got the guards drunk, permitting the prisoner to run away. That scenario is singular, and suspect as wildly fictional.]

new sheriff was elected "there has been men killed often" and "thrown in the river. . . Yesterday Billy Tucubby was killed. We think he was a good man. People would be glad you would have a sheriff that would do right and protect them."[5]

Also, in combing the Choctaw Nation newspaper files for her books, historian Angie Debo made this note: "The *Indian Citizen* has news of shooting all the time. Common as can be. Not treated in sensational manner—just casual news. I can't express how frequent murder is—terrible. Miracle how anyone ever died in bed."[6]

Another note in her file: "The Assassination of a Choctaw Prisoner—This Indian had murdered a man, escaped & had been arrested in Lamar Co., Tex, held by a deputy sheriff, 10 or 12 armed men came up & shot him while he and two young sons of deputy sheriff were hauling corn."[7]

Choctaw courts on occasion were merciful, Angie Debo found. She wrote: "Johnson Jacob, who was convicted of murder & sentenced to be shot to death 'being an orphan boy and destitute was falsely convicted'— to be pardoned by General Council."

In a rather similar case at Kullituklo, two boys were tried for the drunken "wanton murder" of a feeble old Indian they shot in his bed. The jury returned a verdict of not guilty, explaining: "No good, too old, turn boys loose, maybe so he grow up, make good mans."[8]

The bold escape of Willis Jones enraged Chief Jones. He felt his Lighthorse were cowardly or dim-witted. How could a prisoner just run away? He cursed Victor Locke and his men as "outlaws." They would not get away with this insult! His anger was at the boiling point.

But curiously he took no immediate action. The Chief dawdled for a month before he made any attempt to re-capture the fugitive.

Perhaps the weather may have been responsible. A hard winter freeze gripped the Choctaw Nation. Likewise the Kiamichi River was in flood. In any event, Jones waited until the early spring thaw began.

---

[5] Francine Locke Bray papers, unsigned letter, August 27, 1883, Garrard Ardeneum Manuscript Collection

[6] Angie Debo papers, OSU, Box 36, 88-031

[7] Loc., cit.

[8] Loc., cit.

That, too, posed a handicap for riders. Horses almost mired themselves in the soggy dirt streets of Antlers. Boardwalks at the Frisco depot were hazardous, sinking in thick black mud.

Even so, Victor Locke—certain the Choctaw chief would retaliate—gathered nearly one hundred Indians and led them to a high bluff at a bend in the Kiamichi, three miles east of Antlers. Dragging a stick in the ground, Uncle Dick drew the outline for a log-sided fort, and ordered his men to chop down pine trees and build it.[9]

During this February lull, the accused assassins held in the Gaines County jail started throwing a fit. They had been behind bars about six months without trial. Their lawyers, Gardner and McClure, on February 24, 1893 formally protested to the U.S. Indian Commissioner. Defense counsel demanded the prisoners be released on proper bail, or given speedy trial.

No help was forthcoming from the U.S. Government. The prisoners were flatly turned down. The lawyers were notified that unless the Choctaw officials' actions violated the U.S. Constitution, treaties gave them the right of self-government and exclusive legal control over tribesmen.[10]

As tension rose in Antlers among the full bloods in the National Party, dread soared inside the Locke mansion. Susan Priscilla struggled to maintain a measure of equanimity. But she trembled in vivid awareness of the looming peril. Standing in her front door, she could see a mere one hundred yards away the little cluster of stores and offices earmarking the town's main street. When trouble started, she felt, it would begin there, near the Frisco depot and the spring. And their home, she sadly realized, would be perhaps the main target.[11]

Maternal instincts prompted her to gather in her brood. Being together under one roof would provide greatest safety. Husband Victor, she knew, was wise and strong enough to protect his family.[12]

---

[9] Author interview with Dorothy Arnote West

[10] *Report Commissioner of Indian Affairs*, 1893, p 86

[11] Author interview with Dorothy Arnote West.

[12] Author interviews and correspondence with Francine Locke Bray, McAlester and Indianapolis, between April 2001 and July 2004.

Victor Junior, who would turn seventeen on March 23, was pulled out of Austin College in Sherman, Texas. Likewise Dolly, fourteen, left classes at the Kidd-Key finishing school in Sherman, and came home. Ben, nine, and Babe, seven and one-half, were withdrawn from Jones Academy in Paris, Texas. Also in the mansion were Alex, five, and Dude, not yet three. And frail little Hugh, who would be only one year old on March 21. First-born Shub was away, living on a farm north of Antlers with his wife Sinai.

At the height of this treacherous crisis an explosive new threat shattered the Lockes' sang-froid.

Deputy U.S. Marshal William Ellis appeared at the front door on Wednesday, March 8, 1893 to arrest Victor Locke on a federal indictment charging him with illegally cutting timber on Choctaw Nation land.[13]

While it came as a surprise, the accusation did not alarm him. He considered it a "damned nuisance," part of the political feud. His eyebrows doubtless went up when he saw the name of the government's chief witness, Dr. Eliphalet Nott Wright. As "National Agent" in Chief Jones's Progressive administration, Dr. Wright had given an exclusive contract to Green McCurtain to harvest Choctaw Nation timber.

Reading the arrest warrant, Uncle Dick saw that he was charged with cutting on February 13, 1893 three thousand cedar trees, unlawfully because he was "not a citizen of the Choctaw Nation." He turned to his agitated wife, and scoffed. The charge would not stick, inasmuch as he was an intermarried member of the tribe. His lawyers, he promised her, could easily get him off.

Locke went with the deputy by train to Fort Smith to be arraigned in Judge Parker's court. It was a quick formality. He pleaded not guilty; trial was set for May 12. Uncle Dick posted $300 bail and went home.[14]

His return was just in time. Chief Jones was finally going to war!

---

[13] National Archives and Records Administration, U.S. Court, Western District of Arkansas, Criminal Docket #3354, March 2, 1893; March 8, 1893; March 10, 1893; May 12, 1893; Oct. 7, 1893.

[14] *Loc., cit.*

On Saturday, March 11, the principal chief decided to call out the militia to apprehend fugitives Willis Jones and Albert Jackson, and anyone who dared interfere with his troops.

At his home in Caddo, Chief Jones gathered one hundred fifty men, swore them in, and saw to it that they were armed and mounted. He summoned Gilbert Thompson and appointed him captain and commander of the militia.

Captain Thompson recalls in memoirs that Chief Jones gave him official documents authorizing the capture of the fugitives "at any cost."[15]

The militia expedition got off to a slow start. It took time to assemble camping gear, chuck wagons, and other equipment. At length they mounted up and rode about forty miles to Antlers. They arrived on Monday, March 27, and camped one mile west of Antlers.

Unfortunately, the shooting war was about to start without the knowledge of the Indian Agent. Dr. Bennett was in Muskogee, oblivious to the oncoming crisis. Although a "hero" in the earlier McAlester confrontation, this time Dr. Bennett would not hear about the gun battle until it was over.

In fact, his Interior Department superiors would learn about it first in Washington from garbled and exaggerated newspaper telegraph reports, and find it necessary to alert Dr. Bennett, and dispatch him to the scene.

Captain Thompson discovered the first day that he had been given an undisciplined, motley army. His horsemen rode into Antlers, crowding around the railway station, milling officiously in the streets. The militiamen were inclined to swagger and brandish their firearms.

Their commander noted with alarm that some of his troopers had managed to find whiskey. By mid-afternoon some of them were so drunk they could hardly stay in the saddle. To their captain, they looked like a sorry lot as effective fugitive-hunters. He led them back to camp, hoping to get them in hand, and sober.

---

[15] Gilbert Thompson, *Indian-Pioneer Papers,* (Vol. 46, 442-446); *History of the Locke Family,* p 205

On Wednesday, March 29, Captain Thompson ordered fifty of the likeliest-looking militiamen to saddle up. He led them on a more thorough search of Antlers. They could find no trace of Willis Jones or Albert Jackson.

"So we went to the house of Mr. V. M. Locke to see if they were there with him," Gilbert Thompson recalled.[16]

When the militia clattered up to the Locke gate, Judge Givens of Paris, Texas was sitting on the front porch.[17] The horsemen started encircling the mansion. Some rode clumsily and recklessly had rifles in hand; they were drunk again. Judge Givens observed this with some alarm. He got up and went inside. He joined the Locke family and five or six Choctaws who were with Uncle Dick.

"When we got near the house," Captain Thompson said later, "we heard a shot. I do not know whether one of my men shot or whether the men in the house shot—but then the fight started!"[18]

Startled and terrified, Susan and the Locke small children ducked down seeking protection behind chairs, sofas and tables. So did Judge Givens. Victor Junior grabbed a Winchester and joined his father and the Choctaw men.

Victor Locke brandished his rifle and shouted that everyone needed to fight for their lives. The men rushed to the windows and began firing on the militia.

A hail of hot lead rained on the mansion from all sides, bullets zinging through the walls. "The house was all shot to pieces," Captain Thompson wrote later. "I don't think there was any place in the house that didn't have a hole through it."

Crouched at a window, Victor Junior found a militia rider in his sights, and squeezed the trigger. He felt his weapon kick and heard the thud of the shot hitting target. The horse tumbled over dead, and the rider went sprawling.

---

[16] *Loc., cit.*

[17] "The Cloid McCarty Family," *Pushmahata County—The Early Years,* p 260

[18] Gilbert Thompson, *Indian-Pioneer Papers,* OHS, (Vol. 46, 442-446)

Dolly spotted her favorite pony tied to the hitching rail behind the house, in the line of fire. She stood and cried out frantically: "Oh, please, somebody. . ."[19]

Amid the raucous confusion, Mack Hill, the family's longtime black handyman, sidekick, and shadow, heard her. He jumped up, ran out the back door, grabbed the reins and quickly led the pony into the barn.

As he raced back to the house, a militia sharpshooter winged him. Mack staggered inside, blood spurting from a shoulder wound. Susan darted to a cabinet and pulled out a bed sheet. She tore strips and bandaged him. Mack Hill moaned for a minute or two, then struggled to his feet, wincing. He retrieved his Winchester, staggered back to a window, and started returning fire again.[20]

Anxious and inquisitive, Dolly darted from behind a sofa and went to a window to sneak a peek at the action. At once a muzzle flashed and she felt a terrible bee sting burning her forehead, and saw a thick lock of her hair flying away.[21]

Dolly dropped to the floor, realizing that a rifle bullet had grazed the side of her head. There was just a little blood; she wasn't hurt, just dazed and frightened.[22]

Apparently invigorated or inspired by shooting up the Locke mansion, a dozen or so militiamen turned away and rode pell-mell back down the Antlers main street, whooping a war cry, and firing wildly.

Just then a Frisco freight train was pulling into the Antlers depot. The engineer was amazed to "hear rifles going off all over town," he said later. "I just jammed the throttle forward, and got on down the tracks fast as I could!"

When Indian Agent Bennett collected all the facts and summed up the horrendous episode in a starkly critical report to Washington, he wrote:

> It is a fact, almost without denial, that this drunken mob was led by a private individual and not by its proper officers; that many of

---

[19] "To Susan and Her Sisters," Aug. 6, 1949
[20] *Loc., cit.*
[21] *Loc., cit.;* Gilbert Thompson, *Indian-Pioneer Papers,* (Vol. 46, 442-446)
[22] *Loc., cit.*

> the mob were so intoxicated as to be unable to sit on their horses; that they were utterly reckless in the use of their firearms, as they shot into the Methodist church, the Masonic hall, the railway depot, and into the house of the Methodist minister, a white man, where his wife and children were.
>
> That they refused to permit these women and children to leave their home and seek a safe retreat, but forced them to remain therein during the leaden hail which was showered into and about the same for half an hour.
>
> And that altogether the acts of said militia were more those of wild beasts than of human beings. I was and am horrified to think that in our country such an outrage could be perpetrated under the color of law.[23]

Captain Thompson may have been the only sane man in the militia that attacked the Locke mansion. He tried to end the melee but his shouted commands were either drowned out or ignored. It took him until almost 2 o'clock in the afternoon to get control of his men and halt the shooting. Three of his riders suffered gunshot wounds, one of whom died later in the day.

He had no idea how many defenders in the mansion had been killed or wounded.

Amid the new eerie silence that fell over the scene when the shooting stopped, the captain walked onto the front lawn and made an elaborate show of laying down his rifle. Then with open hands he strode toward the front door.

Judge Givens rushed out, his brain spinning for a way to become a peacemaker.

"Quit firing!" Judge Givens shouted. "Mr. Locke is already dead!"[24]

Without attempting to verify Judge Givens's false assertion, Captain Thompson rounded up his men and cleared out. He collected those who had gone back to Antlers, which took a while, and returned to camp—but only to strike it and move his whole band of militia to the

---

[23] *Report Commissioner of Indian Affairs,* 1893, p 89

[24] "The Cloid McCarty Family," *Pushmahata County—The Early Years,* p 260

little town of Goodland, twenty miles south of Antlers. It is unclear why he never went near the Locke log fort on the Kiamichi.

Damage was severe in the Locke mansion. Dolly was shaken by her close call, but not really hurt. Mack Hill's wound was serious, but not life threatening. No one else was hurt. Susan Priscilla breathed a prayer of thanksgiving.

It was not until three days later, Saturday, April 1, that Dr. Bennett reached Antlers. After a quick look, the Indian Agent wired Washington "that the situation was critical, large forces of armed Choctaws confronting each other likely to come in conflict at any time."[25]

On Sunday and Monday, Dr. Bennett conducted an investigation and peace conference at Goodland. Chief Jones came, stomped around angrily, and loudly proclaimed that this controversy was none of the United States' business. Dr. Bennett summoned disinterested eyewitnesses as well as rival political leaders, and heard everyone out.

Chief Jones was totally in the wrong, the Indian Agent concluded. Further the militia started the shooting. Dr. Bennett sent this report to Washington as what he termed his "conviction":

> That calling out of the militia by Governor Jones to arrest Willis Jones was unnecessary and unlawful; that the acts of said so-called militia have been contrary to the laws and the constitution of the Choctaw Nation, and that the conflict precipitated by them was the act of a drunken, irresponsible, and uncontrollable mob, who were banded together as militia for the evident purpose of murdering men, women, and children, thereby removing their political opponents, and so intimidating others that the powers of the present party in authority may be perpetuated.
>
> (This is election year with the Choctaws for their national treasurer, auditor, secretary, etc.)
>
> I know that the present Choctaw government will never bring these attempted murderers [militia] to a trial, but will uphold them in their unlawful acts. I am fully convinced from the pledges heretofore given me by Governor Jones and and his followers that it would be assisting in so-called judicial murder to permit the militia to make arrests in the Choctaw Nation; that where I have heretofore surrendered to

[25] *Report Commissioner of Indian Affairs,* 1893, p 87

Choctaw authorities. . . citizens charged with offenses . . . pledges were violated by Choctaw authorities . . . and the prisoners robbed of their liberties and deprived of their rights.[26]

Despite their continuing enmity, the two sides agreed on Monday, April 3, to a temporary truce. Victor Locke told Dr. Bennett that his men wanted peace, and had only taken up arms to defend their lives. He offered to surrender all their rifles and pistols, if Bennett would protect them.

The Indian Agent turned Locke down, even though he considered the offer "fair, just, and necessary." Dr. Bennett explained: "I am powerless to protect you without military aid, which I do not have at this time."[27] The Indian Agent promptly sought to change that dynamic by wiring the Indian Commissioner to send a U.S. military detachment to put Antlers under martial law.

Captain Guthrie and forty-one U.S. soldiers arrived on Saturday, April 11, set up camp beside the Antlers spring. On his heels came a Special Interior Department Agent named Faison to take charge, and both Dr. Bennett and Captain Guthrie were under his orders.[28]

Straightway Captain Guthrie went to Goodland and conferred with Chief Jones, who resented "the U.S. meddling," and continued to buck. Finally Jones realized he had been out-maneuvered.

"After talking with the captain of the soldiers," Captain Thompson recalled, "the Governor said for me to disband my troop and let the men go home, for he did not want any of our men killed by the soldiers.

"This he said is our own affair but the United States Government has stepped in and sent these soldiers down here to stop us and I guess it would be nothing but right to give in and let the thing go and forget about it.

"We disbanded our men, and Locke disbanded his men and we gave our boys a good handshake and told them to go home."[29]

---

[26] *Ibid.,* p 89
[27] *Loc., cit..*
[28] *Loc., cit.*
[29] Gilbert Thompson, *Indian-Pioneer Papers,* (Vol. 46, p 442-446)

Special Agent Faison ordered Willis Jones and Albert Jackson arrested, and they were placed in jail at Hartshorne.[30] The Kiamichi River log fort was dismantled.

Just days after the horrendous shooting spree, a new tragedy hit the Victor Locke family. The mansion burned to the ground on Saturday afternoon, May 20.

This brief item appeared on page one of the *Indian Citizen* on Thursday, May 25, 1893:

> The residence of V.M. Locke, leader of the National party at Antlers, I. T., burned late Saturday afternoon. It was caused by a defective flue. By hard work on the part of United States soldiers and citizens, much of the furniture was saved. It was the finest residence in the Choctaw Nation. Loss about $6,000, insurance $2,500.

Saddened but upbeat, Uncle Dick told friends he would immediately rebuild, but move his new residence a little further up the north Antlers hill. Most of his valuable papers, including his marriage record, were lost in the fire, he testified at a later date.[31]

Colorful and largely accurate reporting of this spectacular frontier gunfight in newspapers as far away as New York and San Francisco gave Indian Territory in general a black eye.

"Choctaw leaders were very much concerned for fear this disturbance would bring about the loss of their national autonomy," writes historian Angie Debo. "It did, in fact, create a bad impression at Washington, and it strengthened the sentiment in favor of the law recently passed by Congress [the Dawes Act] looking to the ultimate extinction of the tribal governments.

"Green McCurtain, Joe Everidge, C.S. Vinson, and Dr. Wright were dispatched to the Federal capital to explain the riot at Antlers, and J. W. Ownby of Paris, Texas, was employed as counsel to represent the Nation before the United States."[32]

---

[30] *Rise and Fall of the Choctaw Republic,* p 172

[31] *Locke Family History,* p 207

[32] *Rise and Fall of the Choctaw Republic,* pp 172-173

At home, the Choctaw government set about cleaning up loose ends left by the bloody feud. At a special session in June, the Council appropriated $28,000 to pay the militia, and pushed for prosecuting the alleged assassins, still in jail in Gaines County.

The Indians were tried June 17 at Wilburton before Judge Holson of the Choctaw criminal court, with U.S. soldiers on guard. Nine of the Choctaws were found guilty and sentenced to be shot.[33]

Imposing the death sentences caused an uproar. Partisans loudly protested the trials were unfair, and demanded the U.S. intervene. Special Agent Faison asked Chief Jones to suspend the sentences. Angry by this intrusion, the Chief ranted and balked, but finally spared all but one of the convicted men, and his ultimate fate remained in doubt for more than a year.[34]

With the Choctaws' odd-year election still underway, the U.S. troops remained to maintain martial law. The campaign was quiet; Victor Locke's National Party managed to elect four national officers, but the Jones Progressives retained a majority in the House of Representatives.[35]

Tension and dread continued to permeate the Choctaw Nation; most Indians were watchful and suspicious. Although no more riots broke out, the *Indian Citizen* reported that "an appalling number" of political assassinations occurred "among the partisans of both sides" during September and October, according to Angie Debo.[36]

The Federal troops camped out in October 1893 at Tuskahoma during the regular session of General Council, which turned out to be quiet and orderly. Victor Locke was on hand, jaunty, smiling and diplomatically glad-handing his former enemies.[37]

Uncle Dick had a personal reason for smiling. His lawyers had petitioned Judge Parker's court to dismiss the illegal tree-cutting indictment. As an intermarried citizen, they argued, Victor Locke had as much

---

[33] *Ibid,* p 173
[34] *Loc., cit.*
[35] *Indian Citizen,* August 10, October 19, 1893
[36] *Rise and Fall of the Choctaw Republic,* p 173
[37] *Loc., cit.*

right as any Choctaw to cut tribal timber. On October 7, 1893, the court agreed and dismissed the indictment.[38]

The Government troops departed, ending martial law, and essentially terminating the Locke-Jones war.

But the war's last scene would not be played out until one year later.

It was not until late fall 1894 that Chief Jones determined the fate of the nine convicted Gaines County assassins. Eight were turned loose and permitted to leave the Choctaw Nation.

The ninth, fifty-four-year-old Silan Lewis, a full blood who had once served as county sheriff, was ordered shot to death on November 5, 1894.

"He met death like an old-time Choctaw," Angie Debo writes, "refusing to take advantage of the comparative freedom that was allowed him, walking in from the woods in time for his execution. A threatened uprising in his behalf did not materialize, probably because he did not encourage it."[39]

That is only part of the story; for some reason historian Debo ignores the gripping finale and true drama of the execution.

The Indian's death was ghastly.

There are two published versions, both equally bad. In one account, his angry executioner marks an ochre "X" deliberately on the wrong side of Silan Lewis's breast, shoots him but misses the heart, and with his fingers holds closed the wounded man's nose until he suffocates.

A different story was written for the Oklahoma Historical Society by Samuel L. Davis, who said he witnessed the execution and helped dig the condemned man's grave. His version:

> They arrested a good Indian, named Silan Lewis, but he denied having anything to do with their death—and I wasn't the only one who thought he was innocent. They held a mock court at their court ground south of Wilburton. They were in a great hurry and

---

[38] NARA, U.S. Court, Western District of Arkansas, Criminal Docket #3354, Oct. 7, 1893

[39] *Rise and Fall of the Choctaw Republic,* p 174

confusion...so instead of pinning the spot over his heart on the left side they pinned it on the right.

Tecumseh Moore was the one who should have shot him but he said he did not believe it was a just death. Liman Persley was the first deputy. He acted as executioner but when Lewis did not die from the shot they stuffed a handkerchief in his mouth and let him bleed to death inwardly. I helped dig his grave . . .[40]

---

[40] Samuel L. Davis, *Indian-Pioneer Papers,* (Vol. 22: 59-60)

7

Can't Cupid Shoot Straight?

AS THE SUN went down on Wednesday, September 25, 1896 and sent dappled shadows across the jostling streets of Fort Smith, Arkansas, Victor Locke Jr. paced restlessly in a front bedroom of the Main Hotel.

Worried about the time, he doubtless yanked out and looked at his watch every few minutes. Would she come? Why hadn't he heard from her? He began to feel desperate. What if she couldn't get away from the old man?

That same evening in McAlester, Indian Territory, eighty miles west, a stylish young half-blood Indian girl hurried into the Western Union telegraph office just before 7:20 o'clock. At the writing desk, she grabbed a pen and a message form, most likely casting a nervous glance over her shoulder.

She wrote: "Will be on night train." She addressed it to V.M.Locke Jr, Fort Smith, Ark. c/o Main Hotel. She signed it, "Sudie."[1]

Then Sudie McAlester hurried for the railway station, carrying her little overnight grip, feeling certain she had eluded her father.

---

[1] Locke Family Papers, Garrard Ardeneum Manuscript Collection

Sudie, twenty-three years old, was known as "the richest girl in town." She was the only daughter of the famous James J. McAlester, the wealthy monarch of coal mining in the Choctaw Nation.

Sudie had fallen deeply in love with Victor Junior, who now was six months shy of his twenty-first birthday. They wanted to get married. J.J. McAlester thundered, "No!" And he meant it, and wouldn't budge. So they slipped around, and kept their flame of love burning.[2]

Victor Jr. Locke pleaded with her father, and got nowhere. J.J.'s opposition was not surprising. He had what amounted to a feud with Victor Senior. Both men had fought for the Confederacy. But now they quarreled over coal, and Choctaw politics. McAlester vowed no Locke would ever marry into his family. It wasn't an Indian thing. The mining king's wife, Rebecca, was a full blood, her mother Choctaw, her father Chickasaw.[3]

He had invested heavily so his little girl could measure up to the most prestigious husband the Territory might offer Sudie. J.J. sent her to one of America's most elite boarding schools.[4] Along with world culture, art, music, languages, and literature, Sudie learned polite manners and how to embroider and crochet. She was beyond doubt a lady, first calibre.

But she had spunk and an athletic little body. She loved sports, adored baseball, and even played a few games of dangerous Indian stickball. A fast ride thrilled her, but she never learned to drive a motorcar well. Red was her favorite color; everything had to be red, from coats and hats to interior upholstery of any auto she bought.[5]

She and Victor, on the sly, clung to each other desperately. Father finally issued an ultimatum, using his most powerful weapon. Sudie surrendered. She didn't want to be disowned; she had always had money. She didn't think she could stand being without.

Their trysts ended. No more secret rendezvous like in Fort Smith. Sudie cried after their goodbye kiss. [Cupid didn't exactly abandon them.

---

[2] Author interview with Jo Anne Day, Oklahoma City, great-granddaughter of J.J. McAlester, July 12, 2004

[3] *Loc., cit.*

[4] *Loc. cit.*

[5] *Loc. cit.*

They managed a few more secret meetings, and drifted apart. But, lo and behold! Romance was to reunite them thirty-five years later.]

Victor Junior, unable to detect any way around the barrier raised by J.J. McAlester, felt bewildered and heart-broken. His mother brightly challenged his dejection. Losing Sudie would not forever rob him of his chance to taste the wine of life. Susan Priscilla bucked up her son with a sunny smile and frankness.

The boy listened keenly. He welcomed her advice; he admired the way she had tackled misfortune with energy, quick wit, and courage. A model of moral rectitude, his mother spoke frankly about human sensuality, and gave her children candid advice on intimate personal behavior.

Susan Priscilla was drawn to her equally vibrant half-sister, Alice Hodges, a dark-haired beauty whose dress and demeanor always was so elegant that men invariably associated her with "the rustle of silk" and the scent of exquisite perfume. By mail the sisters regularly shared family news and gossip, at times apparently testing each other on sexy jokes. "Guess you do think," Susan wrote her sister, "that I have taken a little offence at the folding bed joke. I have no fear of the folding bed nor nothing."[6]

Her advice to Victor Junior was succinct and sage: *There are plenty more fish in the sea.* Victor Locke Jr. clearly understood; he wiped his tears, and set out to find a new girl.

As for Victor Senior, he was still caught up in his love affair with politics.

Principal Chief Wilson Jones finished serving two consecutive terms in 1894 and was prohibited by law from running for an immediate third. Uncle Dick quickly dusted off his favorite candidate, Jacob Battiest Jackson, for another try to capture the office.

Jackson was opposed by Jefferson Gardner, an experienced politician. He had been a circuit court judge, and national treasurer, storekeeper and postmaster at Eagletown. He was "about 5' 6", bald-headed,

---

[6] Susan Locke to Alice Hodges, Nov. 10, 1894, Locke Family Papers, Garrard Ardeneum Manuscript Collection.

half-breed, a man of few words but very kind," according to historian Peter James Hudson.[7]

Once again Uncle Dick fell short on election magic. Jeff Gardner defeated Jackson.

Just at this point in time, political affairs in the Choctaw Nation again exploded in a dangerous new upheaval. It was over issues felt in every home in the nation, and would keep the people of the tribe in turmoil for the next six or seven years.

What sparked outrage among the Indians was the decision by the federal government to push into high gear its relentless scheme to break treaties signed in the 1830s with the tribes.

Each of the Five Civilized Tribes removed forcibly sixty years earlier to Indian Territory had been solemnly promised tribal freedom and use of their land in common for "as long as the grass grows and the rivers run. . ." Now the Congress and the White House were dead set on extinguishing tribal governments, forcing the Indians to become U.S. citizens under white man's law, and handing out equal-size farms to each Indian.

This was all undertaken with the transparent aim of forcing Indian Territory and Oklahoma Territory to agree to merge as soon as possible into single statehood as Oklahoma. Then the federal government would convert the vast "surplus" Indian acreage into farms for incoming white homesteaders.

The Choctaws, as well as the Chickasaw, Creek, Seminole, and Cherokee nations, were outraged. They protested in vain that the politicians in Washington were callously bent on destroying their sacred heritage and traditional way of life.

Congress began to put on the actual squeeze in 1893. The first step was to send commissioners to Indian Territory to make a roll of all tribesmen. Each would then be given an individual plot in severalty for a homestead. No longer would an Indian be permitted to pick out any place he desired to build his cabin, or to let his livestock run free on the range.

---

[7] Peter James Hudson, "A Story of Choctaw Chiefs," *Chronicles of Oklahoma,* (Vol. 17, No. 2, June 1939), p 207

The Congressional commission, named for its chairman, Senator Henry L. Dawes of Massachusetts, trooped into Indian Territory and immediately encountered serious resistance.

Jefferson Gardner, then Principal Chief and unflinchingly opposed to allotment, refused to even talk to Senator Dawes. Congress, stiffened by the insult, showed no patience with any such resistance. Dawes was authorized to create the tribal rolls and parcel out the land whether or not the Indians agreed.

Choctaw political leaders in the main viewed the situation as an impending catastrophe. A majority vowed to fight against change. Yet a reasonably large number held a differing view. Feeling under the sword of Damocles, these men urged accepting the government scheme quickly in order to obtain the best possible terms.

This ugly clash of opinion among tribal leaders brought staggering discord. Bickering broke out in every county. Old and firm personal loyalties were shattered; party alliances were abandoned. Choctaws who formerly were bitter enemies now found they were of the same mind, and joined hands. The differing views dwelt not only with allotment but such corollary questions as whether to sell tribal coal lands and distribute the proceeds.

While this controversy raged, Chief Gardner ran in 1896 for reelection. For the third time, Victor Locke put Jacob Jackson up for Principal Chief. In all, there were four candidates, the others being former Chief Green McCurtain and Gilbert W. Dukes, a Confederate veteran, who had been a sheriff, judge, and national auditor.

Green McCurtain boldly advocated permitting the United States government to go ahead and impose allotments. Though he won the election, the balloting indicated the tribe actually opposed the Dawes Commission work by nearly two to one. The vote for McCurtain was 1405, but the rival candidates, all of whom opposed the Dawes Commission scheme, topped him as a group, drawing a total of 2384 votes—Jackson 1195, Dukes 613, and Gardner 596.[8]

---

[8] *Pushmahata County—The Early Years,* p 15

With McCurtain disqualified from seeking an immediate third term, Gilbert W. Dukes was elected Principal Chief in 1900, defeating Dr. E.N. Wright and the hapless Jacob Jackson, backed by Locke.

Widespread unrest, uncertainty, opposition, and disillusionment continued rampant on the Choctaw frontier, a clear harbinger of the approach of dangerous new storms.

The July 1902 race for Principal Chief pitted Green McCurtain against a friend of Chief Dukes, Thomas Hunter of Hugo. It was close, and both sides claimed victory in the *Indian Citizen.*[9]

Not unexpectedly, strife and discord again would violently erupt at Tuskahoma in October when officials undertook to tabulate the ballots. For the second time, United States soldiers had to be summoned to keep the peace.[10]

And smack in the middle of the melee was the irrepressible Uncle Dick Locke. This time the fighting would be with fists instead of Colt's and Winchesters.

The debates, fisticuffs, and riotous wrangling in Tuskahoma lasted more than a week. The disturbances were turbulent and vicious—yet at the same time partly sad and pathetic, and in a few instances childish.

When the Council gathered Monday, October 6, Dukes posted armed Lighthorse and wouldn't let the McCurtain faction enter the capitol. The ballots couldn't be counted anyhow because the Supreme Court Justices held fifty of the fifty-one boxes, and feared they'd be stolen if delivered to the capitol.

Anticipating trouble, the federal government had on the scene both Indian Agent Shoenfelt of Muskogee with his Indian police and Deputy U.S. Marshal Hackett of Antlers with his deputies. While these two quarreled about who was in charge, the Senate managed to organize under McCurtain.

On Shoenfelt's appeal, the War Department sent two hundred Negro troops with white officers who arrived Saturday, October 6 from

---

[9] *Indian Citizen,* Aug. 6, Aug. 14, 1902
[10] *Chronicles of Oklahoma* (Vol. 17, No. 2. June 1939), pp 210-211; *Rise and Fall of the Choctaw Republic,* pp 265-267

Fort Reno. Their commander, Major Starr, banished all armed guards and opened up the capitol to the legislators.

Two rival groups staged a tragi-comic panic in the House of Representatives. Each side fought physically for the "Speaker" chair, and finally in the same room two "Speakers" tried to preside while two separate clerks called their rolls. They adjourned after thirty minutes of this farce.

Then the Council began the official count after the Justices, guarded by Shoenfelt's Indian police, carried the ballot boxes to the Supreme Court chamber.

Rival Choctaw factions milled outside and inside of the handsome brick capitol, raucous and jostling, calling out taunts. Eventually men grappled each other, shoving and rolling around on the ground and on the floors. Fisticuffs broke out. The Lighthorse, the Indian police, the U.S. marshals, and the Negro soldiers fixed wary eyes on the melee, and kept their distance. As long as no guns were drawn, they were ordered to ignore the fighting.

About dark, it was announced that McCurtain had been elected, beating Hunter, 1645 to 956.

But Dukes, angry because McCurtain had accused him of peculation, pulled a fast one. Still in office as chief, he filled several phantom Senate vacancies and with the backing of loyal Representatives, declared Tom Hunter elected and had him sworn in by a friendly Supreme Judge as the new chief.

The Indian Agent refused to recognize Hunter, and eventually Green McCurtain took the chief's scepter. It was necessary to spend ten dollars for a new official Choctaw Nation seal. Hunter had walked away with the old one.

ANTLER'S FIRST Catholic priest, a gaunt thirty-year-old beanpole named Father William H. Ketcham, sought out Victor Locke in the summer of 1898 and asked for help.

Uncle Dick knew all about Father Ketcham coming to a strange frontier town with only twenty-five dollars in his wallet, limiting personal spending to about fifteen cents a day, surviving on free meals and shelter in the Frisco bachelor bunkhouse that housed section hands.

That showed true grit. And he admired Father Ketcham for managing to put up three small buildings, a cottage for his residence, a chapel and a classroom for the first students of his projected school. Victor Locke had donated a town lot for Antler's first Baptist church, but in no way was he interested in joining the priest's faith.

"There is one thing that will keep me from ever becoming a Catholic," Locke confided to his friend, Judge Charles E. Dudley. "That is the confessional. I am not going to confess to anyone; they have got to prove it on me."[11]

Father Ketcham, however, was not proselytizing. What he wanted was to get someone to help him learn the Choctaw language.

"I intend to translate our prayer book and catechism into the native language," the priest told Locke. "They say you know Choctaw real well. Will you help me?"[12]

"I'll do all I can for you."

Bad luck dogged the priest in Antlers. The heiress to a Philadelphia fortune who became a nun, Mary Katherine Drexel, sent him $2,500 with which to build his mission school. He deposited it in the nearest bank, at Paris, Texas. The bank failed; he lost half the money. But he cut corners and opened his mission school in the fall of 1897.[13]

Father Ketcham needed a team and wagon, and begged the purchase price from Mother Drexel, explaining: "This is hard country to travel over. It is rough and mountainous country and full of wild animals and some very suspicious people."[14]

"You can count the number of Catholics in Antlers on one hand," Father Ketcham informed Bishop Theophile Meerschaert, who was headquartered in Guthrie. Though Uncle Dick was aloof, he allowed all six of his living children to be baptized.

---

[11] *Locke Family History*, p 205; Days *Gone By,* p 24

[12] Rev. James D. White, "The Saga of St. Agnes," Kiamichi *Journal,* June 2002, pp 3-5

[13] *Loc., cit.*

[14] *Pushmahata County, The Early Years,* p 80

Two of three Principal Chiefs from the Choctaw Nation's fabled talented McCurtain clan are, shown with his wife and child, *(above)* Edmund McCurtain who led the tribe 1884-86, and *(inset)* Green McCurtain, elected in 1902.

All Photos Courtesy Francine Locke Bray Collection, unless otherwise credited.

Victor Locke Sr., circa 1870s, as an up and coming merchant in the Choctaw Nation.

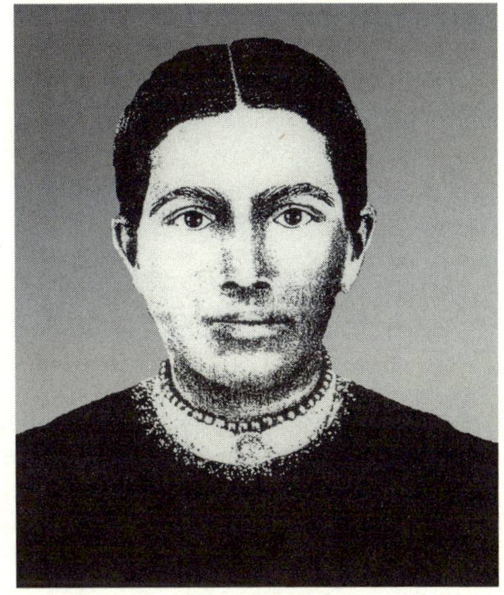

Mary Sharp Locke Foster (1823-1887) Victor Sr.'s mother, who angered him by marrying a Yankee.

Dr. Benjamin Franklin Locke (1851-1900), known as "Dr. Frank," brother of Victor Sr

LEFT: Susan Priscilla McKinney Locke (1854-1898) Choctaw girl who eloped with Victor Sr. in February 1871.

BELOW: Photographed in later years, Victor Sr. and Priscilla were described as the couple who "started it all."

Early day general store in the Choctaw Nation.

Typical residence of affluent Choctaw family in the period before Oklahoma statehood.

Displaying their "catch" are Jesse Nelson (Babe) Locke (*right*) and W. W. Miller, circa 1890s.

D. C. McCurtain, whose involvement in fee scandal opened way for Victor Locke Jr. to be appointed Principal Chief.

Patrick J. Hurley, Choctaw national attorney to Secretary of War, and U.S. diplomat. *(Courtesy Oklahoma Historical Society)*

Cattle roundup time on Victor Sr.'s range near Antlers, Oklahoma. Victor Sr. is believed to be the fourth from the left. Dubbed "The Magnificent Seven" by Locke family members.

One of the pre-statehood Frisco Railroad's trains that gave the Choctaw Nation easier access to the rest of the U.S.–highlighted by the celebrated No. 5 passenger that ran through Antlers between Fort Smith, Arkansas and Paris, Texas—stops near Rodney Mountain while the crew poses May 6, 1904 for photographer.
(Courtesy Oklahoma Historical Society)

This large family group photo was believed taken at Shub Locke's funeral in June 1906. Standing, *left to right*, are Victor Jr.; unidentified woman; Jesse Nelson (Babe) Locke; and Mattie (Shub's daughter). Seated, *left to right*, unidentified woman (thought by Shubs's descendants to be Sinai's mother; Victor Sr., with his hands on the shoulders of Shub's son, Victor B; and Sinai Sherrod Locke (Shub's widow). This is believed to have been taken at the site of the Locke Cemetery in Antlers, Oklahoma.

North High Street in Antlers, early 1900s.
(Courtesy Pushmataha County Historical Society)

Thomson McKinney (Dude) Locke and the frail little Hugh White Locke, circa late 1893. Both died as children, Hugh in 1894, two years, five months and Dude at eight from being hit with baseball bat in 1898.

Susan Priscilla McKinney (*left*, about age 5) and her brother Thomson McKinney, in about 1859.

Mattie Belle Keith Locke, who married brothers Victor Jr. and Ben, holding Curtis, her son by Ben.

Captain Ben D. Locke squats in front of Company L, Oklahoma National Guard Indian Brigade from Antlers, circa 1910.

This "lynching" is merely macabre play-acting in the Kiamichi wilderness.

While attending Kidd-Key College in Sherman, Texas, Mary (Dolly) Locke (*seated in front of Victor Sr.)* is visited by her father who entertains a group of her classmates.

Edwin (Alex) Locke, *(standing, third from the left)* was pitcher on the Sacred Heart baseball team.

Frances Emma (Kit) Philbrook Locke photographed in the 1932 with her brilliant but erratic husband, Edwin Snow (Alex) Locke.

The beautiful Frances Emma (Kit) Philbrook, who left sedate London and barely escaped the *Titanic* sinking, came as the bride of Edwin Snow (Alex) Locke into the Indian Territory wilderness.

Vivia "Bunnie" Locke as she began to grow up.

Victor Jr., circa 1890s, before he became father of "Bunnie."

James Shubetta Locke, whom the family always called "Shub," circa 1890s.

Victor M. Locke, Sr., in his mid-life prime.

Lieutenant Victor Locke Jr in dress uniform for World War I. He eventually retired as a Lieutenant Colonel.

Victor M. Locke, Sr., in his mid-life prime. Victor Locke Jr. as Major in U.S. Army, 1917. *(Courtesy Pushmataha County Historical Society)*

Two Locke brothers in Company L, Oklahoma National Guard Indian Brigade in 1910: *(standing, fourth from left)* Victor Junior, and *(next to him on right)* is Babe.

All photos courtesy Francine Locke Bray Collection, unless otherwise credited.

Victor Junior was confirmed in January 1899 during Bishop Meerschaert's first official visit to Antlers.[15] Then twenty-three, Victor Jr. became an unofficial part-time assistant in the mission school which the priest and the nuns called St. Agnes of the Choctaws. [Financier W.R. Grace is supposed to have sent Father Ketcham $1500 with instruction to dedicate the school to his deceased daughter, Agnes.]

The influence of Father Ketcham was most profound on Edwin Snow "Alexander Hamilton" Locke, who was nine years old when the priest came to Antlers. Alex was confirmed, along with Victor Junior. But he was obviously more inspired or enthralled by religion than his other siblings.

Before he reached his teens, Alex had decided to study for the priesthood. He was enrolled in the Benedictines' Sacred Heart Mission in the Pottawatomie Nation. Much later, on a voyage to Rome, Alex fell in love with an English girl. They married and his life was to undergo a dramatic and tragic upheaval in Chicago.

By 1900, Antlers had one hundred Catholics. In that year the priest was called to Washington, D.C. where he eventually became director of the Bureau of Catholic Indian Missions until his death in 1921.[16]

Before leaving Antlers, Father Ketcham managed to write in the Choctaw language his prayer book and catechism. With others, Victor Locke had schooled him diligently. In the first lesson, Uncle Dick pointed out that the Choctaw language sentence is "backwards," that is the verb comes at the end.

He wrote out an illustration:

In English: "The big white dog looks at that cat."

In Choctaw: "*Ofi* [dog] *tohbi* [white] *chito-vt* [big] *katos* [cat] *ma* [that] *pisa* [see]."[17]

---

[15] *Kiamichi Journal, June 2002,* pp 3-5. [Father Ketcham's resources must still have been meager. He wrote the bishop: "I hope the next time you come, I will be able to offer you something more delicate than possum."]

[16] *Loc., cit.*

[17] The spelling of Choctaw [C*hahta*] varies greatly. Most of the Choctaw words that appear in this book conform to the spellings in John James, "My Experience With Indians, Part II," *Kiamichi Journal,* October 2002; Marcia Haag

In a songbook, Victor Locke found another helpful example. The verse in English reads:

Show pity Lord, O Lord forgive;
Let a repenting rebel live.
Are not thy mercies large and free;
May not a sinner trust in Thee.

The Choctaw version:

Yoshoba ya, Inukahaklot;
Isht Ihak kashofi pulla na.
Chiyoshoba Ilbusa yut;
Ikcha yashfla Chihoya ma, hoke.

Uncle Dick provided the priest with a long list of "everyday" words and expressions with the Choctaw equivalent. Included were:

All right, *ome;* always, *billia*; and so, *ahma*; angel, *enchil*; angry, *nukoa*; baby, *vllosi*; bad, *okpulo*; bathe, *yupi*; be calm, *nuktala-ho!*; be in my pocket, *am-alhto*; beans, *tobi*; bear, *nita*; beautiful, *auikli*; big hunger, *chvffu chito*; black, *lusa*; blanket, *shukbo*; bow, *iti tanampo*; boy, *vllanakni;* bread, *palvska*; breathe, *fiopa*; chair: seat, *abinili*; chicken, *akaka*; clean, *kashofa*; cloth; fabric, *natvnna*; cloud, *hoshoti*; corn, *tanchi*; cow, *wak*; crazy, *tasimbo*; darkness of night, *oklhileka*; deer, *issi*; die, *illi*; doctor, *alikchi.*

Ear, *haksobish*; east, *hvshi akochaka;* eggs, *akakushi*; eleven, *awah achvffa*; eye, *niskin;* face, *nushoka*; fight: battle, *itibi;* finger, *ibbvkushi*; flower, *napakali*; fox, *chula*; good, *achukma*; hair (of the head), *pashi*; happy, *nayukpa*; heart, *chovsh*; hello, *halito*; horse, *issoba*; how are you?, *chim-achukma*; ice, *okti*; it's true, *hikat alhi*; kill, *vbi*; lake, *okhata*; laugh, *yukpa*; lightning, *malahta*; love, *i-hullo*; medicine, *ikhish*; money, *iskvli*; my husband, *ahattak*; my wife, *satikchi*; new, *himona*; no: not, *kiyo*; old, *sipokni*; noon, *tabokuli*; one, *achvffa*; paper,

---

and Henry Willis, *Choctaw Language & Culture (Chahta Anumpa),* Norman, 2001; and various articles by Muriel H. Wright in *Chronicles of Oklahoma.*

book, letter, *holisso*; pig, *shukha*; poison, *ishtilli*; pretty; good-looking, *pisachukma*; put on (clothing), *fokka.*

Rabbit, *chukfi luma*; rain hard, *chitolit omba*; repair, fix, *apoksia*; residence, *aivtta*; rifle; gun, *tanampo*; river, *bok*; run, *balili*; salt, *hvpi*; sanctify, *yohbichi*; say (direct quote), *achi*; stinking, rotten, *shua*; sugar, *hvpi champuli*; teacher, *nanikhvnachi*; teeth, *noti*; thank you, *yakoke*; thin, skinny, *chunna*; thirteen, *awah tuchena*; thumb, *ibbvkishki*; tomorrow, *onnakma*; town, *tvmaha*; tribe, people, *oklushi*; try to eat, *vpat pisa*; ugly, *ikaiuklo*; uneasy, *kamonta*; very many, *lawa*; walk, *nowa*; warm, *libesha*; wash, *achefa*; water, *oka*; west, *hvshi aiokatola*; what is your name?, *nanta chi-hochifo-kvt*; what will I do?, *katiohmi-lachi*; white, *tohbi*; who?, *kata*; why?, *katiumih-o*; wolf, *nashoba*; woman, *ohoyo*; work, *toksali*; wrinkled, *shinofa*; write, *holissochi*; yellow, *lvkna*; yes, *a*; young people, *himmithoa.*

THE MERRY EYES of Susan Priscilla Locke began to lose much of their glitter and sheen during Antler's hard winter of 1897-98. On New Year's Eve she danced, but not as friskily as usual. The years had taken their toll, though she would not be forty-four until the coming November 8.

She felt worn out. For twenty-seven long years, it struck her wryly, she had been a wife, mother, and twice a grandmother, and busy every minute. Susan had suffered too much grief and heartache.

"I am ready to go any time Gabl [sic] blows his trumpet," she had written her half sister Alice Hodges. "This world is nothing but sin and sorrow. And I am tired of it, for it gets no better.[18]

The shadow of the dark angel seemed to hover relentlessly over her household. Often of late she felt recurring anguish over the death of "Little Boss." Never sturdy, but with deep, soulful eyes that still haunted her, Hugh White Locke had died August 21, 1893, barely eighteen months old.

---

[18] Susan Priscilla Locke to Alice Hodges, Nov. 10, 1894, Locke Family Papers, Garrard Ardeneum Manuscript Collection.

Victor Locke had fenced in a small family cemetery on a hill about a mile north of the Frisco depot and the spring. There they buried "Little Boss" in the shade of a cedar tree. Resentment mingled with the parents' sorrow; they hated that this was their third small son to be cruelly snatched away. Charles Guffy had died in 1873 at six, and Japhie in 1883, not yet three.

Now, in January 1898, her two-year-old granddaughter Verna fell desperately ill. Verna was the second child of Shub and Sinai; their first was Mattie Priscilla, born in 1894. The doctors left the sick room with long faces. Recovery was doubtful.

On January 28, Verna Locke died. Once again family mourners bore a small casket to the shadow of the cedar tree on cemetery hill.

In her melancholy mood, Susan was doubly stricken by observing happenings that were blatant evidence of the rapid advance of injurious change on the Indian frontier. The Choctaws already were outnumbered three to one by whites and intermarried citizens. When statehood came—and that appeared foreordained—the Indians would be all but submerged in their own homeland.

She pondered the future for her children. Shub worried her. Now twenty-seven, he had a rambunctious streak. He was too restless and volatile. Victor Junior, twenty-two, had steadied down. Wanting a quality education, he had spent two years at Drury College in Springfield, Missouri. It was an excellent school, founded in 1873 by Congregationalists who came from the East and brought out professors from Yale, Dartmouth, Williams and Harvard. Ben was fifteen and Babe thirteen, both students at Jones Academy in Paris, Texas. At home were Alex, quiet and almost ten years old, and Dude, going on eight.

At nineteen, Dolly had developed, in her mother's estimation, into a conscientious and caring daughter, who had crammed her sharp mind with serious knowledge, an appreciation for culture, etiquette, music, theatre, and language. Dolly, quite plain, was a Francophile and took a spell of signing her name "Tante."

At fourteen, Dolly attended Kidd-Key Conservatory in Sherman, Texas. It was an exclusive finishing school founded in 1893, by the Rev. Joseph Stanton Key and his second wife, Lucy C. Kidd, a noted educator.

Her father enrolled her at Dallas in the Oak Cliff College for Young Ladies, which proved the apex of her educational experience.[19] When Victor Locke visited Dallas, he invited Dolly to spend the weekend at his hotel, the Grand Windsor, and bring along several young classmates.

On one visit her father took her to the Dallas Opera House to see "Carmen," her first such theatrical experience. They were accompanied by a friend, a Captain Miller.

"The stellar role was taken by a beautiful woman," Dolly recalled,[20] "and the house was filled. I sat between my father and Captain Miller.

"I was taken by storm. I had a tremendous attack of stage-struck. I turned to Captain Miller and said, 'If and when I can, this is what I will do.'

"Captain Miller said, 'Oh, don't let your mother hear you say that!'

"If I had told that to my father, he would have said go ahead. He would look at it as a challenge. 'You be a good one—better.' He urged every young person seized with a good desire to go do it.

"That is the only thing in life I ever wanted to really do. As far as looking like the beautiful actress, I knew I could never do that."[21]

News from 'the states" shocked Antlers around the middle of February 1898. Victor Locke hurried home after No. 5 arrived at the Frisco depot, brandishing a New York newspaper. The United States battleship *Maine* had been blown up in the harbor at Havana, Cuba.

It might mean war!

In the parlor, the older boys excitedly quizzed their father, poring over every new paper that came in on the train. If Uncle Sam attacked Cuba, should they join up? They studied the one-time Confederate cavalryman's eyes for their answer.

---

[19] Biography dictated by Dolly Locke Archer to Dorothy Arnote West, Locke Family Papers, dated Aug. 20, 1958, Garrard Ardeneum Manuscript Collection.
[20] *Loc., cit.*
[21] *Loc., cit.*

But just a few days later the *Maine* was totally forgotten! Horror much worse had hit right at home!

On Wednesday, February 23, someone rushed frantically into the house shouting that Dude had been hurt. Susan dashed out and found the boy crumpled in the grass, unconscious, with blood gushing from a savage head wound.

He had been struck with a baseball bat.

His mother got the boy inside, and on a bed. He never moaned or opened his eyes. It was too late. Dude, only seven years and four months old, was buried under the cedar on lonely cemetery hill.

[Whether Dude's death was an accident or foul play is not recorded. The question is intriguing enough that Locke descendants in recent years quizzed each other for clues, and got nothing. As far as scandal went, the Lockes were *tight.* Some suspicion falls, perhaps unfairly, on Alex, who only eleven days earlier had celebrated his tenth birthday. Alex was an avid baseball player.]

Susan was staggered. Two children in the family dying within less than a month! She took to her bed. But the sad days were not yet over. The dark angel still sat on her doorstep.

Susan's normal energy and strength disappeared. Some days she barely managed to get out of bed. Then she sank into a slow and mysterious decline. The doctors took Uncle Dick into the parlor and talked in hushed tones.

On Saturday, May 7, 1898, Dolly sat beside the sickbed, holding her mother's pale hand.[22]

Susan stirred, and weakly asked for a sip of water. Her husband went to get it. Just then Dolly heard a gentle sigh and felt her mother's hand go limp and slide out of her loose grasp.

On cemetery hill, Victor Locke stood beside the fresh dirt mounded on Susan's grave, and announced he intended to be buried beside her. Whatever else is said about Victor, his love for Susan proved true and steadfast. Though only fifty-two when she died, Uncle Dick never married again. That was in sharp contrast to Choctaw custom;

---

[22] *Loc., cit.*

many men remarried when their wives died, some as many as four or five times.

CUPID'S ARROW once again targeted Victor Junior's heart. He fell for a preacher's daughter, Mattie Belle Keith of Antlers. She was winsome, saucy, adventuresome, and quite pretty. On the negative side, sprightly Mattie was extremely flighty and too young for serious romance.

Victor Jr. had just come home from serving six months as corporal in Company E, Fourth Infantry Regiment of Texas Volunteers. He had tried to get into the Spanish-American war. He was too late. Teddy Roosevelt and his Rough Riders stormed San Juan Hill July 1-2, 1898. Spain promptly surrendered, and Victor Junior, who reported to Camp Mosby on June 30, had to hand back his khakis and rifle on November 7 without ever firing a shot except on the practice range.

"Service honest and faithful. An excellent soldier in every respect," was hand-written on his military discharge at San Antonio by First Lieutenant Arnold E. Miller, commanding Company E. The paper noted at enrollment he was 22 3/12th years of age, five feet seven high, with dark complexion and hair, and black eyes, and by occupation a student. He was "paid in full," $58.18.[23]

The little abortive sample of army life was exciting enough to launch Victor Locke Jr. on an important military career that would largely dominate the rest of his life.

More importantly, his ambition and his vision were bursting all bounds, and Fate was catapulting Victor M. Locke Jr. into a meteoric rise in the Choctaw Nation.

Almost unbelievably, the son would within a few years outshine the father as a crucial history-maker among the Choctaw Indians. Much of his record would be good and meritorious, and part of it terrible.

The new object of Victor Jr.'s affection, Mattie Belle Keith lived in "the most beautiful place in town in pre-statehood days."[24] Standing

---

[23] Victor M. Locke Jr. military records, Locke Family Papers, Garrard Ardeneum Manuscript Collection.
[24] *Pushmahata County—The Early Years,* pp 236-237

back from the sidewalk, it stood two stories high, with railed porches bowered in wisteria vine. It was frame, painted white. It was flanked by expansive, manicured lawns and flowerbeds.

This was the hotel owned by her father, William Marshall Keith (1843-1915), a retired Methodist minister who came to Antlers in 1895. His hotel "was an important civic center, attracting salesmen and attorneys" and other travelers.[25] A former missionary to the Choctaws, Rev. Keith had married 2000 Indian couples and baptized 3000 babies. He had been married twice and had ten children. Mattie Belle had five sisters.

On Tuesday, September 12, 1899, the lovers eloped to Sherman, Texas. Grayson County Clerk L. M. Tuck issued a marriage license to V.M. Locke and M.B. Keith. They were married the same day by C.A. Barker, Justice of the Peace.[26] Mattie Belle was seventeen and her husband twenty-three.

Their romance turned out to be a sad mistake.

Barely a year later love captured the hearts of two other Lockes, Dolly and, quite surprisingly, Ben.

Dolly caught the eye of Charles E. Archer, a building contractor from Springfield, Missouri who came to Antlers in 1900 to put up the Harvey House. The sophisticated Archer was ten years senior to twenty-one-year-old Mary Alberta "Dolly"/ "Tante" Locke.

That she was succumbing to his wooing that radiated polished urbanity was no secret in Antlers. This romantic tidbit appeared October 12, 1900 in the *Antlers Democrat:*

> Chas. Archer has been in town several days this week. It is said that when one once drinks the Antlers Spring water he will return again. But we are of the opinion that it is other attractions bringing Mr. Archer back so often and a little bird whispers that he is to become a full-blood Choctaw in the near future.

---

[25] *Loc., cit.*

[26] Testimony of Mattie Belle Locke, Department of Interior, Commission to the Five Civilized Tribes, Antlers, I.T.,Dec. 5, 1902, and marriage, divorce and Choctaw census records, 1899 through 1905, Locke Family Papers, Garrard Ardeneum Manuscript Collection.

On Thursday, January 31, 1901, they were married at noon in the Antlers Catholic church by the Rev. Father Grasian. "They left immediately for a visit to Springfield, Mo. Miss Dollye was raised in this town . . . and was a favorite of Antlers. Mr. Archer is a prominent contractor and is in every way worthy of the prize he has won."[27]

His work ethic interrupted their honeymoon only five days later. The *Antlers Democrat* reported Archer "was in town Tuesday looking after the brick building he is erecting for Jake Easton."[28]

Their marriage, however, was solid and life-long.

Benjamin Davis Locke, only seventeen and a half years old, fell in love with his brother's wife, Mattie Belle!

It was not as disgraceful as it sounds. Victor Junior's marriage to the preacher's daughter had already broken up. They only lived together six months. Propinquity obviously brought Ben together with Victor Jr.'s discarded wife. Their romance did not offend Victor Junior; he quickly went into court for a divorce so they could marry.

On Thursday, February 7, 1901, Victor Locke Jr. and Mattie Belle were granted a divorce. On Sunday, February 10, Ben married her. He fibbed and boosted his age about three years, listing it as twenty-one. Mattie Bell was about nineteen.

Ten months later, Dr. Nic Nash delivered on December 12, 1901 their first and only child, a healthy boy they named Curtis. Mattie Belle's second marriage, too, was doomed. Ben would soon seek a divorce.

THE YOUNG SOCIAL SET in Antlers wanted to dance and have parties despite rigors of the frontier. They built their own pavilion near the depot and the spring. That inspired the opening of a skating rink for more dances, plays, and movies. Then a croquet court and a riverside picnic spot for barbecues and swimming parties. At the hotels, they at times danced till dawn.[29] One rare dance lasted three days.

---

[27] *Antlers Democrat,* Feb. 1, 1901

[28] *Ibid.,* Feb. 8, 1901

[29] *Pushmahata County—The Early Years,* p 311

It was still a raw frontier town of barely a thousand as the Twentieth Century dawned. True, Antlers was linked by a railroad to the outside modern world. Yet as near as five or ten miles from the intersection of Main and High Streets, the thick forests still hid deer, wild cattle, wild hogs, and wild ponies, wild turkey, rattlesnakes, and occasional bear and panther.

Not unexpectedly, the mettlesome Lockes played a vibrant role in the social scene.

Antler's dance craze started zooming in the 1890s, in the hotel lobbies and dining rooms. Many balls took place in the B.I.T. [Beautiful Indian Territory] Hotel.[30] Musicians were mainly locals, among them Victor Locke Junior sometimes at the piano, and his uncle "Dr. Frank" Locke sawing on his popular fiddle.

The young folks in the summer danced about twice a week at the open-air pavilion, twenty by forty feet, ringed by benches, with a side bandstand.[31] Popular were the waltz, schottische, polka and square dance. Many dances went into the wee hours, and young marrieds "parked" their children on pallets in a corner of the dance floor. One of the tots was Ben and Mattie Belle Locke's little Curtis.[32]

Not even a tragic murder-suicide could terminate one dance at the B.I.T. Hotel. Deputy U.S. Marshal Bill Ladd rushed into the lobby and yanked his wife off the dance floor. He dragged her to a room upstairs. Two shots were heard. They found her dead and Ladd dying from his own pistol. Bill was bandaged and the dance resumed. It was five days before Ladd died.[33]

At a Christmas dance given by Mrs. M. E. Berry, an unreconstructed Southerner, Victor Jr., at the piano, played some of her favorite tunes. As a jest, he swung into "Marching Through Georgia." Mrs. Berry exploded. To quiet her, Victor Junior, smiling broadly, switched into "Dixie." Clark Wasson who inspired the joke observed: "Mrs. Berry got

---

30 *Ibid.,* p 167
31 *Ibid.,* p 311
32 *Ibid.,* p 313
33 *Ibid.,* p309

up, lifted her skirts to her knees, and gave as fine an exhibition of the old-fashioned 'back-step' as I ever saw."[34]

The opening of the Harvey House on August 12, 1900 gave social life in Antlers a boost. Established by the Frisco [before dining cars] as a stop where passengers could eat, the two-story hotel-restaurant had a dining room with six long tables and thirteen "richly-furnished" bedrooms.[35]

The Harvey House became known as "the most famous dinner stop on the entire Frisco system. The Antlers restaurant, de luxe in its setting of rugged mountains, spring-fed streams, forests of tall pine trees, and abundant game, offered a bill of fare including venison, wild turkey, fish, quail, wild duck, spare ribs, backbone and country sausage."[36]

A special train brought a throng July 16, 1901 from Paris, Texas to a Harvey House ball. Music was furnished by Mims Carter's black orchestra from Paris. Carter came to Antlers so frequently he wrote a regular opening number called "Antlers."[37]

The Harvey House and the Frisco Depot became the daytime promenade for Antlers' young people. In her *Pushmahata County—The Early Years,* historian Dorothy Arnote West paints the scene:

> Going to the Frisco depot to meet the afternoon train was quite the in-thing to do over a period of a number of years in Antlers. Especially during the summer months was this true for the young ladies of the town.
>
> They spent hours dressing for the occasion. Each must be sure every strand of hair was in place, the face powdered and touched just so, the dress pressed to perfection. Then, satisfied with her reflection in the mirror, the young lady stepped from her home threshold, opened her umbrella to protect her face from the ravages of the sun, and sauntered down a beaten path to the depot for the momentous event—the daily arrival of the afternoon passenger trains, No. 4 and No. 5, which were scheduled for early afternoon stops.

---

[34] *Ibid.,* p 309
[35] *Ibid.,* p 39, p 74
[36] *Ibid.,* p 74
[37] *Ibid.,* p 176

Ever fascinated, the crowd listened for a whistle and watched for the spiraling smoke of the engine. Soon after it was sighted, the train steamed in and came to a braking stop along the depot platform; a porter opened a passenger car door, put down a step-stool, then beckoned to the detraining passengers.

A push-wagon was pushed to the express car to receive the mail and the express freight. In a matter of a few minutes, unless a Harvey House stop was scheduled, the porter called out, "All aboard!" The passengers embarked and the clangity-clang of the bell sounded. As the train faded into the distance down the tracks and the final reverberating "oo-a-ooo" was heard, the flow of pedestrian traffic moved from the platform to the post office to await the "putting up" of the mail. Post office delivery windows were closed until the last letter and card had been distributed to the boxes.

While waiting merchants, attorneys, abstractors, realtors, and others exchanged news and told jokes, the young ladies leaned against the wall, deep in conversation. An inquiring reporter mingled among the crowd gathering news. Once windows opened, a rush to the boxes ensued. Merchants tucked their newspapers (*The Dallas Morning News, the Daily Oklahoman,* or *The Kansas City Star*) under their arms and departed for their offices.

From the post office, the path of the young ladies led to the drug stores to order soft drinks and to while away a little more time. Then, mission—to garner news, to see and be seen—accomplished, the young ladies reluctantly bid one another adieu and slowly walked home, to meet again the following day.[38]

Antlers got its first newspaper when Uncle Dick Locke felt in urgent need of an organ to promote the National Party against the Progressives. By train he brought in from St. Louis and Kansas City a press, a barrel of ink, trays of type, and two or three bales of paper. He was by no means qualified to be printer, publisher, or editor. He employed a newspaperman named J. Y. Schenck and together they put out *The National Advocate.*[39] It was a haphazard operation and the paper did not interest Locke too long.

---

[38] *Ibid.,* p 126

[39] *Ibid.,* p 77

In early 1900, Schenck went into business for himself and launched *The Antlers Democrat,* published weekly. That action apparently got under Uncle Dick's competitive skin. He stomped around, muttering about having all the equipment for a newspaper stored with the hay in his barn.

By luck, Victor Junior encountered a bright-eyed young adventurer named George Warner, a native of Titusville, Pennsylvania, who had come to Choctaw country in 1899 to try ranching. Formerly a reporter on the Rochester, New York *Democrat and Chronicle,* Warner had volunteered for the Spanish-American war. He was a cavalry lieutenant until his health broke, and he was hospitalized for a few months.

President McKinley gave him a new commission, but he was too underweight to qualify. He then went west for a new start.

With the Lockes, he struck a deal and *The Antlers American* was born. In his own *Democrat* issue of May 4, 1900, Publisher Schenck hailed the debut of his new rival: "It is a neat, newsy, well-edited paper and it is pulling for Antlers. The worse thing we see about it is that it is Republican. 'Snooze to you, brother.'"[40]

Antlers hardly was big enough for one newspaper, let alone two. Editor Warner had an immediate struggle keeping *The American* afloat. On June 2, 1900 he sent this note to Uncle Dick at Hamden:

> My Dear Mr. Locke:
>
> Can't very well get down to Hamden this afternoon so come up on this evening's train and spend Sunday with me. I want to talk over some matters with you. Try and bring some money along for the American is nearly "busted." I enclose Grist's bill which please collect for I need all the money I can get in.
>
> Yours very truly,
> George W. Warner
>
> Will look for you on this evening's train.[41]

---

[40] *Ibid.,* p 39

[41] Locke Family Papers, Garrard Ardeneum Manuscript Collection

Friendly and intellectual, George Warner donated an interesting, wide-ranging collection of magazines, pamphlets and books to an embryonic Antlers public library.

Destiny was against him. He didn't live to see whether *The American* could survive [which it did, transforming under several ownerships]. While daringly swimming his horse in the Kiamichi River near the mouth of Water Hole Creek, George Warner, twenty-nine, drowned.[42]

The young editor's body was claimed by his father and brother and taken by train back to Titusville for burial in the family plot.

With dirt streets, with outdoor privies and no running water, Antler residents found life rather rough and tumble. Editor Schenck warned in his paper: "If the people do not organize sanitary regulations, the whole town will be sick this summer. The whole town fairly stinks with dead dogs"[43] [It was not until 1906 that the City Council would order privy contents removed once a month, and the outhouse disinfected with lime or ashes.][44]

When Earl Westmoreland, the abstractor, brought his bride to Antlers she was startled "to see pigs and cows running all over the streets."[45] It may have escaped her notice that dressed panther often hung in front of butcher shops.[46]

Everyone was on alert for horses running away. Typical of such common accidents for one brief period:

Arrival of Frisco No. 1 frightened a two-horse team, which bolted. A man and boy jumped out; the wagon hit a stump. . . A doubletree broke, causing a team in Dora Colbert's funeral procession to run away. . . The Crystal Ice Company team was scared by the blowing off of steam and rammed the wagon into a stump . . . Dr. W. N. John's team ran away near Ten Mile Creek and made kindling of the buggy. One horse fell and rammed the yoke into its breast; the other ran four miles . .

---

42 *Pushmatah County—The Early Days,* p 312
43 *Ibid.,* p 39
44 *Ibid.,* p 45
45 *Ibid.,* p 313
46 *Ibid.,* p 312

. Mrs. J. B. Martin was crossing the railroad tracks at Main Street when her team took off at breakneck speed, and crashed on a stump. Dr. McGinnis was called and took her home in his buggy. Her elbow was fractured.[47]

[It was not until 1914 that Antlers had its first auto accident. A flivver, trying to make a U-turn in deep ruts, flipped. One of the five female passengers was injured, and taken home in a buggy.][48]

Developing friendships with Uncle Dick was important to the boys in Antlers. Joe Taylor Lanham recalled: "The main reason was because of his horses. Uncle Dick had a herd of ponies running wild. Any boy who could catch one of them, and tame it, and ride it, could have it. I wanted one of those ponies; it was a challenge. . . . We also visited Uncle Dick to hear him tell stories of Territory days and to look at his collection of peace pipes, tomahawks, and arrowheads."[49]

ON THE NIGHT of December 31, 1903, the town of Antlers felt perky, anxious to celebrate and welcome a Happy New Year. That was not to be. Instead Antlers was about to be hit by its worst disaster!

Most popular New Years Eve party was a dance in a large two-story wood frame building on Main Street.[50] It was a Thursday night, a bit windy. And with enough winter chill to have wood stoves going.

The large dance crowd was radiant and grew boisterous as midnight approached. With comparable joy, twenty or thirty young men whooped it up a block away in Tom Threlkeld's cafe.[51]

No one at the dance was more bright-eyed and excited than John Hackett. He was the town's Deputy United States Marshal. He had been a key player in the Green McCurtain-Tom Hunter 1902 election standoff at the Choctaw capital. At the stroke of midnight, amid all the kissing and yelling, Hackett dashed out the door onto the building's front porch.

---

[47] *Ibid.,* p128
[48] *Ibid.,* p 128
[49] *Ibid.,* p 134
[50] *Days Gone By,* pp 25-27
[51] *Loc., cit.*

Yanking out his Colt's revolver, he fired six shots into the night sky.[52] The dancers, peeking out, roared approval.

Guns started going off all over town. The bunch at Tom Threlkeld's "shot everything in sight," especially the cafe walls and ceiling. Threlkeld angrily shoved them out so he could close. The boys stood outside, reloading, looking for a target.

Somone yelled, "The phone cable!" They poured lead into the thick cable leading to the telephone exchange that was not yet open. In minutes it was hanging in shreds. The boys dispersed, still firing recklessly at tin cans, trees, owls and night swallows.

At 2 A.M., the music stopped, the dancers sang out final choruses of "Happy New Year," and went home.

Within an hour, someone burst out into the dark of Main Street, and ran up and down screaming, "Fire! Fire! Fire!"

Flames were shooting twenty feet high out of one of the two-story Main Street stores. It wasn't Threlkeld's cafe nor the dance locale. From one building to the next, flames leaped quickly. All of Main Street might burn!

Partly dressed store owners came running. They wrung their hands. Antlers had no water, no fire department. Insurance was too high on wood buildings. They had none. They could only stand and watch the flames ruin them.[53]

By daylight nine buildings lay in ashes. Cause of the conflagration was never found. Only W.P. Cochran was able to immediately rebuild. It took years for one other, C. A. Finley, to again open a store.

Ironically, the following June a cloud burst struck Antlers and did heavy damage on Main Street.[54]

---

52 *Loc., cit.*
53 *Loc., cit.*
54 *Ibid.,* p 28

8

'I'm Mad—Mad as Hell!'

WHEN HIS TRAIN pulled into Chicago on a mid-June night in 1904, Victor Locke Jr. stepped off, momentarily jarred by the persistent clangor of the city of the big shoulders. His ears were more accustomed to the tranquil night music hummed by unseen cicadas in the Choctaw river bottoms.

Now a mature twenty-eight, he had diligently boned up for this important mission to "the states." He was a delegate to the Republican National Convention from the Choctaw Nation.

Teddy Roosevelt would get his vote to run for a second term. He hoped to get a chance to shake hands with the hero of San Juan Hill, look him in the eye and implore him to fix the bad problems back home.

Chicago fascinated Victor Locke Jr. He was thrilled by sight of the $1,000,000 Chicago Orchestra Hall on South Michigan Boulevard; and horrified by ruins of the Iroquois Theatre where only six months earlier fire killed 602 of the audience.

The delegate from the Kiamichi wilderness was not to be mistaken for a scatterbrained rustic. Victor Locke Jr. was as well groomed as the typical Chicago gentleman.[1] Photos of that period show him with the

---

[1] Jo Anne Day interview: "Victor always looked like he just stepped out of a band-box."

regal bearing and mien of a handsome young prince. He stands sharply erect with slightly wavy cropped hair, strong, wide eyes, a Cupid's bow mouth, smooth shaven cheeks, a short neck and a face devoid of typical Indian "moon" shape.

Further, he fully comprehended the day's political issues and accurately assessed President Roosevelt's impressive accomplishments since succeeding the assassinated McKinley in September 1901.

How his Rough Rider hero had locked the chiefs of the miners union and the coal industry in the White House and wouldn't let them out until they settled the crippling 1902 anthracite strike had deeply impressed Victor Jr.

He applauded Roosevelt's maneuvering to get independence for Panama and then grabbing the Panama Canal Zone, and also adroitly fending off Canada's efforts to block corridors to Alaska on the heels of the Klondike gold strike.

In his opinion, Roosevelt showed greatness in becoming the first President to advocate American interference in foreign affairs. "Speak softly and carry a big stick; you will go far." Victor Jr. considered that powerful talk.

His delegate's ticket was marked Entrance B, Section 6, Row N, Seat 11.[2] It bore the portrait of William McKinley. Nothing about the Chicago convention surprised him. Teddy was a lock. The jovial President's flamboyant, popular style was destined to obliterate the colorless and sober Democratic nominee, Judge Alton B. Parker of New York.

On the train ride back to Antlers, Victor Jr. mulled over interesting topics he'd heard discussed in Chicago. Means of travel was exploding. Barely six months earlier the Wright brothers startled the world by flying their little biplane at Kitty Hawk, North Carolina. Somebody in the convention hall told him aghast that surprisingly only three big city newspapers reported that epoch. The flurry of motorcars awed him. Not only was there a Ford flivver, but autos carrying the names Cadillac, Pierce Arrow, Willys, Maxwell, and Reo.

His musical ear caught several popular new songs, including: *Ida, Sweet as Apple Cider; Sweet Adeline; Waltzing Matilda;* and

---

[2] Locke Family Papers, Garrard Ardeneum Manuscript Collection

Frankie and Johnny. Chicago newspapers trumpeted a vibrant new novelist, Jack London, and his stellar "The Call of The Wild." London, Victor Jr. observed with some chagrin, was just his age—and already a big success.

Coming through St. Louis, he felt tempted to stay over and see the much-heralded 1904 World's Fair, but didn't. Later he read about all the scientific sensations revealed there, and was amused by the attention paid to the St. Louis Fair's three gastronomic "firsts"— hamburgers, ice cream cones, and iced tea.

That a son of Uncle Dick Locke would be propelled into the edge of the national political arena as a Republican Convention delegate was no surprise in Choctaw country. Pulling strings and behind-the-scenes maneuvering in tribal government affairs remained the succulent red meat of the patriarch's life.

The Choctaws as a people were in turmoil. Crushing blows relentlessly rained down on the tribe from their Great Father in Washington. Congress and the White House were determined to abolish traditional order and custom in the Choctaw Nation, in fact in all the Five Civilized tribes.

The federal government's intent was clear and simple—take away the Indians' "surplus" land to open the way for white homesteaders, abolish tribal government and convert the Indians into U.S. citizens, penned on individual farms without an open range for their livestock, all under the banner of a new state to be called Oklahoma.

How best to cope with such a dire threat had the Choctaws in disagreement. The issue came down to: *fight* or *surrender*. Even Victor Locke Sr. vacillated. As did everyone affected, he studiously weighed visible merits and the disadvantages. His perennial candidate for chief, Jacob B. Jackson, was violently opposed to change. Principal Chief Jefferson Gardner stubbornly attempted to stymie the Dawes Commission fieldwork on allotting Choctaw land.[3]

With the election of Green McCurtain as Principal Chief, sentiment favorable to allotment began to crystallize among the Choctaws.

---

[3] John Bartlett Meserve, "Chief Benjamin Smallwood and Chief Jefferson Gardner," *Chronicles of Oklahoma,* (Vol. 19, No. 3), p 218

Former Chief Jackson McCurtain's wife Jane, told the Dawes Commission in 1896: " . . .I want to see the land allotted and the United States protect us before it is too late . . .If we could live in quiet and peace . . . as we did in the early years, I would prefer that . . . but allotment and citizenship must come and tribal relations cease." Others shared her view.

Even so, many prominent Choctaw leaders continued to rebel right up to the end.[4] A sizeable group of full bloods was so dissatisfied they proposed selling all the Choctaw land back to the government and going lock, stock and barrel to live in Mexico, or South America. They were aware that the renegade Seminole leader Wildcat *(Coacoohee)* defected in 1850 and took a few hundred Indians and Negro freedmen to live south of the border.[5] [After Wildcat died in 1857, his colony fell apart.] Pro-Mexico Choctaws, led by Jacob B. Jackson, made a trip to look over land south of the border in Winter 1897-98.[6] But nothing came of the scheme.

Despite the steady bursts of tribal in-fighting over the Choctaw future, canny Uncle Dick took full advantage of his still-strong political clout to acquire a share of patronage for his family, in particular his grown sons.

Not only had Victor Jr. embarked on a career in the political field, but two others, Shub and Ben, had patronage jobs, clearly pushed along by fatherly influence.

The lackadaisical Shub Locke was appointed bailiff for the U.S. District Court newly established in Antlers to handle the upsurge in crime ranging from whiskey dealing to murder. [The other bailiff was Will Everidge, son of a powerful tribal leader. Ironically, Shub and Will, close friends, were destined to fall out over politics and duel with pistols aboard a Frisco train.]

Ben Locke, though only nineteen, was sworn in as a deputy U.S. Marshal, and stationed at Talihina. His career as a lawman was brief—and dramatic.

---

[4] *The Rise and Fall,* p 267

[5] Edwin C. McReynolds, *The Seminoles* (Norman, 1957), pp 261-63

[6] *Indian Citizen,* March 17, 1898

How and why he quit his marshal's job Ben good-naturedly related years later to a newspaper reporter in Muskogee. The two-column-long story said in part:

> Captain Locke's story of how he left the marshal's service gives him many a chuckle yet and proves again the great common sense which activated him even in his youth.
>
> He had been sent out to bring back a particularly "bad" renegade from the fastness of the Kiamichi mountains. He knew nothing of the man except by reputation, which was that of a killer. That reputation was attached to the majority of early day outlaws so meant little to the young deputy.
>
> As he neared the district near which the outlaw was supposed to be hiding, he went for counsel to one Colonel Burgoyne, a veteran of outlaw days and familiar with all noted "bad" men.
>
> The colonel, in all seriousness, told Locke to go no farther, that his quarry would stop at nothing, that it was impossible to capture him in his mountain haunts single-handed and that to enter there alone was rank suicide.
>
> "Go back home," Colonel Burgoyne told him, "get a half dozen men and come back, if you must, but come at night. You might have a chance."
>
> The hero of the novel would have pooh-poohed such a suggestion as a slur on his bravery, would have gone into the mountains after his quarry.
>
> "I went back home," Captain Locke will tell you laughingly, "just as fast as I could go and resigned immediately."
>
> And anyone who talks to the captain understands that there was not the slightest cowardice in his act. It was just common sense.[7]

By far the star and most successful politician of the Locke scions was Victor Jr., an astute charmer. Just like his brothers, he was handed low-rung opportunities at the start. But while his siblings' careers were short-lived, Victor Jr. rose steadily, and fairly rapidly, eventually to the Choctaw Nation's topmost position.

---

[7] Locke Family Papers, Garrard Ardeneum Manuscript Collection, *Trench 90,* newspaper published at Muskogee, Oklahoma Veterans Hospital, issue of Oct. 1, 1927

In 1903, Victor Jr. was appointed to a new fifteen-member tribal executive council created to advise the principal chief during the transition into the new realm of citizenship and statehood.[8] At the same time he was, as a skilled Choctaw linguist, authorized by the federal government to serve as interpreter for paying parties.[9]

On July 1, 1908, he was selected by Secretary of the Interior Garfield as District Indian agent for the entire Choctaw tribe. Then came another important appointment that classically exemplified the contrariety of shifting alliances and feuds among tribal leaders. Strangely, Principal Chief Green McCurtain, who had quarreled violently and regularly for years with Uncle Dick, chose his enemy's son to become his secretary. Victor Jr. took the job on February 1, 1910, and of course was extremely well qualified.

He would remain the chief's right hand man until sudden good fortune would shower down all over him!

Back in 1900, Victor Jr.'s first bite of the patronage pie had been inauspicious, but memorable. He was appointed enumerator in the first census district in what is now Pushmahata County. For five weeks he roamed the mountains and river bottoms on a saddle mule. Thirty years later he recalled his experience for the *Oklahoma City Times:*

> It was Indian Territory then. I rode a red saddle mule belonging to my father. Fourteen hours a day for five weeks the animal carried me and he was fatter when we finished than when we started. You can't beat a good riding mule.
>
> My territory was twenty-four square miles containing sixteen townships. Most of the inhabitants were members of the Choctaw tribe. Being Choctaw myself, I needed no interpreter to help fill out my schedules.
>
> Many of the Indians did not know their age in years but could remember their birth by some tribal event taking place at the time. I relied on my knowledge of tribal history to get accurate information in many cases.

---

[8] *Locke Family History,* p 295
[9] *Loc., cit.*

> I wore a large official star-shaped badge. It was the approved insignia of the office. We also carried credentials like they do today. Enumerators in 1900 also carried six-guns, symbols of border law. We were not required to tote guns, but any man who left his persuader at home lacked forethought.[10]

IF ANYONE had asked Shub Locke to spell "joie de vivre," he could not have. Yet blitheness was the very essence of his irrepressible life. And was the death of him—much too early.

Two decades after chopping down the first tree to clear the Antlers town site, Shub was married, had two kids, but happy-go-lucky with no real ambition. He drank too much.

In early April 1906, Shub went to Paris, Texas on a lark with Will Everidge, who had been his fellow bailiff in U.S. court. Shub was thirty-four; Will about the same age. They found whiskey, and drank a lot of it.[11]

They staggered aboard the night train back to Antlers. As the Frisco rocked up the tracks a quarrel broke out "and they had a little battle."[12] Both drew their six-shooters. If sober, they could have taken deadly aim. Shub, of course, already had one notch on his Colts—for killing Deputy Marshal Jim Ashford.

Unsteadily, in the swaying coach, they faced each other only a few feet apart. Both guns roared. Each man began spurting blood. Shub had taken a slug in his left side. Will was winged in the arm. Both fell.

The conductor rushed up and passengers helped him staunch the bleeding with makeshift bandages. Within an hour, the wounded men were in Antlers and under the care of physicians.

Will Everidge's wound healed. Shub Locke was not so lucky. The bullet pierced his left kidney, causing a serious infection. He was put

---

[10] *Oklahoma City Times,* April 17, 1930

[11] *Indian-Pioneer Papers,* Vol. 4:45, May 20, 1937, and *Pushmahata County,* pp 291-92

[12] *Loc., cit.*

to bed. For ten weeks, he lay there. Doctors finally discovered a large abscess on his kidney.[13]

On Tuesday, June 5, 1906, Shub was taken back to Paris to Hermitage Sanitarium, accompanied by his wife and brother Ben. Surgery was advised. A week later, Tuesday June 12, Dr. W. B Chapman of Paris and Dr. I. D. Walker of Antlers operated on the abscess. Recovery seemed likely until he took a bad turn around 6 P.M.

His father took No. 5 to Paris. The doctors told him there was no hope. Uncle Dick returned to Antlers on the midnight train.

Victor Locke Sr.'s telephone rang at 8 A.M., Wednesday, June 13. The message was succinct: "Shub died about 7 o'clock."[14]

The body was brought back that afternoon to his father's house. The funeral took place at 10 o'clock Thursday morning in St. Agnes Catholic Church, where Shub was a member. Then the mourners marched up cemetery hill and buried him next to his mother and little brothers in the shade of the lonely cedar tree.

When his brother died, Victor Jr. was in Idabel in a town site meeting with Choctaw and Chickasaw Indians but got back Wednesday night. Brother Alex, attending Nazareth College at Muskogee, did not arrive until two hours after the burial.[15]

THE STATEHOOD FRENZY created a schism between Locke Senior and Locke Junior. Uncle Dick sided with the Choctaws who struggled to retain their old way of life. These stubborn Indians vehemently did not want to be changed into citizens of the United States, or see created the new state of Oklahoma.

Victor Jr. took the long view. He understood that transformation was inevitable. The Great Father in Washington would not be denied. The seventh President, Andy Jackson, had instigated the Indian removal to the West, and the eighteen statesmen who had followed him into the

[13] *Antlers News-Record,* June 15, 1906

[14] *Loc., cit.*

[15] *Loc., cit.*

White House, including the current Teddy Roosevelt, continued the push to Americanize the tribes.

Congress after Congress was willing and eager to crush the autonomy of the Five Civilized Tribes. Their tribal governments already had been abolished, and the Indians now were being forced to bow to the white man's law.

The free range and ownership of the Nation in common was no more. Each Choctaw was being parceled out 320 "average" acres valued at $1,041.28. If he chose, the allottee might take cheaper or more expensive land thus making his holdings range from 160 to 4,165 acres.[16] The "surplus" territory would be opened to white settlers.

As the Choctaws split into factions angrily debating their forced subjugation to the federal government, Victor Senior actively joined the resistance band. His son more or less sat on the sidelines, listening to the gears grinding behind the scenes, but not publicly outspoken.

Victor Jr. was impressed by the careful and gradual way Chief Green McCurtain swung the Choctaw majority around to "accepting the allotment in severalty of the tribal domain and a policy which was ultimately to lead to the extinguishment of the political status of the tribe."[17]

Green McCurtain was the last elected chief of the Choctaws. Having won the 1902 general election, his term should have ended in 1904. By that time the Indians no longer were holding any elections because the federal government had already started dismantling the tribal machinery.

McCurtain simply was kept in place by the federal authorities to provide Washington a conduit or figurehead through which to negotiate with the tribe. "The power of the chief seemed to grow in importance as details affecting citizenship rolls, allotment deeds and individual disbursements were presented," says historian John Bartlett Meserve.[18] The chief, Meserve writes, "was a great executive, a wonderful administrator and the outstanding leader among his people."[19]

---

[16] *The Rise and Fall,* p 277

[17] John Bartlett Meserve, "The McCurtainbs," *Chronicles of Oklahoma* (Vol. 13, No. 3), p 309

[18] *Ibid.,* p 310

[19] *Loc., cit.*

Meantime, Victor Senior had his hands deep in the scheme which was being pushed by recalcitrant Choctaws, and some Chickasaws, to pull up stakes in Indian Territory and move to Mexico. One prominent instigator of that failed stratagem was Uncle Dick's political protégé, Jacob B. Jackson.

Outsiders were financing the Indians, Uncle Dick revealed in a prospectus he wrote for the venture. This group, most likely investors seeking to acquire Indian land, were to put up expense money and receive a share of the "surplus" acreage that would be left behind. Locke identified them as the "Kansas Syndicate"—misspelling the last word.

Hand-written on his monogrammed stationery, the statement began:

> The Choctaws and the Chickasans are together in moving to Mexico—and the trade they have with the Kansas Synagate is they give 1/4 of their surplus land allotment for 4/4 of land in Mexico.
>
> The Synagate pays all expenses until the trade is perfected and when the Indians receive their land in Mexico—then move all their people at their own expense.
>
> The reason of them wanting to go to Mexico is on account of the two factions which cannot get along. They have had very serious trouble and they want the Government to pay them for what is their due and let them move while they are able to do so—for it will ultimately come to that.
>
> Their object is to own their property in common like they did when they come to the Choctaw Nation.[20]

In the end, the Mexican scheme evaporated. Congress kept tightening the screws, and any effective opposition to statehood was finally stymied. It was goodbye to the way of life the Indians cherished.

The day Oklahoma finally became a state was Saturday, November 16, 1907. Seven thousand spectators thronged the new state capital at

---

[20] Undated, hand-written document in Locke Family Papers, Garrard Ardeneum Manuscript Collection

Guthrie for the historic spectacle. None of the Lockes took part; they remained in Antlers.

In Washington, at the White House, President Theodore Roosevelt picked up an eagle quill pen and at 10:16 A.M. Eastern Time signed the statehood proclamation. Western Union had a direct wire to Guthrie. It took two minutes to flash the official news. The official word arrived at 9:18 A.M. in the new 46th state.[21]

The huge crowd, jamming the stairways and halls of Guthrie's Hotel Royal, the adjacent streets, even sitting in trees, roared approval. Hundreds fired guns into the crisp, sunny sky. People danced in the streets. Governor Charles N. Haskell took his oath in a Prince Albert instead of a sack coat.[22]

Signifying the union of the two, a mock wedding joined Mr. Oklahoma Territory to Miss Indian Territory. Posing as the "bride" was pretty Mrs. Leo Bennett, a Cherokee and wife of the Indian Agent who was the "hero" on the Gaines County assassination episode. William Durant of Durant gave her away. He was the only Choctaw on the program. J.J. McAlester, appointed as a corporation commissioner, was too ill to attend.[23]

"That was the birthday of the proud new state of Oklahoma," Victor Locke Jr. told his father later. "And the funeral of Indian Territory."[24]

IT DID NOT TAKE LONG for the quickie marriage of Ben Locke and Mattie Belle to end. The divorce gave custody of their son, Curtis, to the mother, but Ben would maintain lifelong contact with him. [Subsequently Mattie Belle was to marry twice more, to Dr. J. C. McGinnis and to S. E. Jackson, both of Antlers.][25]

---

[21] Dan W. Perry, "Twenty-seven Years a State," *Chronicles of Oklahoma* (Vol 12, No. 4) pp 393-399

[22] *Loc., cit.*

[23] *Loc., cit.*

[24] Dorothy Arnote West interview

[25] Author interview with Kay Brown Black, archivist, Pushmahata County Historical Society, July 3, 2004

Ben was too outgoing to sit around and pine for romance. He took action even though it meant courting a girl sight unseen, and by mail.

She was, in his thinking, a Seminole Indian "princess," both in beauty and family heritage. Niece of Governor John F. Brown, principal chief of the Seminoles, she was born Ella Maynie Davis, changed her name to Eleanor Maye, and finally called herself just Maye.

In some fashion Ben Locke and Maye Davis heard of each other while she was student at Kidd-Key College in Sherman, Texas,[26] most likely through Ben's sister Dolly who had attended Kidd-Key. The school yearbook identified Maye as "the most popular girl in school."

When they began writing each other in 1905, Maye was twenty, Ben twenty-two. They had common Indian heritage; Maye one-fourth Seminole, and her suitor one-fourth Choctaw.

She was the daughter of one of the most prominent women in the Seminole Nation, Alice Brown Davis, sister of Chief Brown, and George Rollin Davis, who had a North Canadian River ranch and trading post at Arbeka, Indian Territory, twenty miles north of Wewoka. Maye considered herself Destiny's child—seventh child born on the seventh day of the seventh month.[27]

[Oddly, in 1923 it would fall to Victor Locke Jr. to induct Alice Brown Davis as the first woman chief of the Seminole tribe on her appointment by President Warren G. Harding to succeed her brother, who had died. By that time, Victor Jr. would be holding the important government post of Superintendent of the Five Civilized Tribes.]

For two years Ben and Maye corresponded, chatty letters that became warm and affectionate. Both were excellent polished writers. He lived in Hamden, running a trading post. She taught at Emahaka Mission, Seminole boarding school for girls, and lived at Sasakwa.

---

[26] Benita Locke Wagner interview with her mother Maye Locke, undated, Locke Family papers, Garrard Ardeneum Manuscript Collection

[27] *Loc., cit.*

The anxious Ben pressed Maye for a date. Finally she accepted his invitation to a dance January 22, 1907 at the Scott Hotel in Holdenville, I. T., fifteen miles from Sasakwa, on the Frisco line.[28]

Maye arrived first. The three-story hotel, built of rock, had an elevator, and was the largest building in Holdenville. She waited for quite a while, sitting nervously in a corner of the parlor.

A girl came to the door and said, "Your hero."

Maye looked up and saw a smiling stalwart young man wearing a green suit, black overcoat, and a big black hat.

He swept a bow. "Miss Davis?"

"You're late!" she snapped.

"Dammit," he shot back, "I couldn't help it if there was a wreck!"[29]

Ben's easy charm quickly brought her out of her snit. After four more dates, he proposed. Her kiss was an exciting yes. They were married July 22, 1907 in Sasakwa. Her attendants were her sister, Irene, and niece, Pearl Davis.[30]

Their first wedding night was spent in the Bird Hotel in Ada, the second in a hotel in Sherman, Texas. Then they went on to Hamden.

"We somehow lost all our clothes on the train," Maye recalled.[31]

Soon they had two feisty little girls, Allece, born February 23, 1909 in Hamden, and Benita, born November 5, 1911 in Wewoka.

CUPID'S ARROWS once again were about to zing in Victor Junior's direction. Handsome, jaunty, impeccably dressed, intelligent and successful, he stood out as "a catch." Victor Jr. kept his eyes alert and appreciated a pretty face and slender figure. He was not much over thirty and without a known love since his abortive courtship of Sudie McAlester, and his failed marriage to Mattie Belle Keith.

His unattached status was about to change.

---

[28] *Loc., cit.*
[29] *Loc., cit.*
[30] *Loc., cit.*
[31] *Loc., cit.*

First, however, his latent ambition for an active career in the military nudged him into action. Back in 1898 he had rushed to join the United States Army after the outbreak of the Spanish-American war. He was too late to see action; it was all over before he could finish basic training.

But the yen to be a soldier, to command troops in battle, did not die. Luckily, statehood gave him a new and unexpected opportunity. Oklahoma needed to create National Guard companies. Victor Jr. volunteered to form one in Antlers, and did so in 1908.

He was appointed captain, in command, of Company "L," Oklahoma National Guard. Brother Ben was first lieutenant, and Babe a private. The unit consisted of two hundred troops, virtually all with Choctaw blood.

Photos of Captain Victor M. Locke Jr. in dress uniform, slender, erect and virile, with his saber agleam, show him at perhaps the most handsome stage of his entire life.

He was prime for a new romance—and found it.

In the spring of 1909 Victor Jr.'s eye fell on young and comely Maye Cordelia Brown, who had come to Antlers as a schoolteacher. She was from Lee's Summit, Missouri, on the outskirts of Kansas City. Maye for two years attended Baker University at Baldwin, Kansas. Her major was literature and art. She was in the Clionians, a women's literary society.[32]

Victor Jr. was then thirty-three; she was twenty-three. He courted and won her. They went by train to the home of her parents, the McGuire Browns, at Lee's Summit where they were married on Tuesday, July 6, 1909.

Three days later they came back to Antlers and read in the *Antlers News-Record* an account of their wedding in Missouri which included this lavish praise:

> Victor Murat Locke was raised in Antlers and needs no introduction to the people of Eastern Oklahoma. He is known as a young man of integrity and sterling worth; he is one who by his own efforts

---

[32] Archives, Baker University, August 18, 2004

has risen to a position of prominence among his fellow men, and well deserves the distinctions which have been conferred upon him. He is a member of the Choctaw tribe of Indians and has been for years a trusted and valued advisor and guide for his people.

His services have been recognized alike by the Indian and the United States governments. For several years he represented his own people in their councils and then he was drafted by the Department of Interior to assist the Commissioner of the Five Civilized Tribes at Muskogee. He is at this time a special representative of that department.

Mr. Locke has had a military training, and was appointed Captain of Company L., Oklahoma National Guards, about a year ago, a position he now holds, and it may be truthfully said Company L is one of the most efficient in the service.

Captain Locke is also an ardent Republican and is always at the front in the councils of his party. He was a delegate to the Republican National Convention in 1904 and has done much for his party in Oklahoma.

The bride, Miss Maye C. Brown, is well known to a great number of our people, and was loved by all who knew her. A young lady of exceptional talent and grace, she has made friends of all who met her. She, too, has ambition and will make an ideal companion and helpmeet for the man whose fortune she has joined with hers.

Mrs. Locke was educated at Baker University in Kansas, one of the oldest as well as one of the most thorough academic schools in the West.

The happy couple will reside in Antlers, and will be gladly welcomed among our people.

The best wishes of the *News-Record* and a host of friends wish them a happy and prosperous journey through life.

Mr. Locke and bride arrived in Antlers Thursday afternoon and will make their home among us.[33]

Their promise of "a happy and prosperous journey through life" was not to be. Within a short time, Victor Jr. again was single and footloose. [The 1910 census listed Maye C. Locke as a boarder in the home of S. K. Newcomb, whose two-story house across from his livery stable

---

33 *Antlers News-Record,* July 9, 1909, p 5

on Main Street was an early Antlers landmark. In June 1913, she was hired as a teacher at Jumbo.][34]

With two failed marriages before his mid thirties, Victor Jr. himself was beginning to question whether he could be a successful husband. In a letter about this time to his aunt, Alice Hilseweck, he brought up directly overtones of the Oedipus complex, writing:

> You know, Alice, my good Mother was always the real sweetheart of my life, and to this fact I attribute my utter failure to be the husband of any woman. I was often told that I would be the loveliest of husbands because I loved my Mother so well, but this principle won't work.
>
> I was a "beaut" in actual experience, but I console myself by thinking that no man ever accomplished anything without leaving in his wake a string of blunders and mistakes. And I never accomplished in my life except right on the heels of adversity.[35]

A few weeks before marrying May Brown, Captain Victor M. Locke Jr. became close to exploding in anger when his new National Guard company was not called to duty in the Crazy Snake Indian uprising.

"I am mad—mad as hell! Co. L made a dandy muster last Friday. I had fifty-eight men and we three officers present. Besides the whole town turned out to show their approval of the military spirit in our community. Now the first opportunity that arises for my men to have some practical experience I am left out and my telegram offering our services is not even replied to."

Thus began his March 30, 1909 letter to his friend Patrick Jay Hurley, a young Choctaw attorney, who would later become famous as a "hero" in World War I, as President Hoover's Secretary of War, and as major general, and ambassador to China and Australia.

The uprising that ignited Captain Locke's fury was led by a Creek Indian named Chitto Harjo, known as Crazy Snake. With a small

---

[34] *Antlers American,* June 19, 1913

[35] Victor Locke Jr to Alice Hilseweck, March 4, 1911, Locke Family Papers, Garrard Ardeneum Manuscript Collection

band of followers, Crazy Snake refused to accept the government land allotments, and protested the breaking of treaties.

On Nov. 26, 1906 he made a dramatic and eloquent protest before a U.S. Senate investigating committee in Tulsa. He spoke calmly, with no gestures, and held the committee and spectators spellbound, writes historian John Bartlett Meserve.[36]

Statehood came, and unfounded rumors spread that Crazy Snake was about to go on the warpath. The old Indian disappeared. He was thought to be plotting in McIntosh County. The frightened sheriff called in the state militia. No trace of Crazy Snake was ever found, and the so-called uprising evaporated. [Years later a Kansas City reporter discovered that Chitto Harjo died April 11, 1911 at a friend's cabin in the Kiamichi Mountains and was buried there.][37]

None of this was known to Victor Jr. when he was writing Patrick Hurley. In four, hand-written pages, he got a lot off his chest. One of his men heard that the Durant militia company was called up. Captain Locke took it for granted that orders would also come to Company L.

> I immediately assembled all my men. All day long Sunday we lay under arms. . .but no orders from headquarters ever came. You never saw such a disappointed bunch of men. . . The "Snakes" have my deep sympathy in their troubles, but I must do a citizen's and a soldier's duty. . .
>
> I know and you know that a white man is at the bottom of this slaughter or trouble, whether reports as to its magnitude be correct or exaggerated. And I feel that you are bound to feel that the government is guilty of criminal negligence in letting unworthy white men incite our "Injuns" to outbreaks.
>
> The place of origin of this last outbreak of Creeks or "Snakes" is Washington City. The American people are humane but oftimes the exercise of their humanity is misplaced and they forget that there is but one step between savagery and civilization.
>
> I am mad because the government pursues a course toward our people wholly at variance with what is possible and just. For Heaven's

---

[36] John Bartlett Meserve, "The Plea of Crazy Snake," *Chronicles of Oklahoma.* (Vol 11, No. 3) pp 900-01

[37] *Ibid.,* p 910

sake, make haste, Pat, and be President! Make me your prime minister. We will throw aside the Constitution and take the Bible as the supreme law of the land.[38]

"THE STATES" were bustling with population growth and invention by 1910, and Antlers, in a spanking new Oklahoma but still on the edge of wilderness, was showing some progress of its own.

In the *American,* Victor Senior read that the census gave Antlers 1,273, and Pushmahata County almost doubled to 10,118.[39] The United States had grown to 92 million, 4.42 million of whom lived in New York City. Antlers now had a water system, an electric light plant, telephones, more board sidewalks, and one doctor brought in the town's first X-ray machine.[40]

The Locke patriarch kept busy. He built a new Main Street livery stable. Foreseeing the town's growth, for his intermarried Choctaw tribal allotment he acquired a large quantity of "poor" land inside the city limits he could sell as building lots.[41]

Building a railroad from Antlers to connect with the Kansas City Southern in Arkansas looked to him like an ideal means of hauling timber out of the Kiamichi mountain forests. He spent weeks negotiating with the two railroads; they sent engineers to check out the proposed route. In the end it was left for wagons and oxen or mule teams to haul out the timber. The Frisco and Kansas City Southern executives turned him down.[42]

Uncle Dick then gave a lot of thought to oil. E. W. Marland had brought in oil wells on Ponca Indian land in northern Oklahoma, and was rolling in money. He avidly read St. Louis, Kansas City and New York newspapers that arrived by train. Certain items struck him. Americans

---

[38] Victor Locke to Patrick Hurley, March 30, 1911, Locke Family Papers, Garrard Ardeneum Manuscript Collection

[39] *Pushmahata County,* p 49

[40] *Ibid.,* p 48

[41] *Days Gone By,* p 23

[42] *Pushmahata County,* p 44

smoked 8.6 million cigarettes a year. Boy Scouts were founded; in Kansas City, Hallmark Greeting Cards started up.

Any adventure excited him. U.S. Explorer Robert E. Peary reached the North Pole, and other explorers were heading for the South Pole. The Wright brothers had just sold a two-seater biplane to the War Department; it was supposed to stay aloft an hour at 40 m.p.h. The pilot, a Lieutenant Selfridge, was killed in a test flight, but the plane was successfully repaired. Cunard's *Mauritania* set an Atlantic crossing record: four days, 20 hours and 41 minutes.

As a "good" Republican, he approved Theodore Roosevelt's decision to cling to tradition of not accepting a third term, clearing the way for President William Howard Taft. Some of the Antlers politicians irritated him. They passed an ordinance requiring chickens to be kept in pens. Uncle Dick defiantly released all his hens and roosters and paraded the fowl flock down Main Street.[43]

His boys, who were still getting up dances in Antlers, were impressed with some of the new songs just out, especially: *I Wonder Who's Kissing Her Now, By The Light of The Silvery Moon,* and *Let Me Call You Sweetheart.*

In the summer of 1910 Ben Locke sold his 180-acre prairie farm to a man from Joplin, Missouri, F. J. Niles, for $2,250.[44] Ben, twenty-seven, was a highly regarded guide for hunters and explorers in the Kiamichi Mountain wilderness. Deer, squirrel, ducks, and fish were abundant. "Wicked" Smith, a friend of Ben's, bagged 160 squirrels in two hours. Occasional bears were encountered.

The most feared forest beast was the mountain lion or panther (*koi*), a night creature that often hid near streams to spring on deer as they drank. Ben recounted a memorable wilderness incident in a 1926 newspaper article:

> Years ago I was engaged by a party to pilot him through the darkest recesses of our country. We were on the trail, and it was past midnight and very dark although the stars were shining brightly.

---

[43] Memoirs of Allece Locke Garrard, Locke Family Papers, Garrard Ardeneum

[44] *Pushmahata County,* p 50

The constant click, click of our horses' hooves on the rocks and the never ceaseless straining of my eyes trying hopelessly to observe anything unusual was a drain on my nerves. The man, too, was a stranger. I knew nothing of his staying qualities. He was silent and mysterious and played the ghost shadows with his gun in a manner that aroused in me a feeling of uneasiness and anticipation.

The country was wild and one could expect any kind of trouble. Presently the reaction set in. I developed an imaginary leakage of the heart, an enlargement of the spine, and a sincere wish that I was back at my own fireside.

Approaching McGee Creek we drifted down into the bed of the stream when, to my horror, a piercing scream, not more than thirty yards away, sounding just like a woman in distress, was let forth.

Despair and horrified terror seized me. I was insanely frightened and flashed an appealing glance up into the night sky. I registered the Dipper, North Star, Seven Stars and finally centered on Job's Coffin.

Suddenly the stranger's two guns began belching a double stream of fire. The red blaze shooting out from the mouth of the guns told me more than words that something terrible was happening. At the same moment I was conscious of the dull impact of a heavy object falling.

My horse moved fast, we left McGee Creek far behind, crossing Boggy at the halfway bridge. I began to regain my senses and to realize and appreciate the sweetness of life when the stranger turned in his saddle toward me and said: "Boy, that panther sure like to got you!"[45]

EVEN AFTER STATEHOOD, the hulking shadow of Chief Green McCurtain—he was six-two and weighed two hundred twenty pounds—fell frequently across the marble floors of the Interior Department in Washington. Officials still summoned him for consultation on sticking

---

[45] *Muskogee (*Okla*) Daily Phoenix,* July 25. 1926; *Locke Family History,* pp 303-04

points in Choctaw Indian negotiations. They found his "executive direction of the inestimable value."[46]

On trips to the capital in 1910, as well as on daily duty back home, Private Secretary Victor Locke Jr. stuck close to Green McCurtain's elbow. Victor Jr. kept his eyes bright and alert, and his ears open. He didn't want to miss nary a tip on what it took to be in command!

He handled varied executive duties, and thanked his stars for getting a broad education in his three years at Drury College; his classical reading gave him an edge in his work, and, to his surprise, so vaguely did his knowledge of Latin.

Victor Junior considered himself lucky to be the principal chief's private secretary—McCurtain could easily have given the job to his own son.

David Cornelius McCurtain, eldest son of the illustrious chieftain, was better educated, just as competent, and three years older than Victor Jr.[47] Generally called simply D. C., Chief McCurtain's son was born January 29, 1873 in Skullyville, and attended Indian Territory common schools. In 1890, his father sent him to Roanoke College at Salem, Virginia, and on to Kemper Military Academy in Missouri, to Missouri State University, and finally to law school at the Columbian, now George Washington University at Washington, D. C.[48]

Young McCurtain came home, was admitted to the bar, and served as district court clerk and was twice elected district attorney in the Mushulatubbe district. He went to Washington in 1901 as the Choctaw Nation delegate, serving until he resigned in 1907 to become the Choctaws' national attorney.

That was the situation when the year 1910 drew to a close—and so, too, did the old chief's life.

Green McCurtain was the last of the McCurtain dynasty among the Choctaws, the last of the Shak-chi-homa chiefs of that tribe, and the last elected chieftain of this historic tribe.[49]

---

[46] John Bartlett Meserve, "The McCurtains," *Chronicles of Oklahoma* (Vol 13, No. 3), p 310
[47] *Ibid.*, p 311
[48] *Loc., cit.*
[49] *Loc., cit.*

In late 1910, Chief McCurtain awakened with an afflicted face—redness, swelling and itching. His physicians diagnosed his disease as erysipelas, which is life threatening.[50] At his home at Kinta, in Haskell County, McCurtain, only sixty-eight, sank rapidly. With his son and his wife at bedside, he died on December 27, 1910.[51] He was buried at his old home in San Bois, some five miles east of Kinta. A handsome monument marks the grave.

Green McCurtain's demise saddened his private secretary and gave him a shock. Victor Junior's future in tribal affairs was now uncertain. Perhaps the next chief might not retain him. He thought about that deeply. Then a sudden and serious idea came to him. He should try to get himself appointed the next chief of the Choctaws!

He was qualified. He spoke the language. He knew the territory, the people. He knew the ropes in Washington. Why not?

He immediately launched a campaign to influence the selection process. He needed to be recommended to the Interior Department and to President William Howard Taft.

Victor Jr. tried, and failed.

The man President Taft appointed to succeed the old chief was his son, D. C. McCurtain.

---

[50] *Daily Oklahoman,* Dec. 27, 1910
[51] *Loc., cit.*

9

Her Little Roly-Poly Legs!

DESPONDENT AND ANGRY, Victor Locke Jr. saw the appointment of Green McCurtain's son to succeed his father as a crushing blow to his own cherished dream of becoming chief of the Choctaws.

Luckily, Locke was mistaken.

President William Howard Taft abruptly "fired" D. C. McCurtain, only two weeks after putting him in the job. That was triggered by a sensational Congressional investigation into a phony $1,000,000 fee rip-off by the Choctaws' long-time attorney J. Frank McMurray.

In that scheme, McMurray was to hand D. C. McCurtain $25,000.

Seizing the moment, Victor Jr. wrangled the support of the Oklahoma Republican boss, "Big Jim" Harris, and rushed to Washington, D.C. in the winter chill of February 1911 to make his personal pitch to President Taft.

In the capital, he sought help from his old Antlers priest, Father William H. Ketcham, who had been promoted to director of the national Bureau of Catholic Indian Missions, and now was a respected and influential figure in government circles. Father Ketcham readily agreed to intercede for Victor Locke Jr. at the White House and Interior Department, which held power over Choctaw affairs.

The million-dollar scandal had violently shocked Choctaw country. Senator T. P. Gore, the blind "silver-tongued orator" from Oklahoma, exposed the immoral scheme to fleece the Choctaw and Chickasaw tribes in an impassioned speech on the Senate floor June 24, 1910, asserting he had rejected the offer of a $50,000 bribe to assist the calumny.

Senator Gore said the $50,000 offer came from Jake L. Hamon, from his hometown of Lawton, a long-time friend although a back-room political strategist.

The greedy scheme centered on "High Fee" McMurray of McAlester, who had represented the Choctaws as national attorney since 1901. In a nutshell, McMurray was trying to push Congress to authorize claims for questionable legal services to the two tribes amounting to $1,000,000.[1]

Senator Gore's sensational speech triggered a six-month investigation by the House that in the end castigated McMurray, Hamon, and several others including D. C. McCurtain, who had been promised a $25,000 contingent fee if the scheme succeeded.[2]

Of McCurtain's fee, the final House report said: "It is not probable that such overtures come within the statutory definition of bribery or fraud, but your committee believes that the method employed by McMurray to interest the Choctaw chief [Green McCurtain] and his son is reprehensible and should be characterized by a stronger term than 'undue influence.' "[3]

One of several ironies in the scandal was that McMurray's attorney immediately filed charges asserting that D. C. McCurtain's action "disqualified" him from serving as Choctaw chief.[4] Another was that Senator Gore, after being offered a bribe, entertained Hamon with cigars

---

[1] *The Oklahoman,* March 1, 1911

[2] *Loc., cit.*

[3] *Loc., cit.*

[4] *The Oklahoman,* Feb. 2, 1911

and brandy in his Washington home, and got Hamon's father-in-law appointed a postmaster.[5]

McMurray also had retained as associate lawyers former Senators John M. Thurston of Nebraska and Chester L. Long of Kansas, on promise of 10 per cent fees. The House ruled this not unlawful. Hamon also boldly threw around the names of Vice President Sherman and Senator Charles Curtis of Kansas, but they were exonerated.[6]

Former President Roosevelt was tarred by testimony that he ordered dismissal of fraud indictments against McMurray's law firm over strong objections of the U.S. attorney in Indian Territory. Roosevelt took this action after meeting at the White House with a personal friend from Texas, Republican National Committeeman Cecil A. Lyon, who held an interest in the McMurray contracts.[7]

Senator Gore anticipated criticism for opening up the can of worms. "He who digs up a nest of serpents," Gore said on the Senate floor, "needs not be surprised if he hears the serpent's hiss, or if he feels the serpent's sting."[8] The senator felt proud that "I have saved the Indians of Oklahoma between $3,000,000 and $5,000,000."

Victor Jr. could not expect to be a shoo-in for chief. Two other Choctaws were campaigning for the post, Allen Wright of McAlester, brother of the persistent Locke enemy, Dr. E. N. Wright, and Tom Wall of Poteau. In the midst of such fierce partisan politics in Oklahoma, Taft would be expected to act with caution.

But Locke had the edge. On February 13, in Washington he received a night letter from "Big Jim" Harris:

> I have wired strong telegram to President. You will be appointed if you will make no mistake. Good luck to you. Wire me if anything more is necessary. Wall is getting endorsements but not making headway.
>
> J.A. Harris [9]

---

[5] *The Oklahoman,* March 1, 1911

[6] *Loc., cit.*

[7] *Loc., cit.*

[8] *The Oklahoman,* Jan.14, 1911

[9] Locke Family Papers, Garrard Ardeneum Manuscript Collection

Victor M. Locke Jr., just six weeks shy of thirty-four, was formally designated by President Taft on Tuesday, February 14, 1911 as Principal Chief of the Choctaw tribe. He promptly wrote his father the good news. Not everybody was happy about it. Two days later telegrams of protest began "pouring in" on Oklahoma's Congressional delegation, the daily *Oklahoman* reported in a Washington dispatch dated February 16.

> Some of the messages contain vague hints of forthcoming charges against the Antlers man. Indeed it is almost certain that a hot fight will be waged on Locke, the purpose of which will be nothing short of making him an impossibility for the high office to which he has been appointed.[10]

Chief Locke had no time in Washington to either worry or celebrate. Father Ketcham whisked him off to Philadelphia.

There in the Cathedral of Saints Peter and Paul, he sat with Father Ketcham and other dignitaries at the last rites of Archbishop Patrick John Ryan, who was so famous his sudden death was page one news all across the U.S. One Catholic newspaper printed Chief Locke's photo, and ran a story pointing out he attended the obsequies "to pay tribute to the prelate who had befriended his people. . .Chief Locke is a Catholic, Father Ketcham's first convert among the Choctaws."[11]

Then he was off to New York City "for a few days visit with friends," as he told a reporter for *The New York Herald.* He gave a long interview, with this opening remark: "The Indians, like the Irish, take to politics just as naturally as ducks take to water."[12] The reporter, explaining his appointment by Taft, said "Chief Locke became active in the American way of pulling wires and landed the plum."

---

[10] *The Oklahoman,* Feb. 17, 1911

[11] Unidentified clipping with burned edges, Locke Family Papers, Garrard Ardeneum Manuscript Collection

[12] *New York Herald,* February 19, 1911; *Locke Family History,* pp 294-295

Back in Antlers, people who knew him well probably raised quizzical eyebrows at some of his statements in the *Herald* interview, which read in part:

> When he goes back to Antlers, Okla., the 23,000 Indians comprising the Choctaw tribe will hold a big celebration. Chief Locke says the disappointed son of the dead chieftain had forwarded his congratulations and that the best feeling exists between them.
>
> The new chief is a halfbreed Indian and would pass on Broadway for a full blooded white. He had a distinguished bearing. According to his friends, he is the most popular young man in Oklahoma, where he is best known as "Dickie" Locke.
>
> Chief Locke was educated at Drury College, in Springfield, Mo. He is a fluent talker and exercises great care in his choice of words. He served in the Spanish-American War and is a captain in the National Guard of Oklahoma.
>
> "Our state," he said yesterday, "is teeming with politics. The country is peopled with a great variety of citizens, and naturally a chaotic state exists to a more or less degree. But in spite of all that it is the greatest community on earth. The Indians are proud of the part they are playing in the new government. Most of our officials have Indian blood coursing through their veins, including one of our United States Senators.
>
> "I steal away to old Mexico every once in a while. There are parts of that country that I revel in. For the most part Mexico is still governed after the fashion of the American Indians when they had their own country and their own laws. Truth is, they had few laws, but what they did have were religiously enforced.
>
> "I can keep up with the highest clip set in the West, but New York simply swamps me. I arrived here Friday evening last and already I am fatigued from going the pace which my friends are setting. For, you know, I am in the hands of my friends, and I would not be a very good Injun if I cried, 'Hold, enough!'."[13]

---

[13] *Loc., cit.*

THE NEW CHIEF stepped into a dangerous quagmire back home. Conflicts existed of such magnitude some Choctaws talked of going on the warpath. Trying for solutions had frustrated even Green McCurtain and chiefs who preceded him. Some of the snarls had grown beards; they were thirty years old, at least.

Now it was up to Chief Locke to find solutions that would settle down the Indians.

The new treaties that Congress forced upon the Indians so as to create the state of Oklahoma had stripped the nation of practically all judicial and legislative powers. Now they had to ask permission of the Secretary of the Interior or the President to take important tribal action.

A major Choctaw complaint was that Washington was holding in trust millions of dollars granted them by treaties, but would not pay it out prorata to the 20,000 tribe members. Likewise, the tribe was up in arms over the Dawes Commission being given authority to decide who was entitled to claim Choctaw citizenship. They knew thousands of mixed bloods filed fraudulent claims to "steal" Indian allotments.

Three million acres of Choctaw-Chickasaw land covered coal and asphalt deposits worth an estimated $12,000,000. Those minerals presented a huge bone of contention. The Choctaws themselves broke into factions, and were squabbling over whether to sell the mineral rights jointly with the surface. The Interior Department refused to buy the valuable acreage from the Indians, but conversely prevented its sale.

Chief Locke had his own view on this question. He wanted the joint sale, with mineral proceeds dedicated to maintaining tribal schools for Choctaw children. Washington was taking control of education, wanting all Indians to attend "white" schools, to get to know each other.

In the game of politics, Chief Locke had his own Achilles heel, and the very start of his administration exposed it. Appointed by a Republican President, it was up to him to maneuver patronage in favor of his party and to the detriment of the Democrats. He promptly "fired" Choctaw officials who were Democrats.

The veteran speaker of the Choctaw House of Representatives, William Durant of Durant [much later to become principal chief himself], was his most prominent victim. Chief Locke also told Hampton Tucker, mining inspector, and L.C. LeFlore, a townsite commissioner, they were no longer in office unless they could get a recommendation from Jim Harris, Oklahoma's Republican chairman. They, of course, couldn't.

Oklahoma Congressman Charles Carter rushed to the White House with letters and telegrams of protest,[14] but he was complaining to a Republican President. Editorially, the *Muskogee Times-Democrat*, fired this harpoon: "Of course, it is a policy that suits republican politicians well, for so long as they continue Indian affairs in an unsettled state they continue to farm out fat jobs to their friends and henchmen at the expense of the Indians."[15]

Another newspaper criticism: "As a republican governor of the Choctaws, Dick Locke, who is an exceptionally clever politician and manipulator, is delivering the goods to the republican administration that were promised when Taft appointed him."[16]

Not only were white intruders, crooked lawyers, land speculators, and railroads preying on the guile of the Indians, greedy Choctaws were fleecing their own people in this time of confusion and turmoil.

The state's largest newspaper, the daily *Oklahoman,* capsuled the factionalism, quoting another newspaper:

> The full-blood or Choctaw-speaking element is again in control of the Choctaw national government, ousting all the mixed-blood officials at the recent national council. The mixed blood party is made up of Choctaws who do not speak the language and of white men who have married Indian women.
>
> The victory of the council was emphasized by the bodily ejection from the council of William Durant, speaker of the lower house for several terms.
>
> The bone and sinew of the Choctaw Nation is in the full bloods, few of whom speak English and all of whom are intensively

---

[14] Undated newspaper clipping, Locke Family Papers, Garrard Ardeneum Manuscript Collection.

[15] *Muskogee Times-Democrat,* undated, Locke Family Papers, Garrard Ardeneum Manuscript Collection

[16] Undated, untitled newspaper clipping, Locke Family Papers, Garrard Ardeneum Manuscript Collection

> loyal to their own and the United States government, but lately they have been a political minority.
>
> The full-bloods are taciturn and, as a whole, were opposed to the allotment of their lands in severalty and to the abolishment of their tribal government. Unable to stay these changes, however, they girded themselves, so far as their intelligence and experience would permit, to save their tribal property from not only alien spoilers, but from those of their own people who were seeking to enrich themselves at the expense of the nation.[17]

Since the advent of statehood the position of the chief, or governor as some called him, had become a less important position. The chief was required to sign deeds in the transfer of property from the tribe to private parties, recommend transfers and suggest needed legislation touching Indian affairs. Even so, Victor Jr., the brand new chief, would need a strong right arm to guarantee a successful reign.

It brought a smile to his face to realize he knew just the sharp mind to recruit for that task—a friend from boyhood.

BY NO STANDARD, did Edwin Snow Locke fit the Locke family mold. He was a definite throwback. Even among bold siblings renowned for nonpareil eccentricity and the rash quick-draw, his life stood out—start to finish—as the matchless oddball.

Exactly why seems a mystery. As a boy he could not be classified as pixilated, or bonkers, or divaricated—he was just different! Where his brothers were loud, he was retiring and quiet. They loved to explore the wilderness, hunt game, and fish; Alex had no fondness for the outdoors. He did, however, in boyhood play baseball and as an adult would slavishly follow major league action.[18]

Of the lot, only he received a Catholic, not a Choctaw, education; he was most studious and bookish. His photos show a narrow stern face and cold eyes. Something was going on inside his skull that was secret and hidden. In his final years, that would dramatically reveal it-

---

[17] *The Oklahoman,* Oct. 27, 1931

[18] Interviews, Francine Locke Bray.

self. In Chicago, he would become the frustrated philosopher, burrowing into the Newberry Library, ranting as a public park speaker, abandoning his family (apparently in shame) for long periods.[19]

Although his father prankishly nicknamed him Alexander Hamilton Locke, the kid reveled in his new moniker. He retained the name in adulthood, and was usually called "Alex."

With his brothers, he fell under the influence of Antlers' first Catholic priest, Father William Ketcham. For a spell he was an altar boy. Alex developed a deep interest in religion, and seemed to have a desire to enter the priesthood.[20] His parents sent him at an early age to a boarding school in the Pottawatomie Nation operated by the Benedictine monks, Sacred Heart Mission. In that cloistered atmosphere, in herky-jerky periods of class studies, he was superbly educated.

On at least two tragic occasions when an evil cloud hung over his family, outsiders apparently speculated about Alex. The first was when his brother Dude was killed by a baseball bat blow to the head. [*Chapter Seven.*] In 1913, another brother would die of a mysterious pistol wound while Alex, his brother Ben, and Uncle Dick all were at or near the scene. The *Antlers American* would report the gun was fired by accident.

For Alex, the Atlantic Ocean turned out to be his four-leaf clover. Luckily, on the high seas he found love—and escaped death!

From Sacred Heart College, Alex transferred to the American College in Rome to study for the priesthood. He sailed from New York for London.[21]

Aboard ship he chanced to meet an attractive, willowy English girl named Frances Emma Philbrook who was returning home to London. They spent long hours together. Alex was smitten. He was a twenty-four-year-old one-quarter Choctaw male heading for Italy to take up the celibate priesthood. But passion overcame him. He proposed, and Frances accepted.[22]

---

[19] *Loc., cit.*

[20] *Locke Family History,* pp 306-307

[21] *Loc., cit.*

[22] *Loc., cit.*

In London, her father, Albert Francis Philbrook, and her stepmother helped arrange the wedding. Her father was identified on the marriage certificate as a mechanical engineer. Alex gave his age as twenty-four, his occupation as land agent. Frances Emma was twenty-one.[23]

They were married by a Catholic priest at the Church of the Sacred Heart of Jesus in London's Hampstead district. The date was significant—April 10, 1912.

The newlyweds rushed to the dock to sail home on the maiden voyage of the Royal Mail Lines majestic new steamship *Titanic,* departing within an hour on two for New York. They had their cabin reserved for a honeymoon. The purser would not let them board; Alex had no money. He explained that a check he expected from home had failed to arrive; he would be able to pay for the passage on arrival in New York. That promise was unacceptable.[24]

The S.S. *Titanic,* the world's then largest passenger liner and called "unsinkable," sailed on April 10 without Alex and Frances Emma Locke. Aboard were 2,224, including such prominent millionaires as R.H. Macy's Isidor Straus, copper heir Benjamin Guggenheim, and traction heir Harry E. Weidner.

In the North Atlantic on the night of April 15, the 882-foot-long *Titanic* struck an iceberg, which slashed open her side. The liner sank in two and a half hours, with 1,513 lives lost.

The Locke honeymooners were stunned by the tragedy, but sailed home next day, April 16, on the *Mauretania.* Alex took his bride to Antlers to show her off to the home folks.

PICTURE TWO BOYS fishing on a summer day in the Choctaw Nation in the early 1890s. They are Victor Locke Jr., and his new pal, a rugged Irish coal miner's son named Patrick J. Hurley. Idly, they talked of their ambitions.

---

[23] *Loc., cit.*

[24] *Loc., cit.*

"Some day," mused Locke, "I intend to be principal chief of the Choctaws."

"When you are," replied Hurley, "I hope you will make me the attorney for the nation."

"I'll do it," replied Locke, and the incident was dismissed. But, always more of an Indian than a white man, Victor, or "Dick" Locke, as his friends knew him, did not forget. [25]

That scene is taken verbatim from one installment of *The Oklahoman's book*-length biography of Hurley, published after he became famous as a World War I hero and subsequently as Oklahoma's first Presidential cabinet officer, Hoover's Secretary of War.

Written by Parker LaMoore, a noted journalist in Oklahoma City and Washington. D.C., the incident sounds apocryphal, but the writer got first hand facts, interviewing both Hurley and Locke. The newspaper pieces were published also as a book in 1932 by Brewer, Warren & Putnam, New York. [Parker was the elder brother of novelist Louis L'Amour.]

The riverbank scenario came true. Victor Jr. did achieve his ambition to be chief, and he did appoint his fishing pal as the national attorney for the Choctaw Nation.

Pat Hurley had no Choctaw blood; he was strictly Irish. His father, Pierce O'Neil Hurley, fled Ireland with a bullet wound taken in the rebellion against England. In Texas he married another émigré from Erin, Mary Kelly. They drifted to Indian Territory and he became a coal miner at Lehigh.[26]

Pat was born in 1883 on a farm rented from Ben Smallwood, wealthy, educated, bookish, and once chief of the Choctaws. Smallwood took a keen interest in young Pat, encouraged him to browse his library, and bought for him stunning red-topped boots. Pat's mother Mary died when he was eleven and at sixteen he joined his father in the coalmines. He was challenged to earn respect. He did it with his fists, beating the gang bully, as well as a mean balky mule.

---

[25] *The Oklahoman,* Oct. 27, 1931

[26] *The Oklahoman,* Oct. 20, 1931

Handsome, sharp-minded, ambitious, Pat Hurley quit digging coal after the cruel 1898 miner strike. For several months he was a wrangler on the Lazy S ranch. Then he went to Muskogee and worked his way through Bacone College, in five instead of six years, graduating in 1902. He got his law degree at National University in Washington, D.C., where he was a champion debater. He returned to Oklahoma to clerk in the government Indian Bureau. And he got his first taste of military life by joining Muskogee editor Clarence D. Douglas's "outlaw" militia, as sergeant major.

In 1910, the *Lehigh Leader* paid him this tribute: "Of all the boys who have been raised in this vicinity, Pat has achieved the most marked success, and none of the success which has attained, or which he will attain in the future, is undeserved."[27]

It was not until the fall of 1912 that Chief Locke was able to fulfill his boyhood pledge to employ Patrick J. Hurley as the attorney for the Choctaw Nation. It took a bit of maneuvering.

When Victor Jr. came into office, the Choctaw attorney contract was held by Ormsby McHarg, a New York lawyer and politician, who had served as assistant Secretary of Commerce and Labor in the Roosevelt Administration.[28] He was paid $12,000 a year, but rarely left his New York office. Chief Locke arranged for the Choctaw council to cut McHarg's salary in half. In a huff, McHarg resigned.[29]

That permitted Chief Locke to offer the job to Hurley, twenty-eight, at $6,000 a year, plus expenses. He had to route the contract to Washington for approval. Secretary of the Interior William L. Fisher cut the salary to $5,000 and limited expenses to $6 a day.[30]

Then the contract went to the White House. President Taft, who had already been defeated for re-election by Woodrow Wilson, signed the contract on November 28, 1912. [And later President Wilson would extend it.][31]

---

[27] *The Oklahoman,* Oct. 19, 1931
[28] *The Oklahoman,* Oct. 28, 1931
[29] *Loc., cit.*
[30] *Loc., cit.*
[31] *Loc., cit.*

The chief and his lawyer-pal congratulated each other, perhaps cheered themselves by bending their elbows a bit.

Then they rolled up their sleeves, ready for hard work. They would sally forth and slay the dragons then breathing fire on the hapless Choctaws. They would charge into Washington and attack the greedy politicians and crooked lawyers right in their Capitol Hill dens!

HORRIBLE ACCIDENT HAPPENS LAST NIGHT, shouted the headline on page one of the *Antlers American* on Saturday, January 4, 1913.

"Just at six o'clock yesterday (Friday) evening," began the news story, "when the little town of Antlers was just beginning to assume its peaceful slumbers from the day's toil, and another bright and beautiful day had folded its curtain of sunshine and gone to rest, so did the spirit of 'Babe' Locke pass from life's action into the great unknown beyond.

"When the news was flashed over town that 'Babe' Locke was dead, every head was raised in horror, and then bowed in gloom. 'Babe' was dead.

"How the awful tragedy occurred will probably never be known . . ."

On that score, the newspaper was 100 per cent correct. Babe's death was mysterious. It seems clear the family banded together to cover up how he died with a false story. Though implausible, the report was the kind not likely to be challenged since it came from a prominent and famous family.

Many undisputed facts are known. Around 5 o'clock in the afternoon Babe was in Antlers to see Judge Charles E. Dudley, and collect rent from the cotton weigher.[32] He was in a cheerful mood. Dr. L. M. Warner considered him "the light and life of his large circle of Antlers young people. . .a bright future awaited him . . .Presumably he had his faults; most of us do—it is only human. 'There are none perfect—no, not one.' "[33]

---

[32] *Antlers News-Record,* Jan. 10, 1913

[33] *Loc., cit.*

Beyond doubt Babe deserved his popularity. The *Antlers American* pointed out he knew no class distinction: "One might find him in the dazzling ballroom of the fortune favored, the next night would find him in the little mountain hut of the poverty stricken taking part in an old-fashioned square dance. Like us all, he had his faults which were many, but on the other hand he had his virtues, which were legion."

Babe had considered accompanying his brother Chief Locke to Washington on Choctaw Nation business, but decided his lengthy absence would put a hardship on his father, in whose house Babe, twenty-seven and unmarried, still lived.[34]

About 5:30 P.M., Babe mounted his horse and started back to his father's house, which was about a mile north of the Frisco depot. When he rode up High Street, Babe stopped and asked Arthur Kee if he would see him at the dance that evening at the J. Marvin Faust residence.[35]

Ten minutes later Babe arrived at the Locke home to find his brother Ben standing in the front yard. Ben was adjusting the saddle on his horse, getting ready to ride back to his home at Hamden.

Inside the Locke residence, in various rooms, were several people. Significantly present was the honeymoon couple, brother Alex, twenty-five, and the English girl, Frances Emma, he had married in London six months earlier. She was beautiful, and twenty-two years old. Other guests for supper were Mrs. Charles Harrington and Henry Berkham, who were at the table along with Victor Locke Sr.

Babe said a cheerful goodbye to Ben and entered the front door.

Just as Ben was mounting his horse to ride off, he heard the report of a gun.

Mrs. Harrington and Berkham jumped up from the supper table and rushed into Babe's bedroom. They found him, said the *Antlers News-Record,*[36] "lying on his back with his face turned a little to one side. Henry Berkham held up his head as Babe gave two yawning gasps and life was extinct."

---

[34] *Antlers American,* Jan. 9, 1913

[35] *Loc., cit.*

[36] *Antlers News-Record,* Jan. 10, 1913

Summoned from Easton Drug store by phone, Dr. J. C. McGinnis jumped on his horse and raced to the scene. He was too late.[37] The *Antlers News-Record* said flatly "The shooting was an accident," and elaborated:

> The ball entered the left breast about three inches from the left nipple and passed through the body. It could be seen and felt under the skin on his back. It did not touch the heart but it is thought that the ball cut an artery as he bled very profusely.
>
> It is supposed that while Babe was dressing [for the dance] he took a gun out of the dresser. There was a marble slab on the dresser and accidentally the gun fell from his hand and dropped on the marble slab which exploded the cap.
>
> This view is taken of it, or that he was loading the pistol and in loading it, it accidentally fell out of his hand and in striking on the floor or on the dresser, it was discharged.[38]

Among Locke family descendants, the theory that Babe shot himself and did so accidentally has been hard to swallow. Such a story seemed too pat, quite implausible. Uncle Dick and the other witnesses knew the tragic truth, but apparently never cared to reveal it. The mystery has intrigued present day Lockes.

Where were Alex and the beautiful Frances Emma at the time the pistol fired? Alex was known to be moody and troubled over his abortive effort to become a Catholic priest. His name had drawn ominous speculation fifteen years earlier when his brother Dude was killed by a blow from a baseball bat. Is it possible that Frances Emma, a bride of merely six months, could have secretly bewitched the gregarious, fun-loving and handsome Babe, and created the appearance of scandal?[39]

---

[37] *Loc., cit.*

[38] *Antlers News-Record,* Jan. 10, 1913

[39] Personal communication Nelson A. Locke Jr. to sister Francine Locke Bray, May 17, 2004: "I was told nothing about a baseball bat. Please fill me in. I was told Babe was shot jumping out of a bedroom window after being caught in some sort of affair which may have involved Nana [family name for Frances Emma]. The shooter was 'unknown' and the death was chalked up to a 'cleaning his gun' self-inflicted wound. There was a rumor that the shooter might have

Babe's funeral on Sunday afternoon at St. Agnes Catholic Church, said the *Antlers News-Record,* was "the largest ever seen in Antlers." Company L of the Oklahoma National Guard, in which Babe was 2nd Lieutenant, formed ranks at the armory and marched to the home, church and cemetery, led by the Antlers Concert Band. Each time the handsome black casket was moved, the band softly played "Hearts Bowed Down."[40]

At the Locke cemetery upon his flag-draped coffin were placed his military hat and saber. Two Catholic priests read the rites. Company L lined up and fired three volleys, and their bugler sounded "Taps."

"And," said the *News-Record,* "all that was mortal of Babe Locke had been tenderly laid away to await the coming of the archangels."[41]

The *Antlers American* wrapped up its obituary with poetry:

Somebody's watching and waiting for him,
Yearning to hold him again to their heart;
And there he lies with his blue eyes dim,
And the smiling, childlike lips apart.

Tenderly bury the fair young dead,
Pausing to drop on his grave a tear;
Carve on the slab at the top of his head:
"Somebody's darling slumbers here.

ONE OF THE FIERCEST lions in the U. S. Senate, Albert B. Fall of New Mexico, turned red from embarrassment and then white with anger. A flurry of questions from a clever adversary flew at him across the polished tables in the Committee on Indian Affairs hearing room.

Thunderation! The Senator heard himself being called a crook!

---

been our grandfather. Was I close? The thing I liked about our family the most was the way we never got the truth the first time. If your mind reading or time traveling skills were not working, you just never knew what the hell really happened, ever. Or, was it just me? That could also be true."

[40] *Antlers News-Record,* Jan 10, 1913

[41] *Loc., cit.*

Fall leaped to his feet glaring and stammering at Patrick J. Hurley. The handsome attorney for the Choctaw Indians stood up, too, tall and calm, and pointed his long finger at the powerful Senator known as "the terror of Washington."[42]

"You, sir, have a personal interest and will profit from these Choctaw contracts that will rip off the Indians for $3,500,000," Hurley said sternly. "Is that not so?"

At Hurley's elbow, Chief Locke beamed with admiration. Oh, how, surgically his lawyer was cutting straight into the gut of this scandal! Hurley was bold and brave; the other Senators saw that. So did the reporters. "It was one of the bitterest [Senate] fights in recent years," said *The Daily Oklahoman.* [43]

This sensational hearing was taking place in late May 1913. It was the first foray into Washington by the new Choctaw team of Hurley & Locke. They were dead-set on finally rooting out the crooks who could pillage the Indians by hiding in government corridors.

The McAlester attorney with nine lives, J. Frank McMurray, remained the central figure in the rip-off. He still stood to collect a 10 per cent fee when the government sold $35,000,000 in Choctaw-Chickasaw land, in other words $3,500,000 of tribal trust funds for literally doing nothing.[44] Government agents were actually handling the sale.

With skillfully disguised bribes, McMurray bought legislative favors. He needed the Senate to approve his 10 per cent contracts. He got Senator Fall; usually he offered a cut of the loot. They owned neighboring ranches in New Mexico. McMurray had the run of Fall's Capitol office. [Later when Fall was made Interior Secretary he gave McMurray an office next to his.][45]

Startled by the Hurley-Fall clash, the Senate committee expunged their entire exchange from the record, erasing every word. Then, greatly flustered, they immediately terminated the day's hearing.

---

[42] *The Oklahoman,* May 25, 1913
[43] *Loc., cit.*
[44] *Loc., cit.*
[45] *Loc., cit.*

Fall denied having any connection with the McMurray scheme, but the force of Hurley's grilling exposed the truth. In the hallway, other senators crowded around, pumping the Choctaw lawyer's hand, slapping him on the back.[46] Pat Hurley, thirty, had out-dueled the fifty-two-year-old cold and ruthless Fall, a man few in Washington cared to cross.

[Later Albert Bacon Fall had to eat his own bitter fruit. President Harding appointed him Interior Secretary. In 1921 Fall took $404,000 in bribes to secretly lease the Teapot Dome oil reserves out west to oilmen Harry Sinclair and Edward L. Doheney. Exposed by a Senate investigation, Fall was fined $100,000 and sent to prison for a year.][47]

Pat Hurley and Victor Jr. won a complete victory in Washington. The committee adopted a provision that Senator Gore had earlier offered, but was filibustered to death by Senator Fall. It clearly outlawed secret deals made without prior government approval. It read: "No contract with an Indian where such contract related to the tribal funds or property in the hands of the United States shall be valid nor shall any payment for services rendered in relation thereto be made unless the consent of the United States has been previously given."[48]

"This provision in the law," said *The Oklahoman,* "undoubtedly saved the Indians of Oklahoma millions of dollars."[49]

On his return to Antlers, Chief Locke stepped off the Frisco into a welcoming serenade by the band from Company L, Oklahoma National Guard, of which he was captain.

Not everybody was shouting huzzahs for Victor Locke Jr. He had enemies, mostly Democrats, and all vocal. Leaders of the "get Locke" cabal were officials he had fired: William Durant, Dr. E.N. Wright, Hampton Tucker, along with the tainted D. C. McCurtain. They intended to bring charges, it was rumored, accusing Locke of using his office and tribal funds for political purposes, and for incompetence.[50]

---

46 *Loc., cit.*

47 David Stratton, ed., *The Memoirs of Albert B. Fall* (El Paso, Texas Western, 1966)

48 *The Oklahoman,* Oct. 29, 1931

49 *Loc., cit.*

50 *The Oklahoman,* Feb. 10, 1913

One Oklahoma newspaper sniffed: "A Choctaw describes the present contest as an effort of the *outs* to get where the *ins* are."[51] The article praised Locke for lobbying Congress to make a $200 per capita payment to "his people," adding:

> Chief Locke is a man of remarkable personality. Unlike most Choctaw leaders of less than fullblood, he speaks Choctaw fluently, and commonly thinks in that language, rather than English. This has given him marked advantage among the fullbloods back in the mountains, who beam with delight when they meet him, and who familiarly address him as "Dickie."
>
> His sympathies are with the fullbloods, whom he feels are victims of a change that is destructive to their welfare, as they are unable to cope as individuals with the white man.

At the same time, Patrick Hurley also was getting generous kudos for his effective work in the marble halls of the nation's capital. *The Oklahoman's* chief Washington correspondent O. O. Kuhn filed a front page story that included this passage:

> Hurley, though a Republican, probably is one of the most efficient and popular attorneys the Choctaws have had in Washington. He bears the good will of department officials, members of the Oklahoma delegation in Congress, and is not only a worker but has made his efforts count for the best interests of the Choctaws. . .
>
> During his incumbency in office, Hurley has steadfastly refused to play partisan politics at any time, devoting his attention chiefly to Choctaw business. This has made a favorable impression upon the congressmen and therefore they would like to see him retain his position, even though he may be of opposite political faith.[52]

Whatever firepower the Locke enemies could muster, it wasn't enough. He proved immune to puny slings and arrows. Victor Locke Jr. sailed right on, active and busy, proud to be Principal Chief of the Choctaws.

---

[51] Undated clipping, Oklahoma Historical Society, F. S. Barde file
[52] *The Oklahoman,* Feb. 10, 1913

DESPITE TWO FAILED MARRIAGES, Chief Locke was too young, handsome, and virile to remain long a refugee from romance.

Into his life came a pretty young widow, Vivia Nail Robertson of Caddo. Daughter of J. H. Nail, a prominent Chickasaw, she was the great granddaughter of the early day Choctaw Chief Folsom. She had a small son, Wesley L. Robertson II.

As her suitor, Victor Jr. faced a couple of obstacles. First he was still married to Maye, the schoolteacher from Missouri. Second, the Catholic Bishop at Guthrie had decreed that in the eyes of the church his first marriage, to Mattie Belle Keith, remained unbroken. [Through his friendship with Father Ketcham, he apparently was able to wiggle out of that sanction.]

To legally get free, Victor Jr. sued Maye Brown Locke on May 28, 1912 for divorce in Pushmahata County district court. Within weeks, he withdrew his suit and on July 1, 1912 Maye sued him for divorce, which was granted September 13, 1912.[53] Both had prominent attorneys; he was represented by Charles E. Dudley of Antlers, she by Cocke and Willis of Hugo.

On Monday, September 8, 1913, Victor and Vivia were married at the home of her parents in Caddo.[54] About this time, the *Antlers American* reported that his ex-wife had been hired at a teacher in the nearby Jumbo school.[55]

Chief Locke's third marriage started under favorable circumstances. Their only child, a daughter, was born December 7, 1915. Her formal name was Rose, but her father immediately dubbed her *Ba-nat-i-ma,* a Choctaw word loosely translated as "charity." She went through life called "Bunny," and would have a distinguished career as head of the drama department at Oklahoma State University.

---

53 Pushmataha County court dockets [the actual case files have disappeared.]

54 *Antlers American,* September 11, 1913; *Locke Family History,* p 296

55 *Antlers American,* June 19, 1913

The birth of Bunny sent the Choctaws into a mild frenzy, especially the full blood males, according to one newspaper account.[56] The swarthy Choctaw men, coming to do tribal business with her father, "gaze upon her in a stolid manner, but down in their hearts there is the liveliest sentiment of pride, for in all the history of the Choctaw people she is the first daughter ever born to a principal chief of the Choctaws during his tenure in office."[57]

The story went on:

> This very little girl's baptismal name is Vivia Nail, her mother's maiden name, and she is a real Indian princess. Commonly, however, her father and mother call her Rose. Her "pet" name is Bunnie-dim-ah, a close approach in English the pronunciation of the Choctaw word meaning "charity." She is more frequently called Bunnie than Rose.
>
> The wardrobe of Miss Bunnie Locke is costly and elaborate. Her complexion is tinged with the blood of her ancestors, a fact which makes a strong appeal to Choctaw fullbloods who point to her feet and little roly-poly legs and chuckle in Choctaw at the visible evidence that she is of their race.
>
> Both Chief Locke and Mrs. Locke are pronounced Indian types, but neither is of fullblood. Mrs. Locke is highly educated, and a woman of many accomplishments, but never lived along the fullbloods. The latter were eager to see the wife of their chief, and when she first came to Antlers they sought opportunity to look at her as she passed in the streets, standing like bronze statues along the sidewalks. When Bunnie-dim-ah was born, the fullbloods were delighted.
>
> Chief Locke wished for a son, but the little girl has conquered all her father's notions in such matters, and rules him in every way, save when she cries. The chief of the

---

[56] Unnamed, undated newspaper transcript, Oklahoma Historical Society, F.S. Barde file

[57] *Loc., cit.*

> Choctaws then deserts his child, declaring that a man is utterly incapable of caring for a crying baby.[58]

Despite such rosy-hued appreciation of the little princess, she would not be five years old before disaster would wreck another of Chief Locke's dogged searches for marital bliss. Victor Junior may have been lucky at the poker table, but never at love.

BEFORE FIRST LIGHT on March 9, 1916, the Mexican bandit Pancho Villa crossed the Rio Grande with 500 *pistoleros* in a bloody surprise attack on the 13th U.S. Cavalry camp and burned the little border town nearby, Columbus, New Mexico, leaving 14 soldiers and 10 civilians dead.[59]

Though eight hundred miles away, Pancho Villa's savage raid had major life-changing repercussions in Antlers for the Locke clan.

It resulted in happy-go-lucky Captain Ben Locke being promptly ordered to take his all-Indian National Guard Company L of the old 1st Oklahoma Infantry to the border to join other American militia massing with arms to protect American lives and property.

Likewise the Mexican outbreak and subsequent World War I hit with the impact of a hammer blow on Chief Victor Locke. For patriotism and adventure, these conflagrations would prompt him to throw up his cherished position as the Choctaws' headman and plunge into a military career.

President Woodrow Wilson ordered General John J. "Black Jack" Pershing to invade Mexico and capture or kill Pancho Villa and his ragtag revolutionaries. The bandits had earlier massacred American engineers aboard a Mexican train.

Pershing's men, poorly trained, staggered blindly into the wild Sierra Madre Mountains, got hoodwinked by bandit spies, lost their way in deep canyons, and failed miserably.[60] Their American expedition was

---

[58] *Loc., cit.*

[59] *The Oklahoman,* March 10, 1916; Joe Griffith, "In Search of Pancho Villa," *Journal of the Historical Society of the Georgia National Guard*

[60] "In Search of Pancho Villa"

the last to use cavalry, the first to use autos and airplanes—without much success.

"Black Jack" Pershing was pulled out of Mexico shortly after America declared war on Germany April 8, 1917. President Wilson urgently needed him for a more important mission, leading American forces into World War I.

Eagerly caught up in this military adventure, Ben Locke had to resign his job as Chief Locke's private secretary, abandon his trading post at Hamden, his cattle ranch, and leave behind two daughters, Allece, seven, and Benita, five, and his wife Maye.

For two or three years he would be training his command, marching his company up and down such places as Fort Sill, Camp Bowie, and Camp Stanley, Texas. At no time did he or his Indian soldiers get into actual fighting before being discharged February 20, 1920 after the armistice.[61]

Because Ben remained stateside, his wife shared his quarters in some border posts. Her sister, Irene Davis Key, was married to a National Guard company commander, Captain William S. Key of Wewoka, Oklahoma. When both wives resided occasionally at the same post, army humorists made much of the oddity of having present a "Locke and Key."[62]

The advent of America's involvement in war caught Chief Locke when his emotions already were in a swirl from complications of his personal as well as his professional life in Antlers.

The bugler's *charge!* rang in his ears just as it had when he got "mad as hell" because his Company L was not called out for the "Crazy Snake" Indian uproar. Now he held the rank of major in the Oklahoma National Guard, given in 1913 by Governor Lee Cruce when Ben had been elevated to captain and company commander. He craved battle action, and command.

Somehow his "Damon and Pythias" relationship with his closest "buddy," Patrick Hurley, became tinged with, well, jealousy. Hurley, in the Oklahoma National Guard since 1914, had impulsively surrendered

---

[61] *Locke Family History,* pp 303-304

[62] Locke Family Papers, Garrard Ardeneum Manuscript Collection

his post as Choctaw attorney, and already gone into uniform. Hurley would go overseas with the American Expeditionary Force, rise quickly to lieutenant colonel, then general—and eventually to Secretary of War and noted American diplomat.

Victor Locke Jr. also felt his family was sadly being pulled apart. His mother and five brothers already were in their graves. Brother Ben was on the border; Alex was in Chicago. His father at seventy was slowing down, his famed "eagle eyes" dimming slowly toward blindness.

The chief's own romance had withered. He was losing his third wife, Vivia. She would take with her, he realized, darling little Bunny; but he knew no way to prevent the loss of either. He felt estranged from his sister Dolly, who had turned casual, if not unfriendly. He blamed her husband, Charles Archer. To his aunt Alice Hilseweck, he wrote: "Doll seems to grow more exclusive as she grows older. Her husband seems to think he conferred somewhat of a favor on us when he joined the family and for that reason I know very little of their life."[63]

He agonized with his sister in February 1914 when the "palatial" nine-room C. E. Archer residence burned to the ground with nothing saved but two pianos and a couch. The loss, said the *Antlers News-Record,* was $5,000. The cause was unknown, but the Archers would rebuild.[64]

Against his eagerness to pick up his rifle and march off to war, Chief Locke had to weigh the obligation he conscientiously felt was his. That was to continue leading "his people" along the tenuous upward path where predators still lay in wait for the guileless Indians.

He didn't believe he could actually abandon his position as chief, even though he found no joy in remaining a target for a strong phalanx of Choctaw dissidents. They continued to fire arrows of criticism, and to connive to damage his credibility with the President and Secretary of the Interior.

---

63 Victor Locke Jr. to Alice Hilseweck, March 4, 1911, Locke Family Papers, Garrard Ardeneum Manuscript Collection

64 *Antlers News-Record,* February 20, 1914

The conundrum gave him weeks of mental torture. Finally Victor Jr. found a practical solution. He would do both—go into the army and still carry on as Choctaw chief. He thought he could make that work.

From his current post as Judge Advocate in the Oklahoma Guard, on May 9, 1917, Chief/Major Locke entered the regular army at Fort Logan H. Roots in Arkansas in the 12th Provisional Training Company. In the regular U.S. Army he was commissioned a major [serial number 0-141745] on October 30, 1917.[65]

A two-column photo of Major Locke, sober, handsome, his right hand on the hilt of his saber, dominated page one of *The Oklahoman* on October 21, 1917, under a headline speculating that Indians would flock to the Army if they were placed in a separate regiment.[66]

Few Indians had objected to the draft, said the newspaper, and "practically all tribes in the state are represented in the army . . . but Indian leaders are unanimous in the opinion that recruits would be much more easily obtained if the government would agree to form them into a separate fighting organization."

If an Indian regiment was formed, *The Oklahoman* said, "Indians seem to be united largely" on selection of Major Locke to be promoted to colonel as its commander. The page one layout included photos of Captain Ben Locke along with two other Indian captains, Charles Johnson and Walter Veach.

[Ultimately the Oklahoma Indian soldiers were included in the U.S. Rainbow Division composed of National Guard units from all states, and which was an early arrival on the Western Front in November 1917, and did heavy fighting.]

Major Victor Locke was assigned on January 2, 1918 to active duty at Camp Greene, Charlotte, North Carolina. His desire was to go into action overseas; but, as in the Spanish-American war, that wasn't going to happen.

Turning forty, he felt it was time to take stock of his ability to carry out his duties as chief of the Choctaws. If he resigned, was there a competent successor available? He saw good prospect in W. S. Semple

---

65 Locke Family Papers, Garrard Ardeneum Manuscript Collection
66 *The Oklahoman,* October 21, 1917

of Durant, who had Washington experience as clerk of the House Committee on Indian Affairs under Congressman Charles D. Carter of Oklahoma.[67]

As near as he could determine, President Wilson would find no opposition to Semple's appointment.

Victor Jr. made his decision. He would shift his career totally into the military. In July 1918, Major Locke resigned as Chief Locke.

---

[67] *Ibid.,* July 11, 1918

10

'Do Not Worry for One Minute . . .'

I HATE THE GERMANS! Pounding his typewriter despite a sore finger, Major Victor M. Locke Jr. began rag-picking the jumbled thoughts piled high in his emotional cupboard. The War was over. He was back home in Antlers, and glad to be there.

"It was one of the happiest home-comings of my life. I am a private citizen now, and I am happy. I am out of office, out of the Army and broke and yet I am thoroughly sanguine of the results of my future."[1]

It was February 12, 1919 and he was pouring out his innermost feelings in a Valentine's Day letter to his mother's half-sister, Alice Hilseweck; she was his life-long confidante, and conscience counselor.

"The bloody Germans. I hate 'em! The war closed too quick. President Wilson was tricked into premature peace and no doubt in my mind that our little fellows will be called on to finish a job which we have left half-finished. I do not expect you to agree with me. No good woman would.

"But we can only judge the future by the past, and history will substantiate the statement that this is the easiest the Germans have gotten off in a record of blood and thunder in two thousand years.

---

[1] Victor Locke Jr. to Alice Hilseweck, Feb. 12, 1919, Locke Family Papers, Garrard Ardeneum Manuscript Collection

"Their sense of honor is not like ours—the English speaking people. It was no humiliation to them to surrender. They sunk the *Lusitania* and its load of defenseless children—many of them Americans. They did this and more, and yet Germany is untouched.

"They will pay an indemnity like a disturber of the village peace would pay a fine, and then laugh. I hate them and will die when my time comes with bitter disappointment in my heart that I did not get there to wreak proper vengeance.

"In my mind's eye I often picture myself crossing the Rhine with a saber in one hand and a firebrand in the other and scattering death and destruction wherever my horse set foot. I am bitter.

"President Wilson's Utopia will make us shed rivers of blood before this epoch in history is completed.

"Of course I might have had all of this belligerency shot out of me had I been over there, but it will have to be done before the above convictions can be eradicated."

His homecoming was cheered by finding that Dolly had cared well for his horse, saddle and blanket and saved his civilian clothes in "an old trunk my mother gave me." He found "all the folks in good spirits. Papa is getting old but his determination lasts and will probably be with him at the final flicker of life."[2]

Ben was getting out of the army "next week." Alex was in Chicago. "He tried in every way to get in the Army but his eyes failed him. He did his bit by making street-corner speeches for the Red Cross, etc."

Victor Senior "raised the devil" with his grandson Victor, Shub's boy, twenty and married, for "not going to the war." Major Locke made this observation: "There are no slackers in our generations. Our men, most of them, have been booze hounds and bad about making love, but when the emergency arose they had the stomach to go to the front. There! I am guilty of blowing our horn, if this were to come to the eyes of an outsider, but it's true."[3]

Though stationed stateside at Camp Greene, North Carolina, Major Locke felt that "as far as Army life went in this country, I was rea-

---

2 *Loc.,cit.*

3 *Loc., cit*

sonably successful. I went up to Washington city for the holidays and had one of the best times of my life. I danced and drank wine for ten days and then returned to Camp Greene prepared to turn my face toward the setting sun. And here I am."

His father was seventy-three, but obviously had no intention of parking himself in a rocking chair. "Papa and I are going to a dance to-night. We took in one Wednesday night. He still likes a storm, and I guess will until Old Nick takes him in charge."[4]

Major Locke came back to an empty nest. His wife Vivia had deserted to her family home at Caddo. With her she took the Indian princess with the little roly-poly legs. In April 1920 their marriage was terminated when Vivia obtained a divorce decree in Pushmahata County.[5] She was granted custody of little Bunnie, thus forever removing their daughter from her father's everyday life.

[Bunnie's mother moved to San Francisco. As a child Bunny took ballet lessons, and became interested in the stage. Growing up, she received degrees from three universities, Oklahoma, Southern California and Kansas. For a time she was employed in Hollywood by the Cecil de Mille movie studios. She came home and taught high school drama at Holdenville, Oklahoma. In 1950 she joined the faculty at Oklahoma State University and for thirty-one years was drama department head.][6]

[Bunnie developed a close relationship with her half-brother Wesley Robertson II, who became a successful Indian singer and actor, using *Ishtiopi* as his Choctaw stage name. He performed in Town Hall in New York, in Hollywood Bowl, before the King and Queen of England, as a guest of the Roosevelts at Hyde Park, and recorded for Columbia Broadcasting System.][7]

The major's travels permitted him to see Antlers in a new light. He was happy to have a "modern" hot bath at home. "After thirty years of occasional use, I grew tired of the Kiamichi River," he wrote his aunt

---

4 *Loc., cit.*

5 *Antlers American,* April 29, 1920

6 Unidentified, hand-written profile of Bunny, Locke Family Papers, Garrard Ardeneum Manuscript Collection

7 *Loc., cit.;* and *The Oklahoman,* Jan. 26, 1941

Alice, "and I was pleased when this town advanced to the second stage of godliness."[8]

He hated telephones and automobiles, but decided he wanted a Packard "just because my neighbors run up and down the street in anything that will burn gas." On Saturdays he was jolted on the Antlers streets by "the different odors brought in from the country" but felt lucky, remembering a missionary to China telling that Canton had "one hundred fifty different smells."[9]

The Ben Lockes were adding to their home; Dolly and her husband were "growing more and more exclusive." Victor Senior was off testifying as a witness. "He is an oracle . . . He enjoys digging up the dead past."[10] Despite his third failed romance, Major Locke seemed ebullient.

"I am running for office," he told Aunt Alice. "I am hoping to rehabilitate myself in the political world. If the gods hold out in my favor, I am going to soar among the clouds. But that's boastful!"[11]

The gods of politics granted him a mixed blessing. He ran for the state legislature and was elected, the first Pushmahata Republican candidate in several years to go to the statehouse. The House of Representatives elected him chairman of the committee on soldier relief. He had grand plans.

He authored a bill to immediately admit one hundred tubercular soldiers to University Hospital in Oklahoma City temporarily while the state built regional hospitals at Clinton and Talihina.[12] At the same time Congress appropriated $18,000,000 for federal hospitals for war veterans. Oklahoma wanted to be the site of the one designated for the southwest. "A committee of members of the American Legion and other citizens, headed by Victor M. Locke Jr., chairman of the Oklahoma house

---

[8] Victor Locke Jr to Alice Hilseweck, Aug. 30, 1920, Locke Family Papers, Garrard Ardeneum Manuscript Collection

[9] *Loc., cit.*

[10] *Loc., cit.*

[11] *Loc., cit.*

[12] *The Oklahoman,* Jan. 29, 1921

committee on soldier relief, will call on the secretary of the treasury this week to present the claims of this state," said *The Oklahoman.*[13]

"Oklahoma, centrally located, is the logical state," the newspaper argued.[14]

To Major Locke's dismay, both efforts met failure. In disgust, he promptly resigned his seat in the legislature.

Just then came a stunning development. The prairie sky rumbled and on high the gods of Oklahoma politics abruptly decided that after all Major Locke was their fair-haired boy.

His name was submitted for appointment as Commissioner of Indian Affairs![15] That was the most powerful and critical position dealing with tribal matters under the Secretary of the Interior. No Indian had ever held that office.

Oklahoma's newly elected U. S. Senator J. W. Harreld submitted Locke's name to Attorney General Harry Daugherty, who was serving as President Harding's patronage czar. Senator Harreld was a lawyer, oilman, former Congressman—and a bumbler.

Exactly how and why Major Locke became Senator Harreld's nominee for such a powerful government office is not reflected in available records. It was a known fact that the former Choctaw chief was ambitious, and had widespread Indian support and prominent friends in Washington as well as in Oklahoma.

Just as Major Locke's name came into play, a duel to the death broke out among Oklahoma's Republican Party bosses over who was entitled to election spoils. Claiming those rights were the current Oklahoma Republican chairman "Big Jim" Harris, and Jim McGraw, the former chairman, and the 'heirs" of Jake L. Hamon, who had sway despite having been involved in the $1,000,000 Choctaw lawyer fee scandal.

In the end, the squabble reached President Harding's desk. He had personal pre-election promises to keep. The President wound up

[13] *The Oklahoman,* March 7, 1921

[14] *Loc., cit.*

[15] Victor Locke Jr to Alice Hilseweck, April 13, 1921, Locke Family Papers, Garrard Ardeneum Manuscript Collection

slapping down "Big Jim" Harris and splitting about even the patronage jobs between McGraw and the Hamon "heirs."

Senator Harreld was left out in the cold, able to name only one government official, Oklahoma collector of internal revenue. He had trouble even designating new postmasters.[16]

A "lame duck" Senator from South Dakota was given the Indian Commissioner job. He was Charles Henry Burke, who had just lost his re-election campaign. He was a Capitol Hill old-timer, having first gone to Congress in 1899.[17]

[Senator Harreld would be a one-termer. Defeated for re-election in 1926 he would reject any "lame duck" appointment, and return to the oil game in Oklahoma. Attorney General Daugherty would also be out of Washington by then, having been disgraced in the Teapot Dome scandal.]

Major Locke thought he had been "double-crossed" but was sanguine in defeat. "I did not win the commissioner's post," he wrote from Washington's Hotel Powhatan on April 13, 1921 to his Aunt Alice, "but I am not in the least disconcerted as a consequence." His letter continued:

> All that could be done, was done, by friends and people. I myself fought the best fight on record, and like St. Paul in next to last chapter in his second Epistle to Timothy, there is great comfort in having done all that becomes a man. I am proud of my fight.
>
> Therefore, I harbor no ill feeling and in my vaulting ambitions there is no setback. I lost owing to that in politics is called "double crossing." Senator Harreld is certainly responsible for offering the place, and then right at the moment of assured success, he quit me, and went for a man who does not even live in Oklahoma.
>
> Harreld is a Baptist and the Masons of McAlester scared him to death at the idea of supporting a Catholic for office. Miss Alice Robertson [Congresswoman from Muskogee] also took a shot at me because of religion.

---

[16] *The Oklahoman,* May 4, 1921

[17] *The Oklahoman,* April 5, 1921

> This, however, made no difference with the Administration. The trouble there was the fact that Harreld, being a Senator, there are peculiar prerogatives, which go with the office, that the Presidents do not like to disregard.
>
> Harreld realizes now that he played the mischief. His trouble is lack of brains really. He has not yet succeeded in even getting appointments that must be made in Oklahoma, not to mention anything on the outside, like the Commissionership, for his constituency.
>
> Rather than "cuss him out," we pity him for his amiableness.[18]

Major Locke had become a semi-permanent resident of Washington, but was not happy about that. "I am simply crazy to go home," he wrote Aunt Alice on April 13, 1921. "I have not been home but one day since November and I am homesick."

However, he was taking advantage of being in one of the world's most sophisticated cities. He was brushing up on "my imperfect recollections of *Macbeth*" because he was attending Shakespeare plays. He passed up *Romeo and Juliet.* "I care little for such bunk and really I have always side-stepped reading the thing!"[19]

On April 12 he sat in the House gallery to hear and praise President Harding's speech, ten feet from Mrs. Harding. The President's wife bowed when introduced, and struck him as "wonderful and gracious . . .she will be popular." He heard that Mrs. Harding "walks in a storm" and gossips interminably. "There is danger in too much conversation even in high circles, just as it is over the backyard fence down in Antlers."[20]

Major Locke straightway answered the question he expected was in his aunt's mind. "I know you would like to hear why I am still here. I am glad to tell you—even though you had not thought of it. I am awaiting the appointment of a successor to Gabe Parker. I am not a candidate but my friends here are quietly boosting me for the place. I would be glad to get it, for it affords an opportunity for me to do good, or lose a

---

[18] Victor Locke Jr. to Alice Hilseweck, April 13, 1921, Locke Family Papers, Garrard Ardeneum Manuscript Collection

[19] *Loc., cit.*

[20] *Loc., cit.*

reputation & I am willing to take chances. This information, however, is entirely confidential."[21]

Gabe Parker, an outstanding Choctaw educator, was retiring from the most essential "Indian" office in Oklahoma, Superintendent of the Five Civilized Tribes. Parker was picked in 1915 as a "dark horse" to head the federal government office, which disbursed about $50,000,000 a year to tribesmen.

In his six years as superintendent, Parker became, said *The Oklahoman,* "one of the most courteous, efficient and best-liked officials that ever saw service in Oklahoma."[22] Parker, a one-eighth Choctaw, earlier had served as registrar of the U. S. Treasury.

Doping out the wildly shifting alliances among influential Oklahoma Republicans enabled one Oklahoma newspaper, the *Tishomingo Capital-Democrat,* to predict on April 28, 1921 that Victor Locke Jr. would wind up "in the front seat at the patronage pie counter."

His rivals for the Five Tribes post were L. G. "Hell Roaring" Disney, who had been Congresswoman Robertson's campaign manager, and Roscoe Cate, a Muskogee attorney. The latter withdrew, and endorsed Locke. Jim McGraw, the real Republican boss in Oklahoma, tossed "Hell Roaring" Disney overboard, and sent the major's nomination to Attorney General Daugherty.[23]

President Harding on Thursday, May 12, 1921 announced Major Locke's nomination and sent it to the Senate for confirmation.

"I am expecting confirmation by the Senate any day," Locke wrote his aunt on Tuesday, May 12. "In fact, Cooper [Henry Cooper, who was nominated for U.S. Marshal in Eastern Oklahoma] phoned me just now that our names would go through today. He saw Harreld at a late hour last night.

"I am hoping with all of the fervor of an early Christian that this good day will end the fight. It has been the hardest scrap I ever got mixed up in, but there are tougher ones in the future.

---

[21] *Loc., cit.*

[22] *The Oklahoman,* May 29, 1921

[23] *Tishomingo Capital-Democrat,* April 28, 1921

"I must tell you confidentially that as soon as I can get on my feet financially I am going to be a candidate for Governor of Oklahoma. I am going to show the world that Oklahoma is really not intolerant religiously. I am not afraid to make the trial, in any event."[24]

Women in the Muskogee office sent "fine messages" in his behalf. After his nomination was announced, Major Locke went to offer an olive branch to "Miss Alice" [Robertson], who was still displeased. "She did not receive me very kindly. In fact, she insulted me. But being the man that I hope I am, I did nothing to show my chagrin. I wish you had been there, and heard the old lady. I felt greatly in need at that moment of some of my own women folks to talk to Miss Alice as she should have been talked to. I shall not call again."[25]

He "got sick of the hotel" and moved into the old fashioned townhouse at 2021 H Street, N.W. occupied by Father Ketcham's Bureau of Catholic Indian Missions where he had "a bedroom, bath, living room, and library all to myself."

He would not be long in Father Ketcham's townhouse. Major Locke was due back in Oklahoma on June 1, 1921 to be sworn in at Muskogee in an elaborate ceremony as Superintendent of the Five Civilized Tribes.

The major had no idea what a hot potato he had been handed.

SUPERINTENDENT LOCKE entered the Five Tribes office with the avowed intention of totally closing out the federal government's involvement in Oklahoma Indian affairs. Gabe Parker in his six years was credited with doing a masterful job of cutting a lot of snarls in red tape left by Washington's cruel shattering of solemn treaties with the Indians.

The new superintendent wanted to not only complete this but speed it up, stated *The Oklahoman* in a May 29, 1921 full-page layout

---

[24] Victor Locke Jr. to Alice Hilseweck, May 17, 1921, Locke Family Papers, Garrard Ardeneum Manuscript Collection
[25] *Loc., cit.*

headlined: "AFFAIRS OF FIVE TRIBES TO BE WOUND UP BY NATIVE SON."[26] The news story said in part:

> As early as thirty years ago the leaders of the five tribes began to appeal to the government for more business liberty. They wanted tribal property sold and the proceeds divided in severalty so that each Indian could look after his own affairs. They were tired of governmental supervision and the doling out process of Indian payments.
>
> By the terms of the Atoka Agreement of 1898, the federal government agreed to the winding up of the affairs of the Choctaws and the Chickasaws tribes; yet, today, the affairs of those tribes are further from settlement than any other tribe in the group.
>
> This is due in part, however, to the fact that much of their estate consists of mineral deposits—chiefly coal and asphalt—for which no ready market was found.
>
> . . . The Indian bureau was entangled in a mesh of red tape, which could not be overcome. The politician's love for patronage—fat jobs afforded by continuation of governmental supervision of Indian affairs—is believed to have been largely responsible for much of the delay.[27]

The newspaper tossed Superintendent Locke a bouquet: "His acquaintances here, including Parker, are unanimous in the opinion that Locke will make a splendid record in the new position. He has the confidence of the Indians and the general public to a degree not given to most of the Republican aspirants for office, it is said."[28]

From Day One, Major Locke undertook to lift the Indians from bondage, work himself out of a job, and wipe out most patronage—what the Tishomingo newspaper sarcastically called the "pie counter." He stepped into hot water almost immediately when he began eliminating kickbacks, sweetheart deals, and plain stealing that the legion of politically favored grafters employed to fleece the guileless red men.

The Antlers man was honest—a serious threat to the connivers. His enemies at once plotted behind the scenes. They were looking for

---

[26] *The Oklahoman,* May 29, 1921
[27] *Loc., cit.*
[28] *Loc., cit.*

some way to discredit him in Washington, and get him fired. They may have taken a look at nepotism. Major Locke gave a minor clerkship to a nephew, Curtis Locke, the son of his brother Ben and Mattie Belle, who was the divorced wife of the two brothers. He did likewise for another relative on his mother's side of the family. However, when neither young man could measure up to the work, he had them discharged.

He found Muskogee an "up and coming town," in sharp contrast to much of Choctaw country where wilderness and hardship were still commonplace. He carried briefly in his pocket a sad 1922 letter from friends William and Lydia Smallwood, who had moved to a new ranch near the village of Cloudy. Their story:

> With them, they brought 106 head of cattle, five wagonloads of Poland China sows, and a number of horses. The first year 105 of the cows died, and on Thanksgiving Day a tree fell on the 106th cow and killed it. Bulldogs in the community killed the hogs, and three of the horses died. "It was life's darkest moment financially," said Lydia. "A fortune teller at Nelson had told me, 'You are going to trade your smooth land for rocky land, and you are going broke.' Well, it happened."
>
> Next a flood on Cloudy Creek washed out their crop. It was a hard struggle—but they managed to survive, and prosper.[29]

It fell to Superintendent Locke in 1922 to create an unexpected and singular page in Native American history. He selected the first female ever installed as chief of an Oklahoma tribe, the Seminoles.[30]

She was Alice Brown Davis, a seventy-year-old Wewoka widow, chosen to succeed her late brother, Governor John F. Brown, who had been principal chief of the Seminoles for three decades.[31]

Superintendent Locke routed her nomination through the White House in late July 1922 for President Harding's signature; only the President could appoint new tribal chiefs since Indian elections had been abolished along with their governments.

---

[29] *Pushmahata County—The Early Years,* p 298

[30] *The Oklahoman,* August 16, 1922

[31] *Loc., cit.*

Victor Locke Jr. was well acquainted with Mrs. Davis. She was his brother Ben's mother-in-law. Ben's wife, Eleanor Maye—always called Maye—was one of the new Chief Davis's seven daughters. She also had four sons. Her husband, George Rollin Davis, was a North Canadian River rancher and merchant at Arbeka, twenty miles north of Wewoka.

With pomp and circumstances, bells and whistles, and cheers, Mrs. Davis was inaugurated at Muskogee on Wednesday, August 16, 1922 in the United States courtroom, filled with Oklahoma dignitaries and tribal leaders. She entered on the arm of Major Locke.

"Standing amidst a bower of roses and gladiolas," said *The Oklahoman,* "before a flag-draped banner emblazoned with the great seal of the Seminole Nation, blazing a new trail as the first woman ever clothed with the mantle of authority of an Indian chief, Mrs. Davis signed the oath of office.[32] It will be filed away in the government's archives for all time to come.

"The oath of office was administered by W. J. Farver, a Choctaw. The courtroom broke into applause as the full significance dawned on those present that history was in the making and that the age of women had really arrived.

"Miss Alice M. Robertson, America's only woman member of Congress, presented a huge bouquet of American Beauty roses to the new Seminole chieftain, saying 'the queen of roses to the queen of the Seminoles.' "

Installing Chief Davis was a ploy by the Interior Department to gain title to the Seminoles' boarding school for girls, Emahaka Academy. The federal government had taken over tribal schools, but Mrs. Davis as head of Emahaka refused to deed it over.

Asked to do so as the new chief, she still refused. It became a donnybrook. In succession over a few months, three new chiefs, all male, were appointed by the White House. They likewise refused to sign. In the end, the Interior Secretary signed the deed, which probably was illegal.

---

[32] *Loc., cit.*

The Seminole episode didn't cut much ice, one way or the other, in Locke's Five Tribes administration. At all times, he had a lot of balls in the air—enough to keep a couple of men busy.

Now seventy-six, Victor Senior was finding life in Antlers dreary. "Everybody gone. I am lonesome," he wrote "Dear Sister," September 5, 1922. "See, I am somewhat crippled . . . I ride in car every day, but I don't visit anybody, not my own children. You know how it is—nobody cares to be bothered with old cripples."[33]

In 1923 Superintendent Locke finally came under attack from a series of politically inspired bang-bang-bangs intended to drive him out of office. The assault was masterminded by "Big Jim" Harris in a strong effort to reclaim his own influence as Oklahoma's Republican national committeeman.[34]

Secret accusations of wrongdoing were sent from Oklahoma to Indian Commissioner Burke and Interior Secretary Work. Neither was "sufficiently impressed to pay any attention to the allegations," said a Washington dispatch to *The Oklahoman.*[35]

That didn't stop "Big Jim." He worked at restoring himself into President Harding's good graces, hoping to eventually reach the White House with his vendetta.

The charges against Major Locke were never disclosed. Gossip made vague references about "incompetence," and it was rumored two drunk men were seen at his Muskogee home, without precise details.

[Victor Locke Jr. did have a conflicted personality. With brutal candor, he once told the *Tulsa World:* "I have the educated mind of a white man, and the heart of a savage."[36] His savage side was subject to the historic yen of Indians for "firewater," and their inability to handle it. Family correspondence refers to his drunken sprees in Antlers. In March 1932, Locke would be jailed overnight in Oklahoma City for being drunk

---

33 Unidentified letter from Victor Locke Sr., Sept 5, 1922, Locke Family Papers, Garrard Ardeneum Manuscript Collection

34 *The Oklahoman,* June 15, 1923

35 *Loc., cit.*

36 *Tulsa World,* March 7, 1943; *Locke Family History,* p 300

and carrying a gun after his companion, also intoxicated, drove their auto into a collision. Locke was freed under forty dollars bond.[37]]

While Harris kept his tempest heating up, Locke began the year 1923—which would go down as one of his most significant —with an exciting, once-in-a-lifetime adventure. Going to Washington in January on Indian office business, he decided to take along his thirteen-year-old niece. She was charming but naive Allece Locke, his brother Ben's eldest daughter, who was, of course, granddaughter of the new Seminole chieftainess.

The train ride there and taking in the sights and sounds of Washington was eye opening and almost too thrilling for a young girl from rustic small-town Oklahoma. Her diary, from January 18 through February 25, 1923, overflows with wonder and enthusiasm. It reveals her attentive uncle, too, sincerely got a kick out of sharing her experience.

For almost six weeks, Allece was all over the nation's capital, meeting Senators, Congressmen, Interior Department officials, taking in vaudeville, stage plays, her first opera, dining on capon and oysters and other treats at Child's, Harvey's, the Raleigh, Polis, the Senate and House dining rooms.[38]

She shopped the fashionable stores, dismayed that suede slippers —"I have fallen in love with them"—cost $13.50. Sixteen-button brown kid gloves were expensive and a brown taffeta hat cost $18. After looking several times, she bought them all. She got a hair ribbon at Kress, but discovered it was ugly. "I wouldn't wear it to a dog fight."[39]

In idle times, Allece read, finishing the historical romance *Richard Carvel,* and Vol. II of *David Copperfield.* Her uncle bought a set of books on Catherine DeMedici, consort of Henry II, which both perused. He brought in the magazine *House Beautiful,* and "I became house crazy, just like him."

Despite political sniping back in Oklahoma, Superintendent Locke found in Washington that "in official circles everything is serene."

---

[37] *The Oklahoman,* March 30, 1943

[38] Allece Locke Washington diary, Jan. 18-Feb. 25, 1923, Locke Family Papers, Garrard Ardeneum Manuscript Collection

[39] *Loc., cit.*

He told Aunt Alice in a January 24 letter,[40] if anyone was trying to cause him trouble it had not developed yet, adding:

> If they should, is that any indication I am to be dismissed or reprimanded! In the first place, I am not popular with the "grafters" and official Washington is convinced of this fact . . . The *Times-Democrat* at Muskogee is very friendly to me and their speculations are mostly for public appetite. Do not ever fear that the T.D. will get on the wrong trail . . . As to observations about Miss Robertson, she has made herself a liability to the Republicans. The whole capital is laughing at her "squawks."
>
> I am concerned with ambition. I am not interested in anything much except a longing to do a lot of good in this world & build me a house. Alice and I are going to New York one of these days. I am saying to you privately that I had rather be shot than go. . .
>
> Do not worry one minute about what people say. Tell Uncle Bill to ask Charley Wasson on what grounds he bases the statement that I shall be out by March 1. I can guess that deep down in his conscience it is because I didn't give him a job. Why talk about me catching Hell? You should hear what they say about the Indian office here in the East!
>
> My friend the president of Bacone College said in introducing me, "We love him for the enemies he has made." Now wasn't that fine? If you knew all the reprobates who lambaste me, and at the same time were acquainted with the splendid gentlemen whom I call friend, including a batch of rowdy boys, loveable yet full of deviltry, you would not be disturbed for one moment about what a common pig like Wasson has to say. Clarke has kept him out of the penitentiary on divers occasions & why notice the polecat.[41]

When Victor Jr. took Allece to meet Interior Secretary Work, the official engaged the girl in a friendly chat. "I left thinking why should nice, old gray-haired men be put out of office."[42] She made a number of trips to Senator Harreld's office, and was in the company of J. Frank

---

[40] Victor Locke Jr to Alice Hilseweck, Jan. 24, 1923, Locke Family Papers, Garrard Ardeneum Manuscript Collection.
[41] *Loc., cit.*
[42] Allece Locke's Washington Diary

McMurray on the Hill, at lunch, dinner, the theatre, and in her uncle's apartment at the fashionable Portland.

Such subtle exercises in political heterogeneity obviously did not register on her juvenile mind; indeed, others also might find it odd to see Superintendent Locke socializing with the Senator he branded a turncoat and who wrecked his chance to be Commissioner, and likewise with the lawyer he publicly castigated for being neck-deep in Choctaw bribery.

Even Senator Harreld's wife courteously entertained Allece several times. She took the teenager to a reception at the German Embassy, introducing her as "My little Indian friend."[43]

"Ven," asked the Ambassador's wife, "are you going back to Hindia?"

Mrs. Harreld explained about Oklahoma Indians.

Senator William Andrews Clark of Montana was friendly on several occasions and his wife took Allece to dine and the theatre. "I felt very ladylike when the chauffeur helped me into the car." Obviously unknown to Allece was the fact that Senator Clark had millions of dollars, made in copper mining.

Her uncle's three attempts to introduce her to the President failed, but she finally toured the White House. She was stunned by the beauty of the East Room's $3,000 chandeliers, each made with 3,000 pieces of glass. At museums she saw gold nuggets "as big as a wash pan," Napoleon's snuffbox, General Grant's gun, "and lots more."

She accompanied Locke to so many masses at Christ's Church and St. Patrick's "I thought for a time I would like to become a Catholic."[44]

J. Frank McMurray made a hit with the teenager. He alerted them in time to listen to a Senate filibuster, and demonstrated the acoustical trick of standing Allece at one end of the Capitol rotunda while he spoke in a whisper on the far side. "I heard him as plainly as though he were near." He was wise enough to bring her several boxes of candy. Her uncle bought her a dozen roses on Valentine's Day.

---

[43] *Loc., cit.*

[44] *Loc., cit.*

By telegram, Victor Locke Jr. was advised in Washington he no longer was a major in the Army reserves. That was good news. "I am now lieutenant colonel," he wrote his Aunt Alice.[45] "This is a belated promotion long sought, and since it pleases me exceedingly, I am sure it will please you also."

He was aware pacifists were certain there will never be another war, but—

> In my judgment as long as men are selfish there will be danger of wars, and I am going to be prepared until I am too old to wobble.
>
> I had my final interview with the Commissioner this morning and I am returning home with more duties to perform than ever before in my life.
>
> In fact I have never had such a successful trip and I am thoroly happy over the outcome. The last thing he mentioned was the school situation among the Choctaws and since you are now to be one of the members of the conference officially to consider "ways and means," you should put on your thinking cap and do your level best for the little unborn fullbloods.
>
> If I can put over some scheme whereby we can guard against ignorance and illiteracy among Indians in the future, I shall feel that I am fully paid for all the annoyances I have undergone at Muskogee since assuming office.
>
> Incidentally, the Commissioner advised me that Miss Robertson had called while he was out. She complained to his secretary that I had not called. The Commissioner told me that if she ever said that to him he was going to say to the old hen, "Why do you expect him to call!" He made some other comments on her childishness but I said nothing. I am trying to forget the old wretch, and if God will ever forgive me for thinking so little of her as I do, I shall count myself lucky.
>
> By the way, the Commissioner is going to visit Oklahoma this Spring. I want you to have one of your incomparable dinners for him while he is in the state & give him an example of our hospitality.
>
> I must go. I have a little unfinished business to do. I do hate to be rushed at the last moment.[46]

---

[45] Victor Locke Jr. to Alice Hilseweck, Feb. 23, 1923, Locke Family Papers, Garrard Ardeneum Manuscript Collection
[46] *Loc., cit.*

Lawyer McMurray stood them up for lunch on their final day in Washington, February 24, but in the evening accompanied them to Union Station and saw them off for Muskogee on the B. and O. He bowed and handed Allece another box of chocolates.

Superintendent/Lt. Col. Locke left Washington with the aroma of sweet success in his nostrils, but ere the summer sun could cast a single joyous beam on the Oklahoma hills and valleys, all would change.

His success would curdle, and turn sour—bitterly sour.

11

President Harding's Hatchet Job

WHEN OKLAHOMA INTRIGUERS tried to drag the White House into their plot to fire Superintendent Locke, President Harding was much too busy. He was worried sick about his Ohio gang's scandals that were about to pop open, Teapot Dome being the worst. Yet Harding did get involved. Finally, he took direct action.

Oddly, the President also was obliquely prompted into making his decision about the Five Tribes office by two almost extraneous circumstances: (1.) rank dishonesty going on in the Veterans Bureau, and (2.) the outbreak of a catfight right inside the White House.[1]

Everything became so tangled in disparate scenarios that Dick Locke never had a chance.

From the time he was appointed in 1921, Dick Locke's political enemies had been after his scalp. They wanted to fill a plush job with one of their cronies, one who might not be so hard nosed for honest dealing. They bombarded the Indian Commissioner and the Interior Secretary with accusations that Locke was incompetent and a drunkard. Their claims cut no ice in Washington at that level.

---

[1] *The Oklahoman,* Jan. 28, 1923

His most bitter enemies were headed by "Big Jim" Harris, the demeaned Oklahoma Republican national committeeman, who had insisted in 1921 that "Hell Roaring" Disney get the Five Tribes office. Harris's closest ally was Miss Alice Robertson, the former Congresswoman from Muskogee. Joining them, late in the game, were the "heirs" of the late Jake L. Hamon, desperate to cling to part of the state's political power.[2]

It was late Spring 1923 when Locke's enemies managed to go around the lower levels and put their denunciations on President Harding's desk. Despite all his other troubles, the President took a hand in the matter.

First, Harding dispatched Inspector Roberts from the Secret Service to Muskogee to investigate Locke.[3]

Second, and more importantly, he turned to Dr. Hugh Scott, who only a few months before he had appointed head of the Soldiers' Relief Hospital in Muskogee. Dr. Scott acted as a behind the scenes spy; his name was rarely in the newspapers. Political insiders, however, considered him the White House "eye" in Oklahoma.[4]

Dr. Scott was doubly connected. He had been an intimate friend of the late Jake L. Hamon. More importantly, he had earlier been handpicked by Harding and placed high up in the Veterans Bureau in Washington. Dr. Scott was assistant director under Director Charles E. Forbes.

Forbes was a crook, a fact not known until later. In two years, he grafted or wasted $200,000,000 in veterans' funds. [One cited example: he sold as "surplus" 84,000 brand new sheets that cost $1.37 each for 27 cents, and bought 25,000 new ones at $1.03. He took bribes for hospital locations, and committed other misdeeds that finally sent him, in 1926, to federal prison.]

Mrs. Harding, becoming aware of the President's sex scandals with mistress Nan Britton, was so badly stung she tossed around the pots and pans, and took glee in trying to mess up his work. She was a close friend of Forbes' wife, and demanded that Forbes not be fired. On the

---

2 *The Oklahoman,* June 22, 1923
3 *The Oklahoman,* June 15, 1923
4 *The Oklahoman,* June 22, 1923

other hand, the President's sister, Mrs. Heber Votaw, urged him to dismiss Forbes.[5]

Caught in this White House catfight, and intimidated by a wronged wife, Harding felt he had to oust one or the other, Director Forbes or the assistant, Dr. Scott. He kept Forbes, and banished Dr. Scott to the Muskogee hospital. Fully intending to later bring Dr. Scott back to a good Washington post, Harding kept intact their alliance.[6]

What the Secret Service found out, or whether Dr. Scott relayed any damaging tattle-tales to the White House was not disclosed. However, on June 9, 1923 *The Oklahoman* reported that rumors again sprang up in Washington that charges were filed against Locke. The Indian Commissioner hadn't heard of any such charges; neither had Senator Harreld. Interior Secretary Work was off on a weekend trip with President Harding and couldn't be asked.[7]

That Locke was being "railroaded" did not escape the notice of Oklahoma newspapers. The bigger dailies printed editorials deploring what the *Tulsa World* termed "a vicious intrigue within the [Republican] party such as made the party within this state notorious."[8] The newspaper urged Senator Harreld to "stand by Locke" to the limit.

The *Okmulgee Times* was disturbed that no "charges" had been announced. "It would be a great deal more satisfactory to the public . . .if some definite statement were to be given out indicating just why Locke is being removed. If it's a question of morals, perhaps those engineering this 'railroading plot' feel they are doing the 'accused' a kindness by convicting him without a trial in order that the evidence may be kept from the public." [9]

The secrecy, asserted the *Muskogee Phoenix,* "emits an unsavory odor and leaves a distinctly bad taste in the mouth. Locke's cards have been dealt from a deck cruelly stacked against him. . . .[by] these stealthy, whispering politicians."[10]

---

[5] *The Oklahoman,* Jan. 28, 1923

[6] *Loc., cit.*

[7] *The Oklahoman,* June 10, 1923

[8] *Harlow's Weekly,* June 23, 1923

[9] *Loc.,cit..*

[10] *Loc., cit.*

The *Okmulgee Democrat* castigated the "disreputable Republican bosses" who were after the "political spoils. . . .Of course, Colonel Locke made some enemies, but generally speaking these enemies were made by his refusal to permit them to rob the Indians. So it is easy to see just what the real cause of removal is."[11]

"VICTOR LOCKE KEEPS SILENCE DURING PROBE," said *The Oklahoman* June 15, 1923, reporting from Muskogee that Locke "has not resigned as superintendent of the Five Civilized Tribes and has no intention of resigning. He knows of no valid reason why he should be asked to resign.

"While he would not give out a statement in regard to charges being investigated, he did make the above facts clear."[12]

The end of the wrangle came with abrupt suddenness—at the end of a sort of last-minute foot race—in Washington on Thursday, June 21, 1923.[13]

Two or three days earlier Dr. Scott hopped on the train and sped off to Washington. He was on his way to see President Harding. By the time word reached Senator Harreld, who was back home in Oklahoma, it was too late to overtake the physician.

Incensed, Senator Harreld immediately fired off a telegram asking the Indian Commissioner to "withhold action" until Harreld could reach Washington "and present all the facts."[14] He took the next train heading East.

Harreld was too late. President Harding had already made the decision to fire Locke. Indian Commissioner Burke held a press conference to announce Locke's discharge and to appoint his successor. He was Shade Wallen, forty-seven, Vinita's former postmaster, once a merchant, and for twenty years an Oklahoma politico. [Three years later Wallen would be fired on charges of fraud.]

The firing of Dick Locke turned out to be part of the national political agenda. In its June 22 page one story, *The Oklahoman* said:

---

[11] *Loc., cit.*

[12] *The Oklahoman,* June 15, 1923

[13] *The Oklahoman,* June 22, 1923

[14] *Loc., cit.*

"Wallen is now in St. Louis with Harris attending an important conference of Republican chieftains where, it is understood, the factional hatchet will be buried and the machinery put in motion towards swinging Oklahoma for Harding before the next Republican national convention."

That didn't happen. No Oklahoma delegates could vote for Harding. He was dead—just forty-three days after firing Dick Locke.

The President had gone to Alaska, where he seemed to get ptomaine poison from eating crabs. He was still ill with pneumonia when he reached San Francisco on August 1, 1923. He was alone with his wife when next day he suddenly died. He was only fifty-eight. His physician blamed "apoplexy" or "a heart attack." There was no autopsy. Suspicions were published later that either he committed suicide because of his disgrace, or Mrs. Harding may have poisoned him.

Calvin Coolidge took his place in the White House, and quickly cleared away the mud Harding had splattered on it.

[Ironically, before Oklahoma's first 1923 snow fell, "Big Jim" Harris himself would be tossed into the political trash heap, deposed by the Republicans as "undesirable," and replaced by John B. Foster, Tulsa oilman.][15]

Lieutenant Colonel Locke left the Five Tribes office with his head high, and apparently the respect of his staff. At least his secretary, Lola M. Rambo, was able to take up a collection of $150 to buy him a going-away present.

A day or two after Locke had returned to Antlers, Clark Wasson came by Mrs. Rambo's office in Muskogee.

"How is the Major doing?" she asked. "Have you seen him?"[16]

Wasson chuckled. "Yes. I saw him Wednesday out in the yard, bareheaded and barefoot, playing ball with an Indian!"

Mrs. Rambo explained about her plan and asked if Wasson had any idea what Locke would like.

"No, I haven't," Wasson replied. "But I do know he is 'cussing' because you insist on getting a present for him."

---

[15] *The Oklahoman,* Oct. 30, 1923

[16] Lola M. Rambo to Alice Hilseweck, July 7, 1923, Locke Family Papers, Garrard Ardeneum Manuscript Collection

Getting "railroaded" out of a good-paying government position apparently did not greatly disturb Dick Locke. He was back in Antlers by July 5, and, as Clark Wasson observed, was again the happy-go-lucky optimist.

His education, his travels, his understanding of the vagaries of human nature, and being well read stood him in good stead. He remembered one book in his collection contained "The Good Indian's Prayer." In its lines he found so much solace, he made this copy to carry in his pocket:

> Oh, Powers that be, make me sufficient to my own occasions. Teach me to know and observe the Rules of the Game. Give to me to mind my own business at all times and to lose no good opportunity of holding my tongue.
>
> Help me not to cry for the moon or over spilled milk. Grant me neither to proffer nor to welcome cheap praise; to distinguish sharply between sentiment and sentimentality, cleaving to the one and despising the other.
>
> When it is appointed for me to suffer, let me, so far as may humanely be possible, take example from the dear, well-bred beasts, and go away quietly to bear my sufferings by myself.
>
> Give me to always be a good comrade and to view the passing show with an eye constantly growing keener, a charity broadening and deepening day by day.
>
> Help me to win, if win I may; but—and this, Oh, Powers! especially—if I may not win, make me a good loser. Amen.[17]

FOR THE LOCKES as a family, mutual harmony and personal respect was perhaps their most dominant hallmark. They stood as one against the world. Surprisingly, toward the middle of the 1920s, that united front crumbled. In its ruins erupted nasty quarrels, backbiting, and real anger that verged, sadly, on personal hatred.

The question is why.

---

[17] Copy found in Victor Locke Jr. documents, Locke Family Papers, Garrard Ardeneum Manuscript Collection.

For starters, nobody was very happy. Colonel Dick had been scalped, and was pretty much at loose ends. Ben, perennially good-humored, had just been stricken with a mysterious lung disease, and was deeply concerned, if not actually frightened. Old Victor was, well, old and going blind. Dolly was still aloof and snooty.

Most likely booze was the root cause of discord. Both Victor Junior and Ben were drinking heavily. Their correspondence confirms that in this period they hit the bottle with gusto, and frequency.

Also—which comes as a shock—Victor Junior accuses his brother of trying to pull crooked deals on their fellow Choctaws!

Though maintaining his home in Antlers, Dick Locke was frequently away—to Muskogee, Oklahoma City, and Washington, D. C. He was politicking and lobbying for the interests of the Choctaws. He had not given up on trying to induce the Department of Interior to sell the Choctaw-Chickasaw coal and asphalt deposits separately from surface ownership, and place the millions thus derived into a trust fund exclusively for educating the children of the tribes.

By early 1925, the Locke brothers were openly revealing the vicious depth of their personal feud in letters to their aunt Alice Hilseweck.

Writing April 28, 1925 from Washington where he had already spent three months on unfinished "Choctaw business," Dick observed that "in a long, long while," he had not heard from Antlers.

"I guess I am in bad with everybody," he told Aunt Alice, "but it makes little difference to me! I can make out anywhere nowadays—I mean that I can, but I do not say that I want to! I am pretty strong for the soil I have known all my life." His letter continued:

> I know that you do not approve of my viewpoint as regards the Locke family but if you knew what I know, you would probably think differently. For long years I tried my damndest (Pardon some violent language) to keep that mob in a good humor with all the kinfolks, neighbors, friends, and myself, and I was myself out at the job and when I reached my row's end I was through.
>
> The manner in which Doll treated Cousin Sook; her utter brainless fuss with Esther & Dorothy; and the way she acts toward you and Aunt Lizzie— The way she hammered the Ben Lockes and the

Alex Lockes and everybody else who was of any consequence to her is quite inexcusable to me.

Then here come the Ben Lockes with all their fuss & feathers, and at the same time not accomplishing one worthwhile thing in the world.— Parading their poverty around the world, instead of quietly going to work, and making a decent living, and conducting themselves in a high-toned measure, they did just the opposite.

And old man Locke, raising Hell, when anything else would have been so much better. I told him one year ago that he had made me expend my last unhappy moment and I meant exactly what I had in mind.

I told Maye that she and Ben had played their last trick with me, and that when Ben came to my home, drunk, to tell me that sooner or later I would have to come down from my "high and mighty ways"— That prediction cost him my friendship for life.

I have always fought crookedness toward the Indian people and it was some of his crooked deals that I objected to that caused him to utter such prediction for me. Above it all is one infallible truism—if you cannot get along with kinfolks, or friends, or anybody, the thing to do is to get out of the way.

I have gotten out of the way of that gang , and not even death has any weight with me. I am saying this to you—I am ashamed of it all, but Almighty God has something to do with every man's life, and in this I am being directed by a Higher Mind. I have always fled from trouble, and I always will. The man or woman who stirs up trouble from force of habit does not conform to my ideas of life (my ideals, I know I have said) because, happiness to me is the one goal to be reached in this world.

I must tell you I have been quite happy since I have been here. That sounds selfish, but it is true. I have accomplished little, but I have done so much toward an end. Contrary to your suspicions expressed in your letter, I am not expecting anything in the way of political honors for myself.[18]

At that point Ben had already been dangerously ill more than a year. In February 1924 he experienced chest pains at his farm home in

[18] Victor Locke to Alice Hilseweck, April 28, 1925, Locke Family Papers, Garrard Ardeneum Manuscript Collection

Hamden. His wife Maye tried the usual home remedies, some Indian herbs and chest rubs. They didn't work. After a few weeks he was taken to the hospital in Paris, Texas. The doctors diagnosed it as pleurisy. It wasn't. It was worse.

He was in and out, up and down—made no progress. Came a crisis. "To medical science, nurses etc, I was dead," he wrote Aunt Alice.[19] "The priest issued the last sacraments. The priest thought I was on my way—a providential hindrance o' guts and a desire to live a while longer saved me. McCusten the surgeon asked me how it felt to be dead and what did I think about. It was a great fight."

That scare brought him to his senses about whiskey.

"Now that I have cut out booze," his letter continued, "I want you to know that it's not because I'm afraid, but it's the first time I've had the time or taken the time to think what a silly life I was leading."

He apologized for one of the Antlers shouting matches.

> I want to tell you and Uncle Bill that I am sorry about the way Papa talked to Hodges, but the continuous drunk spree at Dick's house that has been the Talk of the Town for a long time was still going on when I was being hauled away to Paris and it just simply drove the old man mad.
>
> He felt it was time to check up on the drunk and instead of jumping on Dick he landed on Hodges. And then Dick turned on Papa. It was awful. Keep Hodges away from that Antlers wild bunch.
>
> Before I left for Paris, Dick came once to see me, stinking drunk. A spade is a spade, Aunt Alice. Dick's big times have bank-busted him. His house isn't his own.
>
> I went ten years. I'm trying to overcome all my past. Please take all this in the right spirit; I'm sure Uncle Bill will. I think Dick has turned against us for good. It's bad business to listen to other people. They hope he makes a big success.

---

[19] Ben Locke to Alice Hilseweck, undated, but doutbless mid-1925, Locke Family Papers, Garrard Ardeneum Manuscript Collection

It would take Captain Ben Locke four terrible years to die. He was the first patient admitted to Muskogee's new Veterans Hospital—and he never walked out. But he never gave up hope.

"When they burned my lung 2 x 2 clear through to the wall, it smelled just like branding a calf," he wrote Aunt Alice.[20] "Dr. Fite said, 'Does it hurt?' And I said, 'Hell, you bet! I'm not going to squawk just to please you!' I have a beautiful silver cross hanging above my bed and when I get to hurting real bad, I think what the Hell! I don't kid where this suffering is. Two major operations, and I'm improving. Nuf sed."

His wife found a small house in Muskogee and lived there with their daughters, Allece and Benita. Money was a problem, but he wrote that he was collecting military pay benefits and insurance. "I'm telling you because I know you won't be broadcasting. I must keep quite until I get all my business concluded. There are people who would piss all over themselves if they knew I was drawing the $100 I am now getting."

In the hospital, he wrote newspaper and magazine articles, mostly recalling his experiences in the Kiamichi wilderness. He had flair, and could capture the silence, grandeur and beauty of the prairie and mountains. He was prone to reminiscence on outlaw days. Referring perhaps to his brief stint as a deputy U.S. marshal, he wrote Aunt Alice:

"Darn those fellows! I used to wish they had made me flash my guns. Pushmahata would have been a better county had I given up my life and took about 15 of those devils along with me. I knew how to handle those wicked guns at close range and I tremble at the thought of my ambitious desires to give them all manner of odds and turn me loose.

"Colonel Fitzhugh Lee at Camp Stoney taught me how to use firearms & how to protect myself & still keep my head. I'm truly glad it's all over. No blood on my shoulders. I've been punished for all other sins. I have paid like a man. God is good to me. I believe now I'm going to get well. And I am truly thankful. No malice in my heart toward no man or party."[21]

---

[20] Ben Locke to Alice Hilseweck, May 7, 1925, Locke Family Papers, Garrard Ardeneum Manuscript Collection

[21] *Loc., cit.*

Locke Ferry, Antlers, which was the only one on the Kiamichi River for miles around.

All photos courtesy Francine Locke Bray Collection, unless otherwise credited.

The Victor Sr. mansion (circa 1889) in Antlers which was "shot to pieces" and mysteriously burned to the ground a few days after the end of the Locke-Jones war. Figures *(left to right)* believed to be Ben, Victor Jr., Mary (Dolly), Susan, Edwin, Victor Sr., and either Shub or an unknown, and J. Nelson (Babe).

Residence of Wilson Jones
(Courtesy Western History Collections, University of Oklahoma)

Bitter political rivalry between behind-the-scenes powers Victor Locke Sr. and Principal Chief Wilson Jones triggered the Choctaw Nation's bloodiest tribal war. It raged intermittently from 1892 into 1893.

Chief Jones recruited and armed a Choctaw militia to descend on Antlers and arrest Locke men. *(Opposite page, top)* Chief Jones poses in front of some of his armed men. *(Below, on both pages)* some of the ragtag army that assembled in the business district of Antlers.

Dr. Leo E. Bennett of Muskogee, the Government's Indian Agent, made a valiant effort to act as peace-maker.

Dr. Eliphalt Nott Wright helped stir up the rebellion by his attacks on "Uncle Dick" Locke.

Dr Leo E. Bennett
(Courtesy Western History Collections, University of Oklahoma)

Dr. Eliphalt N. Wright
(Courtesy Oklahoma Historical Society)

(Courtesy Western History Collections, University of Oklahoma)

(Courtesy Oklahoma Historical Society)

Formally named Rose Vivia Locke, daughter of Victor Locke Jr., was known in the family as "Bunnie" and admired by her father for her "little roly-poly legs."

On one of her regular strolls through Antlers, Dolly Locke with her pet stray, "White Christmas," April 1956.

Victor Locke Sr.'s general store in Antlers.

Choctaw millionaire Colonel Robert M. Jones with his second wife Susan Colbert. He built for her the mansion "Rose Hill," near present day Hugo, Oklahoma. He planted thousands of roses and a long lane of cedar trees, which his slaves called a bad omen. It was. Three of the colonel's first children died, as later did Susan and two of her children. Colonel Jones was stricken by malaria and also died in 1873. *(Courtesy Oklahoma Historical Society)*

Mary (Dolly) Locke on her beloved "Big Rocks" outside Antlers with her husband Charles Archer, circa 1901-1902.

Despite growing old and beginning to lose his sight, Victor Locke Sr. never relinquished his look of command.

Principal Chief Wilson Jones of the Choctaw Nation.
(Courtesy Western History Collections, University of Oklahoma).

On the downhill trail, Victor Locke Jr. steps out of his sedan to gaze over his Kiamichi ranch, April 1943. His ex-wife Sudie ridiculed him in divorce court for hiring a driver "so he could "look important." The cane held by Victor is still in the family.

Choctaw Nation's Civil War veterans gather for a reunion, possibly in September 1923. Victor Locke Sr. is *third from left.*

Typical horseshoe bend in the road through treacherous Winding Stair Mountains. *(Courtesy Oklahoma Historical Society)*

The first railway depot in Antlers.
(Courtesy Pushmataha County Historical Society)

The turn-of-the-century Keith Hotel in Antlers.
(Courtesy Pushmataha County Historical Society)

This photo from the archives of the Oklahoma Historical Society is believed taken in 1903, and is identified simply as "Antler's Best."

Echoes of thwarted romance between teenager Victor Locke Jr. and heiress Sudie McAlester. Her coal baron father, J.J. McAlester *(shown opposite page in two views)*, broke up their love affair because Victor Locke Sr. was his political enemy. Their love was rekindled thirty years later by Victor Jr.'s murder trial and pardon, and they married and are shown *(left)* in Antlers on their 1931 honeymoon. The mansion in McAlester where Sudie grew up survived the decades handsomely as shown *(opposite page)* in 2005 photo.

(Photo, left, of J. J. McAlester courtesy Oklahoma Historical Society and, right, Western History Collections, University of Oklahoma)

Captain Victor Locke Jr. working at his desk with unidentified aide.

All photos courtesy Francine Locke Bray Collection, unless otherwise credited.

On Christmas Eve 1925, the patient in the bed next to Ben's "croaked at 1 a.m. I'm glad for him. An enlarged heart and for days I have listened to his suffering."[22] Still he was upbeat, and eager to tell about Benita going to a school dance party.

> She wore a made-over velvet trimmed in fur, pearl necklace, ten dollar slippers, pale blue silk bloomers and a Marcelle with her mother's ring. I'll tell you, she was a dreamer.
>
> If I've ever had one week's rest from a howling clamor for a damn pair of shoes, I fail to recall. In self-defense, if I ever get any money, I'll certainly get an interest in a shoe factory.
>
> I surely hope this Chrismas finds you all happy and contented. Hell, I'm very much alive, so why worry! Like the boy who had called on his girl. The big rain came so Mother urged him to spend the night. He had to sleep with the Baby. He afterwards said he might as well have gone home in the rain. So why worry about anything.[23]

FROM THE SIDELINES, for a change, Dick Locke watched a flurry of upheavals ripping the tortured Oklahoma political landscape. Two of his most recent enemies were getting their comeuppance. If that gave him satisfaction, he left no record of it. To a degree, however, he must have missed the fray.

Whatever he was doing at the time, he didn't like it. "I am not crazy about this job," he wrote his Aunt Alice.[24] "There isn't enough 'punch' to the thing to suit me. Politics being first cousin to warfare, I like to see things happen with a clap of thunder."

Such a figurative bolt of lightning zapped "Big Jim" Harris, the Wagoner wheeler-dealer, who "railroaded" Locke out of his Five Tribes office. The strutting, confident Harris thought he had the clout to get himself elected to the U.S. Senate.

---

[22] Ben Locke to Alice Hilseweck, Dec. 24, 1925, Locke Family Papers, Garrard Ardeneum Manuscript Collection

[23] *Loc., cit.*

[24] Victor Locke to Alice Hilseweck, May 6, 1924, Locke Family Papers, Garrard Ardeneum Manuscript Collection.

An Oklahoma seat was opening up. Senator Robert L. Owens, a Democrat who had served since 1907 statehood, was sixty-eight years old and tired of the job. He declined to stand for re-election to a fourth term.

The words announcing his candidacy were hardly out of "Big Jim" Harris's mouth before he was butting heads with Senator Harreld. There was nothing personal, Senator Harreld told *The Oklahoman* April 24, 1924, but "it was inimical to the best interest" to have Republican officials who did not "work in harmony.

"I have been the recipient of political favors from Harris and have bestowed favors of equal value on him. He helped make me senator, in turn I helped make him national committeeman."

Despite the polite words, "Big Jim" realized Senator Harreld could sink his campaign. He promptly dropped out of the race. William Bliss Pine, a forty-seven-year-old Okmulgee oilman, tossed in his hat as a Republican and was elected.

The beheading of ex-Five Tribes Superintendent Locke's successor took place at turtle speed. Early on the Interior Department eagle eyes in Washington became suspicious of Shade Wallen. But it took about a year to fire him.

Hunger for illicit wealth led to his downfall.

Indians in the Oklahoma tribes under whose land oil had been discovered, especially the Osage, were piling up royalties amounting to millions of dollars. This gleaming gold usually flowed not directly to the individual red man but went through Government agencies or often was tangled obscurely in Oklahoma probate courts.

Sharpers—especially greedy lawyers— used every known trick, and invented divers new wrinkles, to divert the Indians' money into their own pockets. Many probate judges or their clerks were easy prey, if they got a cut. A clever trickster could manage to slip a few hundred-dollar bills into the pocket of an otherwise honest Indian Agency minion.

Superintendent Wallen, too, was susceptible. So many complaints reached Washington that Interior Department sleuths were dispatched to Muskogee. They reported Shade Wallen had the "Indian welfare problems" in a mess. [25]

In April 1925, Shade Wallen was suspended by the Secretary of the Interior.[26] Washington sent in inspectors to take charge and examine Wallen's records.

Interior Secretary Work was determined to unearth any skeletons in the Muskogee office, and beyond, including accusations hurled at Indian Commissioner Charles Burke. He appointed a blue-ribbon investigating committee, which began hearings in Oklahoma on October 12, 1925.

Reporting from Muskogee, *The Oklahoman* identified as members of the investigating committee:

> George Vaux Jr., chairman, a leading Quaker and an attorney in Philadelphia; Mrs. Flora Warren Seymour, a literary woman and book publisher, and once in the office of the Indian agency here; Frank Knox of Manchester, N. H., editor and newspaper owner.
>
> Backed by fifty-six years of tradition as a government board, the committee of inquiry is expected to make an exhaustive investigation that will divulge the real facts in the charges, counter charges and the welfare of the Indians.
>
> As showing the non-partisan character of the board of ten which is conducting the inquiry, it is said that appointees of Presidents Taft, Roosevelt, Wilson, Harding and Coolidge all are included. Many religions and all parties are represented.
>
> Indian officials here, from Wallen on down, say they welcome the fullest investigation and hope that the inquiry will put a stop to the many unwarranted reports of fraud and deception.[27]

The tale of abuse told by the first witness left the committee "gasping," The *Oklahoman* reported on October 14, 1925. Dr. Samuel Blair, special inspector for Secretary Work, testified that when Exie Fife, a wealthy Creek Indian, paid $50,000 to divorce her husband, $35,000 went to attorneys in the case.

---

25 *The Oklahoman,* Oct. 6, 1925

26 *Loc., cit.*

27 *Loc., cit.*

That proved to be but one example of a wide array of episodes where Indian agency employees either winked or connived in the abuses.

Wallen testified lamely that more money was allowed by Oklahoma's county courts in a single guardianship case than his office dispensed in an entire year.[28]

His whine fell on deaf ears. Based on the inquiry findings, Wallen was dismissed by Secretary Work. But the clean up in Muskogee continued for months. On May 7, 1926 Inspector H. H. Fiske was sent from Washington to replace Wallen. He promptly fired three Wallen underlings, Mack Kelly, C.E. Creager, and Ross Daniels.[29]

Those discharges drew a howl from the Oklahoma Republican committeeman, W. G. Skelly, big shot oilman. Work sent another trouble-shooter to Oklahoma, Joseph H. Gartland, chief inspector in the Interior Department.

Gartland apparently got the political muddle smoothed over and sent back to Washington an inspector named Frank Brandon, who had been on the scene. That was regarded, said *The Oklahoman,* "as another step to get all of Wallen's aides out of the agency."[30] The newspaper asserted that action also cleared the way for the appointment as new superintendent, Irwin Page, Watonga banker who had been active in Senator Harreld's re-election campaign.

The investigation and house cleaning produced only a temporary fix. Shenanigans and problematic decisions and not fully circumspect action by government officials—high and low—would continue to plague Oklahoma Indian affairs for years, fueled chiefly by the glitter of petroleum royalties supposed to go to guileless tribesmen.

Political alliances among the Choctaws remained on a merry-go-round. Old enemies made up and shook hands. Old friendships were shattered, sometimes over trifles.

An echo popped up from the blitzkrieg Dick Locke had launched when he first took over as Choctaw chief to replace Democrat officials in

---

[28] *The Oklahoman,* Oct. 15, 1925
[29] *The Oklahoman,* June 9, 1926
[30] *Loc., cit.*

the tribe with Republicans. He had fired Hampton Tucker as the Choctaw coal inspector.

Now more than a dozen years later Tucker was emerging from the tribe's political trash heap. An attorney in McAlester, Hampton, a tribal member, was appointed attorney for the Choctaws, the lucrative position that Locke had been able to hand to his pal, Patrick Hurley.

Hampton's appointment was made in July 1925 by William Harrison, then chief of the Choctaws, despite bitter opposition from Senator Pine, who complained that Hampton worked against his election.[31]

If this brought him any moment of chagrin, Dick Locke left no written mention of it. His life, his career, his future prospects appeared to be moving forward placidly, from all appearances.

That was not the case. By his own admission, he had not yet conquered the demon rum. Drinking helped turn him into a troubled man. And deep inside, lurked a terrible unchained anger, something of a hair-trigger thirst for wreaking vengeance if wronged or crossed.

Such a crisis was approaching. By September 1927 Dick Locke's anger was destined to burst loose in blazing gunfire in Antlers. He would emerge from the dramatic confrontation with Indian blood on his hands!

---

[31] *The Oklahoman,* July 15, 1925

12

Gobble Gobble Gobble! You Die!

BEFORE DAYBREAK in Chicago, the milkman could hear the tap-tap-tap of Alex Locke at his typewriter in a squalid apartment over a butcher shop. His wife Kit lay miserably ill, clutching a few crumpled $1 bills. Their little boy Nelson slept on a folding cot with a chamber pot underneath, the odor of chicken guts clinging to his hands from helping the butcher.

This was the life that the most eccentric of the Choctaw Locke siblings had fashioned for himself. The handsome energetic Alex spent a lifetime reaching for the stars and an affinity with God—but failed, and failed, and failed again.

In the 1920's his flaming brain churned out brilliant bursts of oddball writing, but wandered, struggled, yearned, and floundered. He wanted God for his pal, but his best and most frequent companion was a 25-cent shot of bootleg whiskey.

What the milkman heard was Alex Locke writing his book manuscript debunking the *Theory of Evolution.* No publisher would buy it. He published it himself, using money he made selling apartments three days a week to Italian sewer diggers moving out of Little Italy. A thousand unsold copies moldered for long years in somebody's basement.

Alex Locke had escaped Antlers, and poverty could not drive him back. "I would rather die a pauper in the shadow of Chicago's libraries than roll in wealth in Oklahoma," he wrote.[1] "I may die before I succeed, but my epitaph will say 'He died a-trying'."

He feasted on knowledge. Holing up in Chicago's fabled Newberry Library, in a single month he read twenty-two non-fiction books. He loved the Newberry, founded in the 1860s, which contained one and a half million books, five million manuscript pages, and three hundred thousand historical maps.

From boyhood he was *different*, yet to clearly define his eccentricity is difficult, explaining it impossible. He had intellect, courage, drive—all that. Perhaps he set his goals too high, maybe because he wanted to "keep a-trying."

The scraps of talent scattered in the detritus of his life's writing show he could have been an advertising agency star. Instead he stayed virtually penniless and fed his wife and son "beans and seven-cent a pound neck bones," pulled cruel "hat trick" disappearances, shoving them onto charity and the county hospital.

Kit's stomach tumor operation caused Alex to sell all their furnishings. "We were literally down to the clothes on our backs," recalled son Nelson Locke, who was born in 1917.[2] "My father's drinking got steadily worse. He would be sober, hard working, and a wonderful person for about three or four months and then start drinking more and more until all the money and sometimes his jobs were gone.

"I witnessed my first case of 'delirium tremens.' He was totally delirious. A doctor came and gave him a strong injection that knocked him out for several days."

When Alex took off, Kit worked as a maid and housekeeper. Her younger sister, Cecilia Philbrook, was governess for wealthy families— the Brachs, Cudahays, Armours, Cummings, in the ritzy neighborhood of Mayor "Big Bill" Thompson. That got Emma and

---

[1] Alex Locke to his cousin Dorothy, July 31, 1935, Locke Family Papers, Garrard Ardeneum Manuscript Collection

[2] Nelson A. Locke memoirs, April 7, 1987, Locke Family Papers, Garrard Ardeneum Manuscript Collection

Nelson at times invited to accompany "Auntie Cis" to theatres and Edgewater Beach Hotel dinners.

Nelson recalls: "I enjoyed the experience and gave no thought to the ridiculous extreme of our poverty at home and this exposure to the millionaire's way of life in the twenties."[3]

Not long after Babe's mysterious death, Alex and Emma had departed Antlers. He worked in Muskogee briefly as a newspaper reporter. In some strange manner he returned to Sacred Heart College near Shawnee. He was known as "Brother Ambrose" and studied with the monks. His wife Kit lived apart in the motherhouse with the nuns.

When this episode ended, Alex went to work in publicity and advertising in Kansas City for Montgomery Ward & Co. He did well. His writing skill is shown in an article published in Montgomery Ward's "Store News" on May 7, 1917:

> MY FLAG
>
> Not because of its particular color or design do I revere my flag, but because it is the emblem of my country. Looking into its folds I see the vast expanse of this beautiful land—I see the spreading prairies and spreading woods, fresh in their green—I see the marvelous mountains, monuments to the glory of their valleys; and all of this is mine.
>
> It tells me I can enjoy creation as it comes within my sphere, drink the pure water, and sustain myself with nature's exuberance. And it stands for my home and my rights—the right of life, of liberty, of happiness—My flag to me is the full exercise of my God-given privileges and I shall defend that flag even to the laying down of my life.
>
> —Alexander H. Locke

His life was in no danger from Kaiser Bill's bullets, of course; poor eyesight kept him out of World War I, despite his "a-trying" to join the Army.

---

[3] *Loc., cit.*

In Chicago for five years he was assistant office manager of Beatrice Creamery, and held other potentially good jobs. Usually he lost them because of booze, or chasing a literary will-o-the-wisp. In later years he stood on a soapbox in "Bughouse" [Washington Square], dedicated to free speech, and orated to passersby. He mingled at the nearby Dill Pickle Club, "a famous hangout for off-beat politicos, literati, and the many later-to-be famous playwrights, authors, poets and intellectuals."[4] He wrote letters to the editor and contributed to magazines.

The noted Beatrice Fairfax reprinted in her nationwide column Alex's tribute to the Philadelphia heiress, Mother Katherine Drexel, who had used part of her $50,000,000 to found the Catholic Church in Antlers. He nominated her for "The Twelve Greatest Women in America." Another published epistle defended Sunday afternoon baseball against priestly criticism.

His brother Victor volunteered to stake Alex so he could move back home, and was turned down cold. The Chicago Lockes made a train trip to Antlers for a few days in the early twenties. Nelson's memoir says he was about five and they stayed with Maye Locke and daughters Allece and Benita. [Ben, not mentioned, probably already was in the Muskogee hospital.]

"I remember the Pullman cars and the trip through the mountains," Nelson Locke writes. "Allece and Benita took me out in the fields and I picked up my first snake. I met Grandfather Locke. He was the town patriarch. They showed me his small, one-story house. It contained the old piano from 1892. They showed me bullet holes in it from the 'Locke War.' He also gave me a pocket knife which Nana [his mother] promptly took away from me as soon as we left."[5]

[Ironies would dog Alex's sad and dissipated footsteps to the end. Even his Gotterdammerung had its own tragi-comic twist. Alex died February 27, 1953 at age sixty-four. He lay in a Chicago flophouse, close by Newberry Library. Nobody knew his identity. It was a week before son Nelson was notified, and arranged a funeral Mass. On the way to the

---

[4] *Loc., cit.*
[5] *Loc., cit.*

cemetery the hearse had a flat. To change the tire, Alex's casket had to be lifted out and set on the roadside! He was *different* even in death.[6]

[His wife Kittie died May 29, 1974 at eighty-two in Clermont, Indiana. Their only child Nelson became a prominent radar air traffic control designer in Chicago, Indianapolis and Saudi Arabia. He married Arlene Pritchard in Chicago on February 14, 1942 and raised five sons and four daughters, one of who, Francine Locke Bray of Indianapolis, became the accomplished family historian.]

FROM HIS HOSPITAL BED, Ben Locke launched an angry war on inept Oklahoma City bureaucrats who refused to give his father a Civil War pension. They could find no record Victor Senior had ever been a Confederate soldier.

What! What! Captain Ben, renowned as the National Guard's cussing champ, doubtless spit out an explosion of swear words that could damage any eardrum within a hundred feet.

The old man had been careless in handling his own case. His application was turned down Dec. 13, 1923. Ben only found out two and a half years later. As soon as he did, on June 24, 1926, Ben demanded the case be re-opened—*at once!*

Ben stated that in 1925 he, as Victor Locke Sr.'s son, was awarded The Southern Cross of Honor by the United Daughters of the Confederacy chapter in Muskogee. "According to your letter," he sniffed, "I am not entitled to this honor."[7]

That set off a flurry of snarling letters between Ben and C. J. Stewart, commissioner of the Oklahoma pension department. They slammed each other with insults.

Stewart bristled that he was unjustly accused of "doing great wrong," and snapped back hinting fraud in Locke Senior's claim of not having $500 annual income, "That puts things in a shady light. There is

---

[6] Author interview with Francine Locke Bray, Sept. 3, 2004

[7] Ben Locke to U.C.V. Pension Dept., Oklahoma City, June 24, 1926, Locke Family Papers, Garrard Ardeneum Manuscript Collection

danger of criminal violation of the law for the purpose of obtaining a pension."[8]

Ben responded that Stewart injured his father with "grave injustice" and explained that disposal of Victor Senior's property for back taxes and mortgages was "terribly complicated."[9]

> He now lives in all that can possibly be salvaged for his grandchildren. He does not have a foot of property . . .The income mentioned must have been a lease which has long since expired.
>
> When a man who has lived in one community for forty years without a stain on his character, has to submit to the indignities of self-over-rated officeholders, then God help the peace and good will of the state of Oklahoma.
>
> In conclusion, three years ago [1923] my wife prepared and served dinner to twelve Confederate veterans, including my father, on my father's birthday. Since that time eight of these men have crossed the river to rest in peace.
>
> I thank God that my business ability will permit me to manage for my father as long as he lives. And I do not have to enter into any further dealings with the pension department.
>
> My dear commissioner, some of these days as you grow older, it may be God's will that you suffer the pangs of cancer of the stomach, tuberculosis of the bone, or insanity of the brain.
>
> Please understand that I am going to establish my father's war record, as well as his eligibility to the claim. The War Record means everything to him and his descendants.[10]

The fight continued. It stayed rough and got nastier. After about a year Ben still couldn't get to first base.

Then occurred one of those startling handsprings that seemed forever happening in Choctaw political alliances. Onto the scene finally stepped the redoubtable Miss Alice M. Robertson. As Oklahoma's first

---

[8] C.J. Stewart to Ben Locke, June 30, 1926, Locke Family Papers, Garrard Ardeneum Manuscript Collection

[9] Ben Locke to C. J. Stewart, July 2, 1926, Locke Family Papers, Garrard Ardeneum Manuscript Collection

[10] *Loc., cit.*

woman Member of Congress, "Miss Alice" had used her hatchet unmercifully on Major Victor Locke—before, during, and after his Superintendency of the Five Civilized Tribes.

They hated each other, in and out of politics, and never tried to hide their mutual enmity. There were several reasons for their feud; one was that "she is said to have made an effort to get the place [Five Tribes Superintendent] for herself," said a Washington dispatch to *The Oklahoman.*[11]

Miss Alice had a soft heart, after all. That's what it took to get Victor Senior his Civil War soldier's pension. Her first letter to Commissioner Stewart disclosed her motivation; she had been designated by the Oklahoma Historical Society with Federal Judge Robert L. Owen [former Senator] to investigate the history of Oklahoma's Civil War veterans.[12]

> A case that has appealed to me perhaps more than any other is that of Victor M. Locke . . . I have in my possession the great history of the Civil War, from which I am able to give the data required to establish his right to a pension, but I am told that the difficulty in his case is that he is supposed to have an annual income of $500 rental derived from a farm. This farm is no longer in his possession.
>
> His son, Captain Ben Locke, whom I see very often at the Veterans Hospital here, where he has been dying by inches for three years . . . is a brave and uncomplaining sufferer . . .and the desire to see his father receive this pension has become almost an obsession with him.
>
> I have made bold to write, asking you if it is not possible for you to not only allow the pension but to let it go back for at least three years; four, if possible.[13]

Commissioner Stewart was smart enough to not rebuff Miss Alice, and also to recognize the clout of a political giant like Robert L.

---

[11] *The Oklahoman,* Nov. 22, 1922

[12] Alice M. Robertson to C. J. Stewart, Sept. 8, 1927, Locke Family Papers, Garrard Ardeneum Manuscript Collection

[13] *Loc., cit.*

Owen. He hopped into action. He granted Victor Senior's pension, and made it retroactive as far back as funds still were available, July 1, 1926.

The check didn't come immediately; it took a few weeks to assemble necessary affidavits. But the pension war was won on practically the very day that a tremendous explosion in the fantastic saga of the Victor Lockes rocked the town of Antlers and the entire Choctaw territory.

Miss Alice commented directly on the sensational episode when she sent a thank you letter on October 18, 1927 to Commissioner Stewart. His action gave her "much joy, especially in the bigness of your conduct in overlooking Captain Ben Locke's impassioned letter to you," adding:

> The family seems to have too hasty a temper, as shown by the terrible situation in which Victor Locke Jr. has recently placed himself. There could not have been a more opportune time for Victor Sr. than now to receive this pension, because he will no longer feel entirely dependent, and he is growing, I am told, feebler all the time.

Miss Alice was 100 per cent right about the Locke "hasty temper," and Victor Junior's *situation.* He had heedlessly thrust his head into the slavering jaws of the most horrendous personal disaster of his life.

TROUBLE SPRANG UP between Victor Jr. and Abner Battiest as early as 1923 over the young Choctaw man's brazen amorous pursuit of four Indian girls who had been entrusted to Locke as wards.

The bloody climax exploded just after frosty dark fell over Antlers on Monday, September 26, 1927.

Abner Battiest, with practiced blandishment, had managed to seduce and impregnate one of the virgins, Alice Gibson, sixteen years old. He later went after a second sixteen-year-old, Rebecca Johns, but was stopped.

In 1923 the dying wish of Alice Gibson's mother was that Victor Locke, a distant relative, would see that the girl and her younger sister, Josephine, were properly educated. Locke accepted that responsibility and placed his wards in Wheelock Seminary. During their second year in the boarding school, Battiest showed up and induced them to run away with him. Josephine resisted his sexual advances, but Alice had a baby.[14]

A little later Abner Battiest married a wealthy Choctaw girl, known as Lena. From a family inheritance, she was receiving a $400 a week allowance. Her uncle, a Choctaw preacher named Silas Cole, became alarmed that Battiest was spending his bride's money "on riotous living."[15]

Cole sought Victor Locke Jr.'s help and they induced the Indian Agency to cut the weekly check to $100. Battiest was, of course, furious. Later it was learned that he privately told several Indians that he felt like killing Locke.[16]

Nevertheless, their mutual enmity did not in that period trigger any confrontation between Locke and the twenty-four-year-old Battiest.

In their personal wrangle, Lena obtained a divorce from Battiest. However, she continued to live with him, and in 1927 was pregnant.[17]

History was about to repeat itself.

An Indian friend of the Locke family, Dick Johns, died in 1925, leaving two daughters, Rebecca, fourteen, and Ruby, twelve. Their mother, Ida Johns, lived in a cottage behind Victor Senior's residence, and kept house for him, as well as working in other Antlers homes.[18]

Ida asked Victor Junior to become "guardian" of the two teenagers, and he agreed. He placed them in 1926 in the Indian boarding school at Goodland, where they did well. In September 1927 they came to Antlers for a brief visit with their mother.

Abner Battiest immediately showed up at their cottage on the Locke Senior grounds. Ida Johns realized that the Choctaw boy, coming around night and day, was hitting on her daughters. She ran to the old

---

[14] Pardon petition presented Gov. W.J. Holloway, Dec. 29, 1930; *Tulsa World,* March 7, 1943

[15] *The Oklahoman,* Nov. 16, 1927

[16] *Loc., cit.*

[17] *The Oklahoman,* Nov. 17, 1927; Governor Holloway petition

[18] *Loc., cit.*

man, eighty-two, blind and feeble, and asked his help. The elder Locke sent word to Abner Battiest to "get off my property, and stay off!"[19]

On Saturday night, September 24, 1927, Abner Battiest stormed into Victor Senior's house and started "cussing him out." The old man, never lacking for courage, grabbed for a tomahawk he kept close by. He couldn't reach it. Battiest leaped forward and knocked him to the floor, and left.

Though he lived directly across the street, Victor Junior did not find out about the attack until two days later when he went to visit his father.

Furious, the younger Locke ran back to Ida Johns's cottage, found Battiest there, cursed him and ordered him off the premises. He grabbed up a Indian stickball bat and hammered Battiest with it. Battiest fled.

Victor Locke Jr. pulled out his six-shooter and fired a shot. The bullet hit a nearby smokehouse. It was later testified that he was "trying to scare the boy."[20]

Then the major stepped back into his father's house and talked to him. It was almost 8:30 P.M. Victor Locke Jr. was excited and angry. Witnesses standing outside suddenly heard him emit from deep in his throat a hoarse cry.[21]

Gobble gobble gobble....Ahrrrrrrr.....gobble gobble gobble!

The Choctaws who caught the sound shivered; they understood its ominous meaning. As *The Oklahoman* later explained: "Since before the coming of the white man it has been a tribal custom of the Choctaw Indians to make a noise that sounds like 'gobbling' before killing an enemy."[22]

Victor Jr.'s heart had reverted to the savagery of his ancestors. He had given warning of impending death to Abner Battiest!

Rushing across the street to his own house, Victor Jr. threw aside his revolver and jerked his Winchester off the wall rack. He ran a short

---

[19] *The Oklahoman,* Nov. 16, Nov. 17, 1927

[20] *The Oklahoman,* Nov. 16, 1927

[21] *Loc., cit.*

[22] *Loc., cit.*

distance to Abner Battiest's house. Three Choctaw boys trailed after him, Ebenezer Wesley, Alfred Johnson, and Jackson Jones. Battiest was sitting on the front porch in a rocking chair.

Battiest saw Locke, watched him bringing up the rifle.

"Don't shoot!" Battiest cried. He turned to run.

Victor Jr. squeezed off a single shot. Battiest stumbled into the house and fell.[23]

Victor Locke Jr. walked inside. The divorced wife Lena, visibly pregnant, was standing over Battiest.

"Is he dead?" Victor Locke asked calmly.

"Yes."

"Victor Locke Jr. walked to the sheriff's office and surrendered," said the *Tulsa World.* "He was a white man again."[24]

The iron door of the ramshackle Pushmahata County jail clanged shut and Victor Locke Jr. spent the night on a hard bunk before he could gain release the following day, September 27, on $25,000 bond. The prisoner remained silent. Victor Locke Jr. would make no statement to Sheriff Nevin Kirkpatrick.[25]

If Locke expected to be hailed as a hero and defender of Choctaw female purity, or for avenging the beating of his father, he was mistaken. The atmosphere in Antlers was tense, and tinged with hostility.

Murder charges were filed; he waived arraignment and trial was set for the middle of November before Circuit Judge Earl Welch. Victor Jr. telephoned Patrick Hurley in Washington, D.C. for advice. He then hired two lawyers, one of whom was Lee Welch of Antlers, incidentally brother of the trial judge. His other choice was Tom Hunter of Hugo, the Choctaw he had helped in Hunter's stormy 1902 losing election fight with Chief Green McCurtain.

Newspaper reporters from Oklahoma City, Tulsa and Muskogee arrived to cover the start of the trial on Monday, November 17, 1927 in what *The Oklahoman* called "a tumbledown frame courthouse."[26]

---

23 *Tulsa World,* March 7, 1943; *The Oklahoman,* Sept. 28, 1927
24 *Tulsa World,* March 7, 1943
25 *The Oklahoman,* Sept. 28, 1927
26 *The Oklahoman,* Nov. 14, 1927

It took all day and into the night to seat a jury—eleven farmers and a cotton ginner. No Indians or ex-soldiers were accepted by Prosecutor Louis Gossett.[27] On Tuesday the state put on a straightforward case; witnesses described how Battiest was shot in the back as he fled.

Locke took the witness stand in his own defense.

"Did you kill Battiest?" asked Tom Hunter.

"I don't know," answered Locke with, according to *The Oklahoman,* "an expression of bewilderment in his eyes."[28]

His lawyers had decided to try for acquittal with a plea of temporary insanity.

Locke testified he had been informed by five Indians that Battiest threatened to kill him because his ex-wife's allowance was cut to $100 a week. He described Ida Johns pleading with him to protect her daughters, and told of his shock on discovering his blind father had been beaten.

The Oklahoman news story continued:

> After that, the major said, he was not aware of what he did until he was told that he had killed Battiest.
>
> Immaculately dressed, as it is the major's wont to be, the defendant answered the questions of the attorneys with the crisp and unemotional manner of the military man and veteran of the World War, until he told of the blow struck his father. Then his voice trembled and he bowed his face in his hands.[29]

To support the claim that Victor Locke Jr. was unaware of killing Battiest, defense attorneys called to the stand Dr. J.E. Fuller, neurologist at a Paris, Texas sanitarium. The physician testified it was his expert opinion that Locke was "temporarily insane" at the time.

On cross-examination, Prosecutor Gossett pressed Dr. Fuller to describe symptoms of insanity. The physician said he could not describe insanity in general terms as reactions would be individual.

The prosecutor smiled and attempted to twit the witness.

---

[27] *Muskogee Phoenix,* Nov. 15, 1927

[28] *The Oklahoman,* Nov. 16, 1927

[29] *Loc., cit.*

"Take me as your subject," said Gossett. "Tell us whether I have symptoms of insanity."

With a broad grin, Dr. Fuller leaned forward.

"I must decline," he said. "I might not be able to get out of town."[30]

Other witnesses testified that Locke had been virtually penniless for the last four years since dismissal as Five Tribes superintendent, and had become morose from loss of his property. That caused him, argued his lawyers, to lose his reasoning powers.

Informally, the courtroom learned that Battiest's ex-wife had borne his baby since his killing. Likewise a letter was shown around from Alice B. Davis of Wewoka. She was Ben Locke's mother-in-law, whom Victor Locke Jr., as Five Tribes Superintendent, had appointed as the first female chief of the Seminoles. Her letter said:

> Tomorrow I will be with you in spirit. I expected to attend the trial, but circumstances will not permit and I will wait with bated breath the outcome.
>
> I only write to let you know that I have not forgotten and my prayers will be with you through the trying ordeal.[31]

In summing up to the jury, Tom Hunter referred to the help he got in the 1902 election fight. "Sometimes," he said, "I have been asked as to whether the defendant has paid me to defend him. I reply that he has paid me enough long ago."[32]

The other defense lawyer, Lee Welch, told the jurors:

"Do not send Major Locke to the cold gray walls of the penitentiary. Major Locke has told me to ask you to send him rather to the electric chair, if you find him guilty!"[33]

Judge Welch pushed the trial along by holding night sessions, and brought testimony to a close Wednesday night. He gave the jury three options: one of finding Locke not guilty on the grounds of tempo-

---

30 *Loc., cit.*

31 *Muskogee Phoenix*, Nov. 15, 1927

32 *The Oklahoman,* Nov. 17, 1927

33 *Loc., cit.*

rary insanity, guilty of murder, or guilty of manslaughter. If Locke was in his right mind at the time he killed Battiest, the motives offered for the deed by witnesses were not sufficient to justify homicide, Judge Welch instructed the jurors.

It was already dark when the jurors began deliberations Wednesday night. At midnight, Judge Welch called them back to the courtroom. They seemed to be having trouble making up their minds. "Go to bed," the judge said, "and resume tomorrow."

On Thursday, November 17, the verdict was manslaughter; Judge Welch sentenced Locke to ten years in prison. His attorneys filed an immediate appeal. They had found a technical error; one juror, Charlie Lewis, was not qualified because he had failed to register as a voter on return from living in Arizona.[34]

The *Tulsa World* found pithy significance in "the sensational trial," observing:

> The judge who heard the testimony was the brother of one of the defense attorneys and also a close friend of the defendant. So was the prosecuting attorney. All these factors availed him nothing in court.
>
> The fact remained that Locke had put aside the white man's law in order to conform to an antiquated code of honor. A jury of farmers found him guilty . . .The verdict was regarded as a triumph of written law over unwritten law and duty over friendship.[35]

Again, Locke posted bond and walked free. The threat of ever going to prison was a long ways off; he knew his appeal could drag on for several years.

Victor Locke Senior, who sat in the courtroom through the trial, wrote Ben at the Muskogee hospital that his brother was convicted "by the sorriest looking men in the country . . . Another trial will be declared. Don't let this bother you in the least. The people will think more of him than ever for committing this deed."[36]

---

[34] *The Oklahoman,* Nov. 18, 1927
[35] *Tulsa World,* March 7, 1943
[36] Victor Locke Sr. to Ben Locke, Nov. 18, 1927, Locke Family Papers, Garrard Ardeneum Manuscript Collection

Ten days later, the father returned from seeing his son in the hospital. "It was a pleasure, and I'll never forget. Maye appears to be the noblest woman God ever made. I thank her for those two little girls. They're all I've got to be proud of. . . .We had a hurried trip home. Was held up in Kiowa for fast driving. But finding out we was from Push County, they said we didn't know any better and let us go without a fine."[37]

AS THE YEAR 1928 DAWNED, the waters were running deep for Captain Ben Locke. The ex-Congresswoman Alice Robertson knew what she was talking about. He had been dying by inches in the Muskogee Veterans hospital.

Always a realist, he was too smart not to know his time was short. The family knew, too. Victor Locke Jr. decided that his brother deserved a full military funeral. He had already drawn up a list of American Legion riflemen to fire the salute. As Ben would wish, the service would be in the Antlers Catholic church.

In his letters and hospital conversations, Ben expressed great sadness in having to leave scant resources for his wife Maye and their two daughters, Allece and Benita. His son, Curtis, from his marriage to Mattie Belle Keith, was old enough at twenty-seven, to make his own way.

Death was overtaking a brave adventurer who had a lifelong love affair with the Choctaw wilderness, the green mountains, sparkling streams, and the limitless bluestem prairie. As the *Antlers News* would comment later, Ben Locke "longed for the great out-of-doors, of which he had been a part since childhood."[38]

In the predawn hours of January 4, 1928, his flame of life flickered and dimmed. At 3:35 A. M., he quit breathing.

Most of Antlers turned out to say goodbye. From the Catholic service he was borne up the hill to the Locke Cemetery. As the acrid odor of gunpowder from the soldiers' rifle salute drifted away, he

---

[37] *Ibid.,* Nov. 27, 1927

[38] *Antlers News,* Jan. 6, 1928

joined his mother and siblings in eternal sleep beneath the shade of the big cedar.

OUT OF THE FROZEN NIGHT AIR hanging over Antlers floated the voice of the Kingfish haranguing Lightnin' and Madam Queen. Old Man Locke listened. Once his woodsman's ear was keen enough to catch the delicate whisk of a doe's tail as she bent to drink at the spring. No need tonight to strain; this vocal racket was loud enough for him to understand Kingfish's every word.

Someone down the street had bought one of those new-fangled Atwater-Kent or Stromberg-Carlson seven-tube radios with super-magnetic speakers. When sunset quieted the sky you could tune in this *Amos and Andy* broadcast from as far away as Chicago. Or on the NBC Blue Network get Rudy Vallee crooning *Carolina Moon* or *I Can't Give You Anything But Love, Baby.* Maybe listen to Graham MacNamee's NBC sports broadcasts. Or on the Red Network hear Duke Ellington from the Cotton Club.

The rattle of a passing Model T jiggled his brain to recall that now some 15,000,000 were on the road, and the Model A was just out. And by this year's end 20,000,000 phones. His electric refrigerator hummed—Lord knows how many of those! He was stunned when Victor Jr. told him airlines criss-crossed America's skies with 180,000 passengers last year.

On this December 1928 evening Christmas had come and gone. The fireplace was briskly aglow, and the wood box piled high. Feeling, not seeing, the dancing flames stirred memories of early days in the Kiamichi wilderness. Sixty-two years ago when he first came to Choctaw country, who would have believed such inventions were even possible?

It was hard to realize that Henry Ford earned $264,000 a day! No wonder he was America's first billionaire. Everything had become big. There was no end to newness—and bigness. Forty-three billion cigarettes smoked in a year. A million dollar gate to see Jack Dempsey kayo Georges Carpentier in the fourth round. And talking pictures—Al Jolson in *The Jazz Singer.*

Time was overtaking the proud monarch of the *old* Choctaw hills. Blind, feeble, tottering with his cane into his eighty-third year, his doughty Johnny Reb bravado of six decades ago had leaked out and left a powerless human shell. The dark angel's breath was close enough to ruffle Uncle Dick's hair. Ben was not quite a year in his grave, and the father would join him sooner than he imagined.

But the old warrior's wit, and kind heart, remained intact. His charming answer to an in-the-family letter:

> Tell Daisy I'll write her a letter. He mother says for her sixteenth birthday all she wants is a dog, a pony, a gun and four bits in money. Tell her I have her pony, I have a dog, a gun, and I have four bits for her. So I'll try to make her happy when she comes to see me.[39]

The old man coughed, pretty hard. Pain flashed deep in his throat, and his chest felt tight; sore, too. Might be a good idea to mention this to Vic Jr. He didn't know how he could do without Victor Jr. The New Year was just around the corner, and Victor Jr. might have to leave Antlers and go elsewhere to make more money. He'd heard him say the Battiest trial had busted him; Victor Jr. gave his last hundred dollars to his lawyers—"I am broke at the worst time in my life."[40]

Victor Jr. was his father's eyes. He read the newspapers and passed on the interesting stuff. The last Presidential campaign fascinated both of them. Al Smith, the New York governor, running as the Democrat, was a Catholic. How would the "solid South" react to that? Victor Jr. would squint, and look puzzled.

Herbert Hoover made an upbeat speech and Al Smith's folks twisted it to have the Republican promising "A chicken in every pot and two cars in every garage." But Hoover won, getting 58 per cent of the popular vote and 444 to 87 in the electoral college. Victor Locke Jr. was glad to see Hoover go into the White House, thinking it would enhance

---

[39] Victor Locke Sr to Ben Locke, Nov. 18, 1927, Locke Family Papers, Garrard Ardeneum Manuscript Collection

[40] Victor Locke Jr. to Alice Hilseweck, May 28, 1928, Locke Family Papers, Garrard Ardeneum Manuscript Collection

the career of Patrick Hurley. [It did; Hurley became Hoover's Secretary of War, the first Oklahoman to ever get a cabinet post.]

Newspapers were rife with crime news, Victor Jr. told his father. Chicago had 498 murders last year, a lot of shooting between Bugs Moran hoods and the Al Capone gang. Even New Orleans had 111 killings.

More than his father, Victor Jr. noted new books published in 1928: D. H. Lawrence's *Lady Chatterly's Lover,* Thornton Wilder's *The Bridge of San Luis Rey,* and Agatha Christie's *Mystery of the Blue Train.* New celebrities emerging included Mickey Mouse, Fats Waller, Lawrence Welk, Fannie Brice, Guy Lombardo, Eddie Cantor singing *Makin' Whoopee.*

The old man could hardly believe that J. C. Penney now had 500 stores and A & P about three times that many, that the German dirigible *Graf Zeppelin* arrived at Lakehurst, New Jersey after covering 6,630 transatlantic miles in 121 hours, that the New York Yankees took the World Series in four straight games from the St. Louis Cardinals.

By New Year's Day 1929, the Locke patriarch was not interested in hearing any news, talking to anyone or having visitors. He had taken to his bed, and the doctors' diagnosis was bronchial pneumonia. His condition, they told Victor Jr. and Dolly Archer, was grave. Considering his age—hopeless. They made no attempt to move him to the hospital in Paris, Texas. He had made clear he wanted, when the time came, to die in his own bed.

On Saturday night, January 5, 1929 his time came. Two doctors hovered over him, and came away with grim faces, shaking their heads. A Choctaw full blood keeping vigil with the family stepped outdoors. Cognizant of Indian folklore, he listened for the legendary owl hoot.

The courageous old warrior's used-up heart stopped at 10 p.m.

The *Antlers American* devoted its entire page one lead column to what it termed "the passing of one of the most outstanding men active in the affairs of Oklahoma and one who had become a center around which much of the history of Pushmahata County was built."[41]

---

[41] *Antlers American,* Jan. 10, 1929

Hardly any phase of his life from the Civil War through the "Locke war" to his recent retirement was denied lengthy recounting. The news story pointed out he died just one year and a day after Ben.

Victor Jr. was fully aware his father had resisted becoming a Catholic, was in fact seldom a churchgoer, though his pocketbook had been opened time after time for Christian ventures. Even so he arranged for Father Martin to come from Durant and conduct a funeral mass in Antlers Catholic Church on Monday, January 7.

After daybreak that Monday, the son went up cemetery hill with two strong-armed full blood friends who carried shovels. In the shadow of the cedar tree, Victor Jr. took a stick and outlined for them the gravesite. Their shovels bit into the sandy loam. Susan Priscilla's husband was being buried next to her.

Staring at his mother's headstone, Victor Jr. doubtless was struck by the fact that she had been gone thirty years and four months, almost to the precise day.

No telling how many crowded into and around the Catholic Church, and trailed the cortege up cemetery hill. By the time the winter sun sank beyond the western horizon, stillness had fastened itself on the Locke graveyard. The rip-roaring saga of Victor Moreau Locke Senior was over, its end heralded by a long mound of raw earth.

But never was this grandee of the wilds to be alone. Choctaw spirit gods would chant his praise on high. Moonbeams were already streaming down to dance on his grave.

13

'Just Cut Your Dogs Loose!'

IN HER WIDE-SPACED dark brown eyes glittered the appetent passion of a love denied them thirty-four years ago. Victor Locke Jr. had found his first sweetheart Sudie. They both were older, wiser, heavier—and hoping to make up for lost time. He took her in his arms and kissed her vigorously.

Their wedding photos in *The Oklahoman* on January 22, 1931 were separate mug shots of handsome but stern, or at least serious-looking, individuals well into middle age. He was turning fifty-four, and she was almost three years older. She looked truly Indian, being half blood, with a broad face, large nose, staring eyes, close-coiffed black hair, and a bulky frame. His hair looked graying; he wore rimless glasses, a white shirt and dark business suit, and had his mouth clamped as tight as if he had just decided to shoot somebody.[1]

A lot of water had gone over the dam since the Choctaw coal baron J. J. McAlester back in 1896 thwarted the elopement of his wealthy daughter with the then twenty-year-old son of his Choctaw business and political enemy, Uncle Dick Locke.

---

[1] *The Oklahoman,* Jan. 22, 1931

Sudie McAlester afterwards married twice; Victor Locke Jr. three times. Her husbands died, one struck by lightning, the other of heart attack. Each of Victor Jr.'s wives divorced him, determinedly and perhaps quite eagerly.

Ironically, the Abner Battiest murder trial re-ignited their love story. Sudie, a widow in McAlester, read about his arrest. Empathy seized her. Regret-stained remembrances swam immediately in her brain, reawakening the almost-forgotten yearnings of a younger heart. The ex-lovers arranged to meet, and fell in love all over again.

With Victor Jr. in the shadow of a ten-year stretch behind prison walls, they wisely decided to hold off the nuptials to give him time to conjure up some courthouse magic.

Sudie grew up the spoiled "richest girl in McAlester."[2] She played dangerous Indian stickball, loved baseball, the color red, and dashed about in fast cars. Her father, with some struggle, got a bridle on her, and turned Sudie into a confirmed "lady," skilled in exquisite needlework. She always lived in family mansions, replete with many fireplaces, servants, vast landscaped grounds with caretakers.

"She always addressed her first husband as 'Mr. Fitzgerald'," recalled Sudie's great niece, Jo Anne Capps Day.[3] "He was at a water well and lightning struck and killed him. She grieved about that for a while and then she married 'Uncle Barnes.' I don't know his first name. He was always just 'Uncle Barnes.' Good-looking young man. Conductor on the Katy."

During her first marriage, the Fitzgeralds adopted a daughter, who died in the 1918 flu epidemic. Sudie and "Uncle Barnes' also adopted a girl from an unwed mothers home in Fort Worth. That turned into a disaster.[4]

"They called her Hazel," remembered Mrs. Day. "She was a wild thing. Got drunk as a teenager, thrown in jail. . .about 12 or 13 when Victor Jr. married Sudie. Victor Jr. put her in a Catholic school in Fort Smith, but she ran away.

---

[2] Author interview with Jo Anne Capps Day, July 7, 2004

[3] *Loc., cit.*

[4] *Loc., cit.*

"Hazel had seven husbands. They all beat her up. The last one broke both her arms and both legs. That put her in the hospital a long time. She was in jail a lot in McAlester."

When they rediscovered romance, Victor Jr. was living handsomely in Oklahoma City. He was associated with a small group of financiers and oilmen in the Farmers Mutual Royalty Syndicate, a highly speculative venture.

Both openly and behind the scenes, Victor Jr. was struggling to avoid having to go to the penitentiary. His lawyers were requesting a new trial, and that appeal inched along in the customary snail's pace of most such cases. [It may have actually got lost because a 2004 search of Oklahoma appellate court archives produced not even a sniff of Battiest or Locke, and all that remains in the Pushmahata County district court clerk's office is a docket entry of about thirty words setting the trial date.]

No matter; Victor Locke Jr. was going a different route, anyhow.

He made use of his courtly charm. Jo Anne Day had seen that first hand. "If you complimented Vick on something he was wearing, say a scarf or a necktie, he'd take it off and give it to you," she recalled. "He was very generous. Oh, I loved him! He liked kids. He was a snappy dresser."[5]

The scheme Victor Locke Jr. undertook was to make an end run around the criminal court of appeals by going straight to Governor William J. Holloway to ask for a pardon.

He played his cards like he held four aces. First of all Governor Holloway was on the eve of going out of office; if anyone complained, the Governor could safely brush the criticism aside.

On the afternoon of December 29, 1930, Victor Locke Jr. walked into Governor Holloway's office with his pardon petition in hand, and, more importantly, accompanied by an aristocratic delegation of sixteen prominent Oklahoma women of Indian blood. They all had signed the petition saying the killing should be pardoned because "it was a question

---

[5] *Loc., cit.*

of honor wherein Victor M. Locke Jr. sought to protect the honor and sanctity of his family" after Battiest had seduced one of his wards.[6]

Governor Holloway observed that he had received "a large number of personal letters from prominent citizens" urging him to pardon Victor Locke. At his request the state Pardon and Parole Attorney investigated and approved a pardon.[7]

Almost smothered by the cheerful chatter of the Indian ladies, Victor Locke Jr. walked away with a full pardon bearing Governor Holloway's signature and the official seal of the Secretary of State of Oklahoma.

No mention was made in the newspapers that the ladies included Alice Brown Davis, his late brother Ben's mother-in-law, two of her daughters, five of his cousins, his Five Tribes secretary, and three or four lifelong friends from Antlers, Hugo and Durant.[8]

What mattered to him was freedom—from the threat of prison, and a chance to revitalize his love affair from 1896.

From her room at Oklahoma City's Huckins Hotel, Sudie telephoned her niece Lura McAlester in McAlester. "Lura," she said, "come and bring your blue dress. Vick and I are going to be married and I want you to wear a nice dress."[9]

Mrs. Day recalled the newlyweds "did have a nice home. They always had a lot of people around . . .They had a lot of friends, and many, many parties."[10]

Along with "a lot of friends," Victor Jr. Locke also had his share of naysayers. One from Choctaw country was Muriel Wright, daughter of Dr. E. N. Wright, a longtime political enemy of the Lockes.

---

[6] Petition to Governor Holloway, Dec. 29, 1930, Locke Family Papers, Garrard Ardeneum Manuscript Collection

[7] *Loc., cit.*

[8] *Loc., cit.;* Signatures on the petition were: Mrs. R. L. Fite, Tahlequah; Alice B. Davis, Wewoka; Mrs. J. P. Jones, Chickasha; Mrs. W. K. Hilseweck, Margaret Lewis, Esther Hilseweck, Mrs. A.E. Perry, Irene Davis Key, all of Oklahoma City; Lola M. Rambo, Muskogee; Mrs. A. J. Arnote and Elizabeth Griggs Nash of Antlers; Mrs. A. J. Cline and Czarina Conlon of Durant; Susan Thomas of Talihina, and Mrs. Hattie Wilson of Durant.

[9] Jo Anne Day interview

[10] *Loc., cit.*

Writing January 18, 1931 to her parents on stationery of the Oklahoma Historical Society, where she was a researcher, Miss Wright made these snide observations:

> Another excitement of the week was Victor Locke Jr.'s marriage to Sudie McAlester Barnes. People shake their heads at his fourth marriage to a rich woman just after he has been pardoned for the murder of Abner Battiest.
>
> I saw him in the cafeteria one noon after his pardon and before his marriage. His attitude was clearly puffed up and braggadocio; it seems as if he still has to atone for his actions. Certainly a kind Providence is giving him every chance to redeem himself.
>
> Perhaps now that his wants for money, position, and a home are given him again, he may fool us. However, what is that old proverb about an old dog new tricks?[11]

Although the stock market crash of 1929 staggered the American economy, Victor Locke Jr. continued to live in *grand seigniorial* style. He had a fine Oklahoma City home, occupied offices on the ninth floor of the high-rent Petroleum Building, was president of the Farmers Mutual Royalty Syndicate, employed a secretary, kept his influential hand in Republican politics, and traveled and dined with Oklahoma's upper echelon. He maintained a studious and strict gentlemanly stance and signed all his correspondence "V.M. Locke Jr."

His fortunes went up and down during the mercurial 1930s, but his spirit never seemed to sag. Nowhere did he leave any comment on the tragedy of the dustbowl exodus of the tattered Okies, even though some of them were departing from the northern reaches of Choctaw country. He obviously watched this in agony.

For posterity he wrote no comment on the Lindbergh baby kidnapping, or the bullet-riddled finale of the crime spree of Bonnie and Clyde, or about the "lady in red" leading John Dillinger out of the Chicago movie house into the FBI's fatal fusillade, all of which made page one of *The Oklahoman* in this exciting period.

---

[11] Muriel Wright to Dr. and Mrs. E.P. Wright, Jan. 18, 1931, Muriel Wright Papers, Oklahoma Historical Society

Victor Jr. would, however, sit in the Oklahoma City courtroom alongside his friend U.S. District Attorney Herbert Hyde at times as he prosecuted "Machine Gun" Kelly and his red-haired gun moll Kathryn for the $200,000 kidnapping of oil millionaire Charles F. Urschel. The kidnappers were convicted in 1933 and given life in prison. Victor Jr. was startled but not impressed by Kathryn Kelly's spitfire behavior, as he told his sister Doll:

> I sat at the table reserved for counsel for the prosecution and I heard every whisper, even Kathryn's cuss words . . . Kathryn hardly possesses the courage of a Belle Starr. I think she is somewhat of a 'sawmill fusser' rather than a woman of spirit. I knew Sallie Norris, Sallie Durant and that Harkins woman all very well and they could have backed Kathryn off the stage when it comes to real courage.
>
> She is a typical woman of the underworld, and showed miserable judgment yesterday when she slapped a federal agent. Belle Starr would have put on her lady airs under similar circumstances, and to have offended her jailors would have been fartherest from her mind.
>
> This world is so full of cheap stuff, even among thieves.[12]

Disgusted, Victor Jr. at the noon break left the courtroom.

The female who most troubled Victor Jr.'s thoughts was Sudie—his old sweetheart/new wife. They were in deep water. After only a few months of marriage, Sudie was out of his bedroom, but not out of his life. Considering the apparent, and early, discord of his three previous marriages, perhaps that did not come as a surprise to his Antlers friends.

Sudie was not one to let down her hair in public. Few people ever glimpsed Victor Locke stepping out of a shower. Thus their bitter breakup was intensely private—and exceedingly fierce, and lengthy, lasting almost nine or ten years.

Oddly enough, despite the fury, Victor Jr. occasionally tried to get Sudie back. One factor in the rupture of their 1931 romance appears to be Sudie's adoped "wild" daughter Hazel. Late in the divorce struggle, Victor Jr. wrote one of Sudie's aunts:

---

[12] Victor Locke Jr. to Dolly Archer, Oct. 11, 1933, Locke Family Papers, Garrard Ardeneum Manuscript Collection

> As for a history of our few months actually together, I am going to tell you how Sudie avoided her Indian kin and friends. How she would pick up the strangest characters to be intimate with and shut out the few real women that I called to show friendship and interest in our welfare.
>
> I do not mind telling you that these "strange characters" are the ones from whom I revolted. I couldn't stand that class of trash . . . When Andrews wrote me a blackmailing letter threatening all sorts of embarrassments, I never was so shocked in my life than to know that Sudie would be a party to such representations.
>
> She and I never had any fusses. As late as September 25, 1939, I demanded that she get rid of her entourage and come live with me. No, she had to bring Hazel's baby along. That settled it. She phoned me herself and offered to come providing—but there could be no proviso.[13]

Before the end of their pathetic divorce contest, a ton of nasty words had been flung back and forth, lawyers on both sides racked up hundreds of billable hours, and the Choctaw sun rose and set a few thousand times. One thing was clear, Victor Locke Jr. was not the least interested in trying a fifth trip to the altar.

However, in retrospect their breakup was not all one-sided. In her letters from McAlester to Victor in Oklahoma City in 1933 and 1934, Sudie's salutation was "Dear Sweetie." Her signature was "lovingly, Sudie."

When once she phoned Victor Jr. asking to come visit him, he begged off as too busy. She wrote: "I want to know what day we can come. I never failed to see you when you wanted to come and was always glad to see you."[14] Legends that J. J. McAlester had buried money under his mansion caused her to write Vick asking him to send her "the gun (pistol) automatic at once. . . .I need it. We are having prowlers at

---

[13] Victor Locke Jr. to Mrs. W.B. McAlester, Feb. 5, 1940, Locke Family Papers, Garrard Ardeneum Manuscript Collection

[14] Sudie McAlester Locke to Victor Locke Jr., Jan. 6, 1933, Locke Family Papers, Garrard Ardeneum Manuscript Collection

night. They have made several holes under the house, looking for the money they think is buried."[15]

THE ESTRANGEMENT that existed for thirty years between Mary "Dolly" Archer and her brothers began to heal with Victor Jr. about a year before her husband's death.

It may have been because he was so wounded by his failure with Sudie that Victor Jr. undertook to revive their childhood soul mate relationship. He succeeded.

Charles E. Archer had created this chasm in 1901 by his aloof attitude. The Locke men, or anyone else, perceived they were expected to feel personally lucky just to know someone of such superior calibre. "Just stuck up," Ben had groused.

Archer died January 1, 1934 in St. Joseph's hospital at Paris, Texas—and not pleasantly. He was sixty-four years old and ill with diabetes and nephritis. For a month the doctors tried to save his foot, which had turned black. They waited too late to amputate. He died of gangrene.

As early as July 1933 Victor Jr. had launched a lusty chitchat correspondence with Dolly. He tried to get her car repaired, and must have been rooked. "I have a disposition to look on friends as 'pure gold' and oftimes they turn out to be brass. Such is the case at Antlers and I am trying to forget. I have been the victim of 'grafters' until I am sick."[16]

Victor told her of his visit to a Creek Indian conference at Okemah. "We reached the table and I swallowed three big bowls of Tom Fuller, cleaned up a plate of sour bread, made a big dish of golden brown 'Injun' cooked pork look like a tramp had had access to it . . . I wish you knew the Creek people. They are a superior race to all other members of the Five Civilized Tribes."[17]

Though Victor maintained his friendship with Patrick Hurley, he managed to get crosswise with Mrs. Hurley, the perhaps too haughty daughter of an admiral, as he told Doll:

---

[15] *Ibid.,* Dec. 8, 1932
[16] *Ibid.,* July 6, 1933
[17] *Ibid.,* July 25, 1933

> I have a long letter from Colonel Hurley. He invites me to his Virginia home, which I could hardly accept as Mrs. H— amuses rather than interests me. I have an idea that she frowns on the friendship that exists between Pat and myself. I have this intimidation from H— himself. It seems that someone told her that myself and several others had said, or agreed, that Pat got married just like he would buy a dresser for his room, or a table to dine on.
>
> If some long tongue told her this, I don't blame the woman for being "blowed up." However truthful it may be, it was a bad thing to say.[18]

With the Great Depression slamming Oklahoma, Victor Locke Jr. organized a committee of Indian women to "hustle jobs for Indians" and had success. His "Aunt Alice" had become a drag. She was involved in court "and her demands on my time, pocketbook, and patience is almost unbearable."[19]

He was clinging to his Choctaw political niche. "I want to go up to Talihina, Wilburton and McCurtain . . . to see about the chief's appointment. I am not a candidate, but I want to be in with the man who gets the place."[20]

After Charles Archer's death, Dolly, in her mid-fifties, became Antler's certified town eccentric. Their brick home on the hill had burned twice, last in 1928. Patched up with a log addition, it was her haven for living alone, since she had no children. Each day she trudged a mile to the post office, "elegant" in long dress, gloves and parasol. She neither acknowledged greetings nor spoke.

She was followed by a pack of dogs, strays she collected. Her pet, "White Christmas," whelped often, once with a litter of twelve inside the First Christian Church which had just started an "open door" fad. On Antlers streets, old nesters obligingly and silently cleared her a path; newcomers and travelers gawked, and had rude thoughts. Historian Dorothy Arnote West wrote:

---

[18] *Ibid.,* Aug. 21, 1933
[19] *Ibid.,* Oct. 11, 1933
[20] *Ibid.,* Jan. 22, 1934

> "She loved every tree, rock and shrub on her hill . . .She told me: 'It means a great deal to me to live so near the old Kiamichi river, the playground of my youth. It still flows on, the prettiest stream in the state'."[21]

"She is quite a personage," Victor wrote new friends in Chattanooga, "and once known she is never forgotten. Read *Gone With The Wind* and keep in mind Scarlett O'Hara. You will have a good picture of my sister."[22]

Grumbling that he was broke, Victor Locke Jr. tried to get Dolly to sell for him his house on High Street in Antlers. Instead she fixed it up, rented it, and mailed him the checks. Also he wanted her to sell his vacant lots for $350. "I am broke."[23] Later: "I have built up an income that will keep me out of the poor house all my life, but you know when possible I have lived extravagantly."[24]

He tried to buy part of her hill, wanting four blocks, enough for "a garden and room to raise chickens and pigs. . . I am living in the Skirvin Hotel. It is fine. I would hate to die in such surroundings."[25] She turned him down. He suggested she sell his ranch on Big Cedar. "I cannot stay there. When I am away, everything goes to rack and ruin."[26] In the end, Curtis Locke, Ben's son, took over the ranch.

Trouble about the size of Winding Stair Mountain, and almost as fierce, fell on Victor Locke Jr. in the late 1930s. Investors in Farmers Mutual Royalty Syndicate, Inc. went on a rampage, yelling for some promised profit.

Eight people from four different states filed suit in federal court at Oklahoma City demanding an accounting. "Dividends of 1 percent a month were paid during the stock sale," reported *The Oklahoman,* "but

---

[21] *The Early Years,* p 302

[22] Victor Locke Jr. to O.L. Davis, April 24, 1940, Locke Family Papers, Garrard Ardeneum Manuscript Collection

[23] Victor Locke Jr to Dolly Archer, Sept. 30, 1940, Locke Family Papers, Garrard Ardeneum Manuscript Collection

[24] *Ibid., March 7, 1941*

[25] *Ibid.,* July 31, 1941

[26] *Ibid.,* Aug. 20, 1941

these were cut down to only 3 percent for the entire year of 1933, and none at all have been paid since."[27]

Vick wrote Dolly: "I am worried sick. Never so worried in my life."[28] And with good reason. He had hopped on a courthouse merry-go-round that would keep him spinning two or three years. Then came more bad luck, as related to Dolly:

> I am afoot. Fortunately I was not in my car when the wreck happened. Colbert is the best driver that I ever had but as Scarlett O'Hara would say. "He must have been going like a bat out of hell" when the accident occurred. I just thank Almighty God for being spared the thrill.
>
> I am having difficulties in our business, but like all things that are evil, it will pass. There is nothing of the despondent in my nature, and I will be happy under any and all circumstances.
>
> I can live on nothing, or I can live like the King of England, so that's that.[29]

It would have taken hard looking to find a more staunch and loyal Republican in Oklahoma than Victor Locke Jr. Wild horses could not have kept him away from the 1940 Convention in Philadelphia. Leaving Oklahoma City on the evening of June 18, 1940, he wrote Grady Lewis, his Antlers friend who had become a prominent attorney in Washington, D. C. he was "not for Gannett or Hoover or Willkie. There will be many a twist before the situation comes to a head."

Victor was hoping the convention would "do something" for Patrick Hurley, but grumbled that the latter hadn't let his friends know what he wanted. "I feel Pat has as good a chance for something as anyone. But he must make the first move. . . Hyde is strong for Pat, and he is temporary chairman of the resolutions committee. John Nicholas is against Pat, but that is a decided asset. I do not see how Pat stood that fellow. I can't."[30]

---

[27] *The Oklahoman.* May 24, 1940
[28] Victor Locke Jr. to Dolly Archer, Oct. 28, 1941, Locke Family Papers, Garrard Ardeneum Manuscript Collection
[29] *Ibid.,* Nov. 10, 1941
[30] Victor Locke Jr. to Grady Lewis, June 18. 1940

That fall's Presidential election broke Locke's heart, with Franklin Delano Roosevelt defeating Republican Wendell L. Willkie for an unprecedented third term. [The end of Victor Locke's life spared him from seeing F.D.R. in 1944 win a never-again fourth term, turning back Governor Thomas E. Dewey of New York.]

THE CROOKED DAGGER of hate forged from sweet love gone sour was jabbed back and forth between Sudie and Victor with cruel vigor.

They exchanged numerous letters, plus phone calls and visits, over an amazing period of eight or nine years after their marriage breakup.

Their hippety-hop communication ran the gamut from high to low, quizzical to direct, sugary to acidic. She coyly suggested reunion and then months later made a curious negative statement. "A man with your disposition," she wrote, "don't need a wife, only young men around you."[31] [Victor Locke Jr. saved much of this correspondence, and it remains in Locke family historical archives, some letters undated.]

By the end of their dueling, they were trying to literally tear each other apart.

Early on she wrote in friendly fashion that her quilts were the hit of a Catholic charity show, clearing $300. She mentioned money which Victor had sent a friend. "She was so pleased with your letter but she can't read your writing, so I read it to her."[32]

She hammered away from her home in McAlester at not seeing him. "Have tried several times to get you over the phone but you would not talk." "What does it take to make you happy?" "You come to town and you won't come to see me."

Still, most of her letters started: "Dear Sweetie," and closed "Lovingly, Sudie." A few were "Dear Dick" [his nickname] or just "Dick."

---

[31] File of Victor Locke correspondence with Sudie McAlester Locke, 1933-1940, mostly undated, Locke Family Papers, Garrard Ardeneum Manuscript Collection. [Two Antlers historians asked if the author's research unearthed any evidence that Victor Locke Jr. was bisexual or homosexual. It did not.]

[32] *Loc., cit.*

Sudie twitted him about the Republican defeats in national politics. "Dick, since the country has gone to the devil, will that make a difference in you getting to be chief? Now don't cuss the Democrats any more. They have done a lot for you."[33]

"You said you were going to buy a car," Sudie wrote, "and give it to me for a wedding present. I didn't ask for it, but was mighty glad to have a new car." Later: "Had to put the car up. Takes too much gasoline."

They jousted over Victor's only child, Rose or Vivia, called Bunnie, born in 1915 during his marriage to Vivia Nail Robertson, his third. He had largely ignored both his ex-wife and their child; much of Bunnie's childhood was spent in California.

Sudie got in a hard jab: "As for giving your daughter your attention, I thought it due for the last seventeen years. I have told you so, and you have often said she was no more to you than any other child. I have not kept you from her. You have had all these years to do for her. Blame her mother."

In early 1934 they started swinging haymakers.

"I don't understand your attitude toward me," Sudie wrote. "Now write and tell me what you want to do. I am at a loss to know what to do. Do you want a divorce? I won't give it to you. You even asked me to leave Mr. Barnes, and I thank Heavens I didn't. Since you have treated me, you have to support me. And get that in your head right now."[34]

Within a short time, she had taken a new tack. She would sue for the divorce. Her brisk letter:

> Dick:
>
> Yes, I phoned you *COLLECT.* I wanted you to come over and let us get this matter settled one way or the other.
>
> I am going to get a divorce. Everything was all right until you had E----- H----- [*her slanted handwriting is undecipherable]* in our home and I'm going to name him.
>
> Sudie

---

[33] *Loc., cit.*
[34] *Loc., cit.*

Within a few days another letter demanding Dick take action:

Dear Major:

Please send my belongings before you leave for China. My rings. Cameo. Indian. The gun belongs to me. In the first place you had no business to take it. I don't care whether you believe it or not, it is so. Hazel wants her dictionary.

Your sister and I are friends and always will be.

As ever, Sudie

P.S. Send everything you have that belongs to me. Please.

On March 15, 1934, Victor Locke Jr. wrote a stinging response:

Sudie:

I have sent your pictures. Mrs. Thomas is expressing your jewelry today. She is having it insured. Curtis should have sent your automatic by now. If not, it will be done as soon as I return to Antlers.

I will send Hazel's dictionary as soon as I can get it out at Aunt Alice's. I am surprised that you would think of the book. The Lord knows Hazel needs it!

This leaves nothing but your cut glass, which is at Mrs. McKee's in Antlers. I will have it sent to you as soon as I get to Antlers.

In the meantime, you have some things of mine that I want. Please return the silverware given me by the employees in Muskogee. Also the picture framed (of myself) which really belongs to Aunt Alice. And those two keepsakes of mine of my childhood days, the bonnet and the baby shirt. This is all. Please do these things as promptly as I have complied with your request.

I wish to say that as soon as the financial world gets on its feet, and I get some money, I will arrange for you to get your divorce and settle up with you in full. If you have any family pride left, you will follow a dignified course in this matter, and keep your own counsel.

I have no fear of anybody or anything, and if you choose to raise Hell, just cut your dogs loose!

I hope this is the end of a nightmare.

Yours, V.M. Locke Jr.

For reasons not clear, this cat-and-dog fight fell into a lull. About five years elapsed with no action, no divorce suit, no letters that survive in the Victor Locke Jr. collection in the extensive family archives.

The appearance of a vacuum was totally deceiving for the poisonous crooked daggers were still unsheathed. The wily combatants were merely waiting to have another go at it.

If Sudie wanted Victor to pay plenty for her pain, suffering, and claimed disappointment, she may have concluded, or her lawyers may have concluded, it was precisely the wrong time to rummage around in the Locke cash register.

It could be empty. Victor had proclaimed himself broke several times. That could be true. America was still caught in the jaws of The Great Depression which had the sharpest teeth felt in many a lifetime. Oklahoma bled probably more than most states; the frantic flight of the dustbowl Okies was ample proof of that.

As Victor Locke might say, "You can't get blood out of a turnip. And I don't even have a turnip."

Of course, he was clever and adroit enough to get by in some fashion. He was scrambling to make a living in the oil investment business. The stockholders in Farmers Mutual Royalty Syndicate kept yammering in lawyers' offices and courtrooms for their money back. That fight was about as draining on Victor as his squabble over a divorce. The royalty fight seemed to end in a sort of draw; at least, Victor Jr. didn't get tarred and feathered, or have to shell out a heap of money he didn't have.

Victor Locke Jr. had a sharp, fluid and creative brain, bolstered by years of literary reading and the study of languages and history—as well as observing and contemplating the devious antics of *homo sapiens.*

In this slack period of his life, Victor Locke undertook to put this cranial talent to use as an author, or storyteller. He decided, apparently, to pull together the Patrick J. Hurley saga. He wrote his friend about his effort and, on October 10, 1939, got a response from Hurley that included this:

> I know that whatever you have said about my family is okay. I disagree with your estimate of your own. No man ever was endowed

> more bountifully by nature than you. The reason you and I have not gone far is because we enjoy life too thoroughly to devote ourselves completely to public achievements.
>
> Your family is a family of warriors. The men of you family have always been tough as a boot, courtly as Lord Chesterfield, and generous as Mark Anthony.
>
> The women of your family have not in all the generations left one dark spot on the family tradition. Entertaining this opinion, I could not agree with you that the family has gone to seed. If you and I live to see the development of the next generation of your family we will have some pleasant surprises coming to us.[35]

Ice was crusting on weak stretches of the Kiamichi River in December 1939, one of the hardest freezes in recent years, when the Sudie-Dick Locke marriage squabble abruptly burst into flame again. He finally filed for divorce.

Then began two or three years of brawling in the Pushmahata County courts—not actual confrontations from the witness chair before the judge, but through a flurry of paper. In petitions they accused each of deceit and misconduct at various stages of their romantic entanglement stretching back to its beginning forty-four years earlier!

They tried to make up during 1931-1939. For a few brief periods, they lived as man and wife, in Oklahoma City and McAlester on weekends. Only three months before filing for divorce, Victor urged Sudie to come back to him. But when they got to court she accused him of being a drunkard and dumping her because she no longer was rich.

Their brutality toward each other is documented in a sad sheaf of documents more than an inch thick left in the Pushmahata County district court clerk's vault, as Case No. 4311.[36] The initial filing was Victor's divorce petition December 7, 1939, on routine grounds. They were married January 12, 1931 and "on or about" December 1, 1931 Sudie "abandoned and deserted" him "without any cause, excuse or provocation."

---

[35] Patrick J. Hurley to Victor Locke Jr., Oct. 10, 1939, Locke Family Papers, Garrard Ardeneum Manuscript Collection

[36] All legal docments quoted are in Pushmahata County District Court file No. 4311, Victor M. Locke, plaintiff, vs. Sudie Locke, defendant, initial filing on Dec. 7, 1939, and numerous subsequent dates

Sudie, ready to fight, got lawyers and went on the offensive. She was entitled to the divorce, and alimony. Both of them ripped down their privacy curtains and exposed scenarios typical of the pages of *True Confessions* magazine.

In her "early girlhood," she conceded in her cross-petition, Sudie fell for his "pseudo-chivalry' and agreed to marry Victor in 1896. Her father objected, investigated her suitor and "convinced her that he was a wastrel given to excessive drinking and gambling and inclined to be too free with his amours." Sudie first believed she could reform him, but finally dropped the idea, and never thought of eloping, as Victor claimed. If she answered letters he sent in the Spanish-American war it would have been "to only to relieve his home hunger."

When she heard Victor Locke Jr. had taken his first bride she didn't care because she had married James Fitzgerald. One year later Fitzgerald was killed by lightning in Little Rock. Victor's claim that she called him one year later to come to her, Sudie said, was a figment of Dick's "overly lurid imagination." She married S.H. Barnes and did not carry on a "friendly correspondence" with Victor.

> She admits, however, that the plaintiff [Victor] often in an attempt to further his political fortunes about matters concerning the Choctaw tribe . . .was especially anxious to obtain the influence of her father. . . On visits to the home of her father, he was treated with generous courtesy . . . but never as a suitor . . .Her father would not have permitted it and she would not have allowed it.[37]

Victor had claimed she borrowed $200 from him while married to Barnes and never repaid it. She admitted getting the "emergency" loan, and said Barnes repaid Victor. She accused Victor of making accusations to cause her "humiliation and embarrassment, or to feed his overgrown self-esteem and to perpetuate a pretended conquest."

Sudie "regretfully admits" that "she was probably to blame" for their 1931 marriage because she believed his promise to "forego whatever remained of the bad habits of his youth." Her petition said "she

---

[37] *Loc., cit.*

should have been warned by the story of the lives of four other women, each of which was darkened by previous marriage to the plaintiff, and each of which divorced him because of his misconduct." Yet mutual friends urged her to marry Victor.

> She had long believed that the plaintiff was capable of worthy things. That his vices and unconventional conduct were not of the essence of his life, but the ephemeral exhibitions of the moment. And it was only after years of excuses that she made to herself for him that she became wholly disillusioned. She expressly denies that there was any excitement of the hour upon the inauguration of a governor that excited her. [*As* Victor *claimed about their 1931 marriage.*] That she had seen governors come and go, as had the plaintiff, for many years in Oklahoma.
>
> And defendant especially denies that she was thinking in terms of 1896. She was thinking and planning in terms of years to come, hoping their lives could be lived together in respect, in harmony, and in affection till at the end one might look upon the other's still face, while tears of regret fell upon the coffin's lid.
>
> And defendant especially denies that the difference between them has arisen because the fires of youth have burned out. She realized at the time of her unfortunate marriage to the plaintiff that she had passed her youth and believed that the plaintiff through age and experience had learned the futility of confusing love with lascivious desire, a mistake that youth doesn't always avoid.[38]

Sudie conceded she went to Antlers with Victor on election day in 1932 in a Buick sedan he claimed he bought her as a wedding present, but he traded in her car as down payment. Then the Buick was wrecked in Calvin while he was returning to Oklahoma City, and she had to trade it in for a cheap second-hand car.

She challenged his claim of being too old to learn to drive. "His paranoiac imagination induces him to believe that it is beneath his dignity to indulge in the physical exertion of driving a car. That it is more becoming his egotistical self that he sit the dominant master over the subservient underling, who does his driving for him."

---

[38] *Loc., cit.*

At Christmas 1938, Sudie spent three days and nights with "Dick" "as his wife" at the St. James Hotel in Oklahoma City, she conceded, and they talked of "reestablishment of their home." Then he lost interest, she claimed, when he found her property was tied up in a trust.

Even so "her feelings . . .were tinged with regret. . . because there were so many possibilities in his mental equipment." But when she read a petition he filed February 20, 1940 she realized he was trying to cause her "shame and embarrassment" and also "how utterly wasted her regrets had been."

She waited "through weary years" but was "always his wife and aware of her conjugal obligations," while Victor Locke was determined "to just live and get along and sooner or later die out of the tragedy of youth."

For whatever reason, Victor chose to unburden his reaction, in full detail, to Sudie's aunt in McAlester, Mrs. W. B. McAlester. Apparently she had written to him. Under date of February 5, 1940, he replied:

> Dear Mary:
>
> Your letter of January 15th came in due time. . .As for the divorce, that is settled. She can have that at the drop of the hat; in fact, it has gone too far to take back. The whole thing now rests upon property settlement. . . and she knows that she is lost when it comes to that feature of divorce suits. I am now having every check that she endorsed tabulated . . . to show that she committed a sin of omission when she alleged (so the lawyer tells me) that I had never done anything for her in a financial way but to buy one dress Christmas two years ago.
>
> Now the thing that I am grasping at is could and would it be possible for you and Doll to join together and get Sudie's ear over and above the lawyers, J. J. McAlester Jr., and all other agencies engaged in airing this painful situation?
>
> If it could be done quietly and secretly, I would be glad to abide by whatever conclusions you all may arrive at. I would be glad to help Sudie in her financial difficulties, but I am not going to provide Hazel Barnes, J.J. Jr., and the rest of that gang of leeches. I could name them all, but they are well known, so it is unnecessary
>
> I do not want to impose on you or anyone. But Sudie is making a mortal and lasting mistake and she is the one who will suffer in

the long run. I am sending a copy of this letter to Doll, and I shall see her tomorrow.

I pray that all will be well with you and your family.

Most sincerely yours,
Victor M. Locke, Jr.

Rather than go quickly to trial, Sudie's lawyers kept lobbing paper complaints against Victor. Sudie wanted $150 a month alimony, $100 expense, and $100 for her attorneys. The court gave her $50 temporary alimony and the expense and lawyer money. But court records do not show Victor ever paid it.

Victor Locke Jr. had been "living in luxury, driving the most expensive cars, having always his private chauffeur and valet . . . is accustomed to and does wear the finest apparel," she alleged. Over the years he bought her only "two inexpensive house dresses and one medium-priced suit." She claimed he had an annual income of $10,000 and a worth of $20,000.

Sudie said Victor accepted her adopted daughter, nine when they married, paid to send her to a Catholic school in Fort Smith, then rejected the girl, asserting she should "be a hasher in a restaurant or something of that sort." [Hazel apparently was first married at fifteen.]

When she left Victor, Sudie went to her rundown small farm in McAlester. Dick, she said, came on weekends "invariably drunk." One weekend, she said, he stayed at the McAlester hotel. She went to tell him he had a phone call, and he came to the door drunk. "What the hell are you doing here?" She turned and left, she said.

In answering her allegations, Victor said Sudie agreed to marry him before he joined the army for the Spanish-American War and also when he came back in 1899, and stood him up both times. He said over the years they stayed in touch "by letter and visits of the most friendly kind."

As to the governor's inauguration in 1931, "perhaps it was the excitement of the hour, perhaps the actions of some occult powers" that caused them "to think in terms of 1896" and get married. That was a mistake, Victor asserted. "Thirty-five years had come and gone, and the fires of youth had burned out. That statement is the truth, rock bottom of these proceedings."

"As for living in luxury," said Victor Locke's petition. "evidently defendant was in a dream when she made the statement, like Maud Muller's dream of *Her narrow kitchen walls, stretched away into stately halls."* Victor retorted that he lived in one room at Judge Baxter's and in a 14 x14 room at St. James Hotel.

Curiously, there is no record that the divorce case was ever concluded. They were definitely through as man and wife, and the "fires of youth" had become ice cold.

Docket entries and petitions in Pushmahata County district court just simply trail off with no explanation. When author made a search of those records in September 2004, the Court Clerk's office said they had nothing to show that a divorce decree was ever granted either Victor Jr. or Sudie. [A curiosity is that in wire service stories about Victor Locke Jr.'s death, Sudie Barnes Locke was identified as his wife. She was not mentioned at all in his obituary published in the hometown *Antlers American.*]

Obviously, if Victor Locke chose to quote from John Greenleaf Whittier's "Maude Muller" in a legal response, he must have been impressed by the poem, the tale of the girl with "briar-torn gown" and "graceful ankles" and "long-lashed hazel eyes" who on a summer's day "raked the meadow sweet with hay."

He might have contemplated adding other stanzas appropriate to his stretched-out romance:

> Then she took up her burden of life again,
> Saying only, "It might have been."
>
> Alas for maiden, alas for judge,
> For rich repiner and household drudge!
>
> God pity them both! and pity us all,
> Who vainly the dreams of youth recall.

The Pushmataha County Historical Society identifies this photo as "Street scene after Antlers got exciting."

All photos courtesy Francine Locke Bray Collection, unless otherwise credited.

An avid rancher, Victor Locke Sr. was an expert horseman and rider. Here, *left,* he is shown directing one of his cattle roundups before the turn of the century.

The strength and serious determination of Victor Locke clearly shows in this photo from his early manhood.

The tailored and handsome Victor Locke Jr. when he was operating the oil royalty syndicate in Oklahoma City.

Characteristic pose by happy-go-lucky Babe Locke *(seated, with legs crossed)* with standing, *far left,* brother Victor Jr., and *(far right)* Major Niles.

The Frisco Railroad's official photo of the Harvey House, which became the social center of early-day Antlers.

All photos courtesy Francine Locke Bray Collection, unless otherwise credited.

14

In the Shade of the Old Cedar

WITH *CITY BOY* written all over him from the narrow brim straw sailor to his polished black lace-ups, Nelson Locke emerged from the sunny banks of Big Cedar Creek with a terrapin in his hand.

"I found an *amphibia,"* he announced, thrusting the little creature before Victor Locke.[1] His uncle's eyes flicked wide, and then he smiled, and felt a warm glow. The lad's superb Chicago Catholic education only enhanced his wonderment at making touch-and-feel discoveries in the Choctaw wilderness.

Their Indian companions shrugged off the strange word, and flashed wide grins. They knew what a terrapin was, regardless what this *alla nakni* from the states called it; anyhow, the white man's tongue was *ilaiyuka aiimoma.*

This was middle of May 1941. Alex's only child Nelson was spending a week exploring the green forests and wide plains on Victor's Big Cedar Creek ranch. That turned out to be the lone dividend of Victor Locke's long and vigorous effort to restore the economy and dignity of

---

[1] Victor Locke Jr. to Dolly Archer, June 2, 1941, Locke Family Papers, Garrard Ardeneum Manuscript Collection

his wastrel brother. Despite months of recent rescue offers, Alex rejected any help. Nelson, friendlier, eagerly had accepted this genuine invitation.

"The thing I like about that young man," Victor wrote Dolly, "is that there is no gush about him. He takes his time about everything, and creates an impression of stability.

"He amused me very much with his lack of knowledge of outdoor life, but there was no pretense of manner. What he called a terrapin is all right. The boys who helped him to have a good time liked him very much, and to me that was a sign of quality."[2]

For Victor Locke Jr., this was a time of continued uncertainty, worry and stress. Though he could still practically taste his sixty-fifth birthday cake, fancy and green and white, the shadows were beginning to lengthen for him, and at awesome speed. He may have sensed that his time was short, because he made a hurry-up first-time visit to ancestral haunts.

With his niece Benita Locke and a driver, he spent three or four days in Tennessee, to see the old Locke plantation at Ten Mile Stand, and, as he told Dolly, "see the grave of the original émigré, Thomas Locke, before the whole world thereabouts is inundated."[3]

His Farmers Mutual Royalty Syndicate was still under legal attack, his back pain persisted from a fall in the snow, he was short of money, and his economic future none too bright. Along with these pressing concerns, Victor worried about the war in Europe.

As a military man, still a lieutenant colonel in the Army reserve, he gained optimism by Winston Churchill's hard resolve to withstand the blitz of London, and overcome the fall of France, and the British humiliating retreat at Dunkirk. Referring to the possibility that America would be drawn into the conflict, Victor wrote Dolly: "I feel that England has won her fight, and there will be no war, which suits all situations, political as well as financial."[4]

In early 1941, however, he changed his mind. Hitler had started his invasion of Russia. The winds of war were beginning to ruffle the

---

[2] *Loc., cit.*
[3] *Ibid.,* July 31, 1941
[4] *Ibid.,* Oct. 5, 1940

leaves on the cherry trees in Washington, D.C. Since it looked like the Yanks would, in the end, have to go, Victor Locke Jr. was ready to put on his colonel's cap and strap on his saber. Reading about the German blitzkrieg combining tanks and warplanes, he may have felt chagrin when he remembered saying not too many years ago there would never be a better battle force than soldiers on horseback—cavalry.

"I am really tired of my work," said his letter to Dolly. "I want to relax. Either that or get in the big world which means war right now. I have written Colonel Knox [William F. Knox, Secretary of Navy (1940-1944)] to find me a place. He said he would. This is a secret, however."[5]

No call to duty ever came to Lieutenant Colonel Victor M. Locke Jr. Before year's end America would be sending ships, planes, tanks, and fighting men to two fronts. But Fate did not intend that Victor Locke join in the action or the celebration of the victory America was to achieve in 1945 under a mushroom cloud.

He had wanted Dolly to hop on the Frisco with him and sally forth to Chicago, find their derelict brother, help him straighten up and re-establish him there with his wife and son, or bring them home to Antlers. That didn't happen. He felt he had accomplished a worthwhile feat in getting Nelson down to Antlers.

Nelson was nineteen in 1936 when Victor had come to Chicago as a delegate to the National Republican convention. The Oklahoma Choctaw invited his nephew to join him at the Palmer House for lunch. "My big memory of the lunch," Nelson recalled later, "was his having five martinis and not showing any effects. I had two and could hardly see. I was nineteen."[6]

Victor took him to meet Frank Knight, managing editor of the *Chicago Daily News,* and on to the Heidelberg Restaurant on Randolph Street.

"Uncle Dick did not drive. He had a young man from Antlers along. The Antlers boy was expert in birdcalls and whistling. He put on a

---

[5] *Ibid,* March 19, 1941

[6] Nelson Locke, "The Early Years," April 7, 1987, Locke Family Papers, Garrard Ardeneum Manuscript Collection

show during the audience participation part of the Heidelberg floorshow. It was a big success."[7]

In 1941, when he was twenty-four and accepted Victor's invitation to visit Oklahoma, Nelson boarded the Sante Fe streamliner *The Texas Chief* in Chicago at 8 A.M. and arrived in Oklahoma City at midnight.

"I stayed with Uncle Dick and his driver at a small hotel," Nelson wrote later. "He was chairman of the Farmers Mutual Royalty Syndicate and Benita was his secretary. Allece was teaching in high school.

"After a few days we drove to Antlers. Uncle Dick had a new Mercury sedan every year then. It was the wildest 170 miles I ever rode. The driver prided himself on his speed and Uncle Dick just sat in back and enjoyed it. In Antlers he had a room in Nevins Kirkpatrick's house and I slept on a cot."[8]

One Big Cedar Creek character who stuck in Nelson's memory was an Indian wearing a blue slack suit and a baseball cap who he encountered at "a beautiful spot" in the woods. In a memoir called "The Early Years," Nelson explained:

> He had a shotgun and was hunting. We met him again a few days later and he was carrying a bow and arrows. He said he had had only two shells for the shotgun and no money to buy more. So he used the bow and arrow. The bow was of Bois d' Arc (Ironwood). The arrows where long with no feathers. They had brass shell cases instead of points. He demonstrated his ability to hit a target with amazing accuracy and force.
>
> Our camp had a log lean-to kitchen and "two half-wooded tents." We borrowed a pickup to get there because the road was too poor for a passenger car. The Eyachubby family lived there in a log and frame farmhouse. It was papered inside with pages from old issues of the *Saturday Evening Post.* Rufus, his wife, and their new baby were distant relatives. Rufus had to register for the draft in Finley, which was seven miles away through the forest. He walked there and back.

---

[7] *Loc., cit.*
[8] *Loc., cit.*

> In the evening, Rufus' wife would cook cornbread and fry large amounts of beef. Choctaws would just drift in from the forest and join us for dinner. Uncle Dick was in his element. They chattered in Choctaw and made jokes over me coming from the big city. As Uncle Dick's nephew, I was considered one of them—a Choctaw Indian.[9]

Out on Cedar Creek, Victor and his Choctaw friends gave the Chicagoan an intensive short course in Indian lore, vigils in the pristine moonlight that were so silent you almost dared not to breathe while you listened to hear and interpret the "conversations" of the wild creatures. Spending daylight hours delicately fingering the bent grass, scattered leaves, and broken twigs, and sniffing for precise scents—all to develop tracking skill. Above all how to take a "snake's sleep"—as Victor said his father called it—which was a quick nap any tired Indian might need. Nelson really mastered this skill.

After their outdoors excursion, Victor introduced him to the denizens of a different world. "We came back to Antlers," says his memoir, "and Uncle Dick spent most of his time in the backroom of the speakeasy, visiting with old-timers and friends."[10]

Dick Locke could not resist subjecting his nephew to a little tomfoolery. Nelson wrote about the incident:

> We were sitting in the speakeasy (Oklahoma was dry) when he told me that Mrs. Archer (Tante) was coming out of her building across the street. I should go over and introduce myself.
>
> I left the restaurant/speakeasy and went over. She stopped, looked me over, and said, "I don't speak to anyone who comes out of that place." Then she turned and walked away.
>
> Uncle Dick just shrugged it off. The next morning he told me to take the car and visit her on the hill. She was very gracious and acted like nothing had happened. We drove around the area visiting her tenants.[11]

---

[9] *Loc., cit.*
[10] *Loc., cit.*
[11] *Loc., cit.*

Victor Locke Jr., father of only one child, counseled his nephew on advantages of siring a large family. He explained later to a Tennessee relative: "Of the descendants of my father, Nelson Locke is the only one on whom we pin faith. I have advised him fully that the Locke family is going to seed unless he shows some speed in the better things of life. He appeared to understand."[12] [Obviously, he did; Nelson fathered nine children.]

On his return to Chicago, Nelson wrote his thanks for a "wonderful vacation. It was the best I ever had. I will never forget it."[13]

THE BANG AND CLATTER began at 2 o'clock in the morning, rousing an infuriated Victor Locke from sleep. It happened every night. They were loading the trucks at the nearby Arkansas Transportation outfit. "It is terrible!" he roared. "It's criminal!"[14]

Even in daylight the passing trucks on High Street were driving him crazy.

"I'm giving up my house," he told Dolly. "It's too close to town. I'm going out to my place [the ranch on Big Cedar] and live. Alex and his wife will go with me to do the heavy work.

"I am having the house repaired, and when I vacate I want you to take it and find a renter. I haven't the patience to fool with renters."[15]

The sand was pouring furiously down in the hourglass of Victor Locke Jr.'s life. Perhaps, as smart as he was, that fact was dawning on him. He grew increasingly pensive and nostalgic. Bits of his past popped up in unexpected places. He blinked over this item in *The Oklahoman:*

> LOST 'TIME' FOUND—Seventeen years ago while Walter Ferguson, Tulsa banker, was on a train in Virginia, a $100 watch presented to him

[12] Victor Locke Jr. to O.L. Davis, April 24, 1940, Locke Family Papers, Garrard Ardeneum Manuscript Collection
[13] Nelson Locke to Victor Locke Jr., May 27, 1941, Locke Family Papers, Garrard Ardeneum Manuscript Collection
[14] Victor Locke Jr. to Dolly Locke, March 19, 1941, Locke Family Papers, Garrard Ardeneum Manuscript Collection
[15] *Loc., cit.*

> by Victor Locke, principal chief of the Choctaw tribe, mysteriously disappeared. C.W. Kemp, police lieutenant in charge of the stolen goods department, discovered the watch, which bears Ferguson's name, in a city pawnshop where it had been taken by an old gold dealer.[16]

Into Dolly's convenient ear, Victor Locke moaned some of his most painful regrets. He was frank about misadventures and mistakes in his life. The past experiences, good and bad, seemed to fascinate him. "I recall those events with an overflow of sentiment that beats all things in life."[17]

There was a dedication of the Doaksville Cemetery; that gave him "the strong suspicion" that he and his sister were "probably the only people still alive who were born in Doaksville."[18]

His intention to create a residence for himself that high-flown architects would envy was gone; too much time had been wasted on dreaming, though he once hired a draftsman to make preliminary sketches.

The written record does not show Victor Locke Jr. paying much attention to his baby girl with little roly-poly legs who grew up to become a celebrated college drama department chair. He regretted that he was not closely involved in her growing-up years. That was one of the confidences he shared with Dolly, which his sister discussed in later years with Ben Locke's widow Maye, and with Nelson's wife Arlene.

"Children can have but one mother and one father," Maye wrote Dolly. "They do not govern this law of nature, they can't change it. With man-made laws, wives and wives, and husbands and husbands, form such an intermingling caravan one can't say 'who' belongs to 'who.' There follows strife, hate, bruises, hurts that are everlasting for the children involved.

---

16 *The Oklahoman,* Jan. 9, 1936

17 Victor Locke to Dolly Locke, March 24, 1941, Locke Family Papers, Garrard Ardeneum Manuscript Collection

18 Victor Locke Jr. to Dolly Archer, May 8, 1939, Locke Family Papers, Garrard Ardeneum Manuscript Collection

"Just looking at Dick's daughter, she reflects the tangibility of lack of prior parental contact. It was a great mistake for both. If she can honor his name in the life she has yet to live, 'it will be well.' "[19]

To Arlene Pritchard Locke in Chicago, Dolly voiced regret no effective reconciliation was achieved, writing: "We are considered most undemonstrative—have it related how Rose Vivia (Bunnie) expected her very absent father (a broken home) to embrace, etc., etc. When as he extended his hand fault was found with him by someone he loved very much, in fact a niece—his way—-but think the daughter unforgiving. Their last meeting & very few—they were just getting acquainted."[20]

The schism between father and daughter was dictated by the extreme bitterness that broke up Victor and Vivia Nail Locke when their child was only barely two years old. Vivia grew up in a proud heritage and wealth. Her backbone had as much iron as Victor's. She was bound to dominate the upbringing of their daughter—named Vivia for her mother, known variously as Rose, *Ba-nat-i-ma*, and chiefly called "Bunnie."

Vivia's strong character is well delineated in an early 1900's book, *History of Oklahoma:*

> Mrs. Vivia Locke was educated in the North Texas Female College at Sherman, completing courses in music and art besides the literary course. She inherited the beauty of her mother [a white Tennessee aristocrat] and the business-like ingenuity of her father. In connection with her education there is a reflection of the Indian Territory romance.
>
> She learned in school that she possessed unusual beauty, that it was out of the ordinary for one to be of Indian extraction, and that her father was "the wealthiest man of the Chickasaw Nation," all of which had no power to lead her into rapturous dreams of diverting those qualities into a career of useless fastidiousness.
>
> Rather, the discovery put her on the defensive against deceit, and kindled an ambition for the most profitable use of her talents. Many

---

[19] Maye Locke to Dolly Locke, March 16, 1943, Locke Family Papers, Garrard Ardeneum Manuscript Collection.

[20] Dolly Locke to Arlene Pritchard Locke, Aug. 1, 1956, Locke Family Papers, Garrard Ardeneum Manuscript Collection

> a white man courted pretty Vivia Nail, but Vivia Nail was never deceived by any of them. She was proud of her Indian blood, proud of her beautiful mother and her mother's aristocratic ancestors, and proud of her successful father.
>
> These were stronger ties than the proffered or feigned affections of her suitors. She was only eighteen when her mother died, and she returned home to become her father's helper. She was married July 14, 1900 to Albert M. Robertson. By that union she has a son, Wesley Leroy, aged fourteen.
>
> In 1913 she became the wife of Victor M. Locke, Jr., principal chief of the Choctaw Nation. They have a daughter, Vivia, now one year old.[21]

Both father and daughter toyed with feeble efforts to close the rift. But it was late in the game. In 1932 there is an indication she may have attended his fifty-sixth birthday party in Oklahoma City. At least next day he wrote his Aunt Alice: "Well! We are on our way—I am going to propose an engagement to Rose today, and have her come back before graduation, and get some clothing."[22] His daughter was then a student at the University of Oklahoma.

Bunnie seemed to have taken pride in her father's military achievements; at least she somewhat emulated him. In February 1943 she was among the first to join the Women's Army Corps—the fabled WACs—and was commissioned a second lieutenant.

Victor Locke Jr. wasn't just pleading poverty, actually he was broke. He bought a 1941 Lincoln Zephyr Sedan at Fred Jones Motor Company, 200 South Harvey, Oklahoma City. It was under a mortgage from the First National Bank for $1,377, which was in default. The mail brought him the sad notice that the car would be seized and sold at public auction on January 29, 1942.

---

[21] Joseph B. Thoburn, *A Standard History of Oklahoma, Vol. III,* (Chicago, 1916) p 1335

[22] Victor Locke Jr. to Alice Hilseweck, March 24, 1932, Locke Family Papers, Garrard Ardeneum Manuscript Collection

Hard times, a certain amount of enforced idleness, and depression or acute weariness arrived together and camped on Victor Locke's doorstep.

Just around the corner, the dark angel approached.

It had been a glorious life for Victor Murat Locke Jr., healthy and vigorous child, accomplished scholar, teenage political rifleman, Choctaw agent and interpreter, principal chief of the Choctaw Nation, Superintendent of the Five Civilized Tribes, delegate to two Republican national conventions, state legislator, friend of the famous, convicted killer, etc., etc. etc.

In several respects he outshone his doughty father, but some would say the sum total of Victor Senior's exploits, largely under more hazardous circumstances, left this son in the dust, in fact surmounted the combined achievements of all his boys.

History will decide. The two Victors will be hard to equal.

It is sort of ironic that Bunnie Locke signed up for the WACs in mid-February 1943. One morning not quite two weeks later at his writing desk, Victor Locke Jr. leaned forward to get a sheet of paper. Of a sudden he couldn't see. He felt numb, lost his balance, and crashed to the floor.

His housekeeper found him and by that afternoon, Friday February 26, 1943, he was in the Government Indian hospital at Talihina, about fifty miles northeast up the Kiamichi River.

He had suffered a cerebral hemorrhage, doctors said. It was devastating. He had predicted years earlier he would die alone, but to his bedside came five family females—sister Dolly, sister-in-law Maye Locke and her two military daughters, Allece, hostess at Camp Gruber at Muskogee, and Benita, attached to 14th Air Depot, Oklahoma City, and Maye's sister, Irene Key of Oklahoma City, wife of General William S. Key, head of the Oklahoma National Guard.[23]

Dr. E. S. Patterson of Antlers and the Talihina hospital's Dr. Russell Schull tried but could not rectify the damage. Victor Locke lingered until 1:30 A. M. Monday, March 1, and died. In twenty-two more days he would have been sixty-seven years old.

---

[23] *Antlers American,* March 4, 1943

They gave him two funerals in Antlers, one traditional Choctaw service at home, the other at the Catholic Church, where the Rev. Everest V. Foix officiated.[24] Then his casket was wheeled up cemetery road to his place beneath the shade of the sad old cedar tree, to be in eternity with the others of his remarkable family.

The book was now closed on what perhaps was the most exciting and incredible father-son chapter in Oklahoma Indian history.

---

[24] *Loc., cit.*

Afterword

DEATH CAME ingloriously to the last two Locke siblings who survived Victor Jr.

Alex, as detailed in Chapter 12, died as an unknown in a Chicago flophouse in February 27, 1953 at sixty-four, leaving only Mary Locke Archer, the eccentric "Dolly," living alone in her hilltop home on the north edge of Antlers.

To Dolly, her "hilltop" was the passion of her life. She told Antlers author Dorothy Arnote West she "loved every shrub and tree on her land," and the vista of the not too distant Kiamichi River kept alive "beautiful childhood memories."[1] Yet the Devil was sneaking in the shadows to relentlessly pursue her with his most destructive weapon.

Fire broke out in 1917 and destroyed the frame house she and her husband Charles Archer had built on the hilltop after their 1901 marriage. Undaunted, they lived in a tent near the ruins, entertaining friends with parties while they rebuilt--with brick. In 1928, six years before Charles Archer died, the brick home burned, but the walls remained standing. The Archers refused to leave the hilltop, partially rebuilding the brick ruins, adding a log annex.

After her husband's death, Dolly lived there alone, a happy recluse, with "White Christmas" and her other stray dogs, daily making the long walk to the Antlers post office, keeping up her correspondence, principally with nieces. She cared little that the townspeople considered her a "character," a benign eccentric.

On Wednesday, December 11, 1957, high school students passing by on their way to lunch saw flames shooting through the roof of

---

[1] *Antlers American,* December 12, 1957

Dolly's house.[2] Their phone call brought Antlers firefighters. While others were stringing four hundred feet of hose, Fireman Andy Taylor found Dolly, badly burned, in a crumpled heap twenty feet outside her door. She died within a few hours, at age seventy-eight. The fire was believed to have accidentally started from a wood heater or an oil cook stove.

A headline in the *Antlers American* pointed out Dolly was able to achieve her desire "to live to the end on 'her hill.' " She was buried in the Locke family cemetery. Dolly willed her real estate holdings--which included the family cemetery--to a grand niece, Susan Locke, who had been named for Dolly's mother, Susan Priscilla. Little Susan was the granddaughter of her brother Alex, and one of the nine children of her nephew Nelson and his wife Arlene.

The arsonist spirits that seemed to inhabit Dolly's hilltop did not pack up and leave. Even after her death, their evil lurked for eight years beside her old house, which had been restored and was occupied by Peck Bloodsworth, his wife and five children.

The fourth fire to hit Dolly's old abode came on Friday, November 19, 1965. At noontime, flames shot out of the Bloodsworth cook stove. Before the fire trucks could arrive, the house and all contents burned to the ground.

Fortunately, the Bloodsworths did not meet Dolly's fate; all escaped safely.

---

[2] *Loc. cit.*

Acknowledgements

I AM INDEBTED to many people for helping to provide material for this work, but to none more than Francine Locke Bray of Indianapolis. For twenty-five years or longer, she has collected data, photographs, oral histories, papers and documents on the Locke clan—not only from Choctaw Nation days but from Tennessee and before. Her passion for the story of the Lockes from Day One springs from being one of them, great grand-daughter of Victor Locke Sr. I met Francine while researching another Indian book that involved both Victor Jr. and Ben Locke. I discovered her through my visits to the Garrard Ardeneum in McAlester, Oklahoma. She proved extremely knowledgeable, helpful, efficient, and charming. In searching her marvelous material at the Ardeneum—*what a clever word!*—I stumbled into the realization that the Locke saga had all elements for a fascinating biography. The usual lengthy research would not be required because Francine had already assembled such a wealth of family and historical information. Likewise, Francine is smart, an articulate storyteller, and has fabulous organizational skills. If free of her duties at the Indiana University School of Medicine, she could have written this Locke saga

Francine Locke Bray dancing with husband Michael.

herself. In addition to providing data and photos, Francine helped edit the manuscript.

The most valuable published source of information was the *Locke Family History,* an impressive compendium by Betty J. Broyles of Chattanooga, Tennessee. Her 532-page book begins in 1750s London and explodes into tracing several thousand Lockes through arrival in Virginia in 1775 and migration on to Tennessee. For details on the Lockes in the Choctaw Nation the most eminent publication proved to be *Pushmahata County—The Early Years*, by Dorothy Arnote West of Antlers, Oklahoma, privately published in 2002 when Mrs. West was one hundred years old. It is a thorough and well-written work of 336 pages, containing her exciting historical narratives as well as several hundred memoirs of Choctaw Nation families. [I was fortunate to be able to interview both Dorothy West and Betty Broyles.]

Two officers of the Pushmahata County Historical Society, Myrtle Edmond and Kay Brown Black, graciously and generously assisted in my Push County research, for which I am most grateful. Other Oklahomans who helped as guides through the hard facts and rich myths of the Locke saga, and deserve my thanks, include:

Jo Anne Day, Oklahoma City; Dr. James Milligan, Durant; Marcia Haag, Norman; Henry Willis, Moore; Dolores Cary, sculptor and artist, Yukon; Mary Ann West, Edmond; Olin Williams, Bennington; Bob West, Idabel; Margaret Kymes, Muskogee; City Librarian Carolyn Trimble, Wewoka, and her assistant, Barbara Crelia; Gwen Walker, Confederate Memorial Museum, Atoka; Becky Lujan, Wewoka, for careful copy-reading and editorial assistance; Lisa Bowles, University of Oklahoma Law Library, Norman; Western History Collections at University of Oklahoma, Oklahoma Historical Society, University of Oklahoma Press; also Carol Ann Nordheimer, Wilmington, Delaware; Rita Dunn, Fort Worth, Texas; Daniel Coleman, Kansas City (Mo.) Public Library; William Garvin, Drury University, Springfield, Missouri.

Also, I express my appreciation for Chief Gregory E. Pyle's astute recognition of the importance of detailing the authentic and historic struggles of his people on the Indian Territory frontier.

Bibliography

Books

Anderson, Edwin Alexander, *Choctaw English Dictionary,* Oklahoma City, 1978

Bearss, Ed and Arrell M. Gibson, *Fort Smith,* Norman, 1969

Broyles, Betty J., *Locke Family History,* Collegedale, Tenn., 1995

Byington, Cyrus, *A Dictionary of the Choctaw Language* [Bureau of American Ethnology, Bulletin 46, Washington, 1915]

Debo, Angie, *The Rise and Fall of the Choctaw Republic,* Norman, 1934.

————————*And Still The Waters Run,* Norman, 1940

————————*The Road to Disappearance,* Norman , 1941

Dudley, C.E., *Days Gone By,* Pushmahata County Historical Society, reprint 1988

Foreman, Grant, *Advancing the Frontier,* Norman, 1933

————————*The Five Civilized Tribes,* Norman, 1934

————————*The Removal: The Emigration of the Five Civilized Tribes of Indians,* Norman, 1932

Haag, Marcia and Henry Willis, *Choctaw Language & Culture: Chata Anumpa,* Norman, 2001

Imon, Frances, *Smoke Signals from Indian Territory,* Wolfe City, Texas, 1976.

Kidwell, Clara Sue and Charles Roberts, *The Choctaws: A Critical Biblography*: Bloomington, 1980

McReynolds, Edwin C., *The Seminoles,* Norman, 1957

Morris, John W., Charles R. Goins, and Edwin C. McReynolds, *Historical Atlas of Oklahoma,* Norman, 1976

O'Beirne, Harry, *Leaders and Leading Men in the Indian Territory,* Chicago 1891

Stratton, David, ed., *The Memoirs of Albert B. Fall,* El Paso, Texas Western 1966

West, Dorothy Arnote, *Pushmahata County—The Early Years,* privately printed, 2002

Wright, Muriel H., *A Guide to the Indian Tribes of Oklahoma,* Norman, 1951

Leading the Way, Oklahoma Bar Association, 2003

Newspapers & Journals

Antlers American

Antlers Democrat

Antlers News

Antlers News-Record

Griffith, Joe, "In Search of Pancho Villa," *Journal of the Historical Society of the Georgia National Guard*

Oklahoman, The

Harlow's Weekly

James, John, "My Experience With Indians," *The Kiamichi Journal,* October 2002

Muskogee Daily Phoenix

Muskogee Times-Democrat

New York Herald

"Love and Marriage: Ancient Choctaw Style," Bishinik, December, 1980.

Indian Citizen

Indian Champion

Oklahoma City Times

Tishomingo Capital-Democrat

Tulsa World

West, Mary Ann, "The Locke-Jones War," *Real West,* October 1986

White, Rev. James D., "The Saga of St. Agnes," *The Kiamichi Journal,* June 2002

Government Documents

Report Commissioner of Indian Affairs, 1892, 1893

National Archives and Records Administration, Fort Worth, U. S. Court, Western District of Arkansas, Criminal Docket #3354

Other Sources
Baker University archives
Blanche, O. L., *Indian-Pioneer Papers,* Vol. 61-258-361.
Davis, Samuel L., *Indian-Pioneer Papers,* Vol. 22:59-60
Debo, Angie, Papers, OSU, Box 36, 88-031
Locke, Allece, Washington Diary 1923, Francine Locke Bray
Papers, Garrard Ardeneum Manuscript Collection
Locke, Nelson, Memoirs, Locke Family Papers, Garrard Ardeneum Manuscript Collection
Locke, Mary E. (Dolly), collection of letters and stories she sent in the 1940s and 1950s to the daughters of her nephew Nelson A. Locke and his wife Arlene, owned and catalogued by Francine Locke Bray as "To Susan and Her Sisters," Locke Family Papers, Garrard Ardeneum Manuscript Collection
Oklahoma Historical Society, F.S. Barde file
Pushmahata County District Court, Civil Case #4311, filed Dec. 7, 1939
Meigs County, Tennessee cemetery records.
Victor M. Locke Jr. pardon petition presented to Gov. W.J. Holloway
Thompson, Gilbert, *Indian-Pioneer Papers,* Vol. 46-442-446
Wright, Muriel, Papers, Oklahoma Historical Society, "Notes on E. N. W.," April 22, 1926

Chronicles of Oklahoma
Baird, W. David, "Spencer Academy, Choctaw Nation," Vol. 45—Spring 1967
Badinelli, Don F., "Struggle in the Choctaw Nation: The Coal Miners Strike of 1894," Vol. 72—Fall-1994
Balyeat, Frank A., "Joseph Samuel Murrow, Apostle to the Indians," Vol. 35—Autum 1957
Benson, Henry C., "Life Among the Choctaw Indians," Vol. 4—June 1926
Bobo, Lacy Pierce, "Reminiscences of Pioneer Days," Vol. 23—Autumn 1945
Brown, Loren N., "The Dawes Commission," Vol. 9—March 1931

Bruce, Michael L., "Our Best Men Are Fast Leaving Us: The Life and Times of Robert L. Jones," Vol. 66—Fall 1988

Bryce, J. Y., "About Some of Our First Schools in Choctaw Nation," Vol. 6—September 1928

Caldwell, Norman W., "The Red River Raft," Vol. 19—September 1941

Carter, Kent, "Tams Bixby: Doing Government Business in the Gilded Age," Vol. 78—Winter 2000-2001

Christian, Emma Irwin, "Memories of My Childhood Days in the Choctaw Nation," Vol. 9—June 1931; "Memories of My Childhood Days in the Choctaw Nation," Vol.11—September 1933

Coleman, Louis, "Cyrus Byington: Missionary to the Choctaws," Vol. 62—Winter 1984-85

Conlan, Czarina C., "David Folsom," Vol. 4—December 1926; "Peter Pitchlynn: Chief of Choctaws, 1864-66," Vol. 6—June 1928

Corbett, William P., "Rifles and Ruts: Army Road Builders in Indian Territory," Vol. 40—Fall 1982

Debo, Angie, "Education in the Choctaw Country After the Civil War," Vol. 10—September 1932; "The Location of the Battle of Round Mountain," Vol. 41— Spring 1963

Graebner, Norman Arthur, "Cattle Ranching in Eastern Oklahoma," Vol. 21—1943

Hall, Arthur H., "The Red Stick War," Vol. 12—September 1934

Hayes, Jerry G., "Ardent Spirits Among the Chickasaws and Choctaws, 1815-1856," Vol. 28—Fall 1991

Hofsommer, Donovan L., "Bawling Cattle and Barking Brakemen: An Oklahoma Railroad Memory," Vol. 54—Fall 1976

Hudson, Peter J., "The Reminiscences of Peter J. Hudson," Vol. 12, No. 3; "A Story of Choctaw Chiefs," Vol. 17, No. 2; "Choctaw Indian Dishes," Vol. 17—September 1939; "Recollections of Peter Hudson," Vol. 10—December 1932

Johnson, Walter A., "Brief History of the Missouri-Kansas-Texas Railroad Lines," Vol. 24—Autumn 1946

Kagey, J. N., "Jones Academy," Vol. 4—December 1926

Langley, Mrs. Lee J., "Malmaison, Palace in a Wilderness, Home of General Le Flore," Vol. 5—December 1927

Lewis, Anna, "Nunih Waiya," Vol. 16—June 1938
Locke, V. M. Jr., "Governor Cole," Vol. 4—September 1926
Mackey, Alice Hurley, "Father Murrow: Civil War Period," Vol. 12—March 1934
Maxwell, Amos, "The Sequoyah Convention," Vol. 28—Summer 1950; "The Sequoyah Convention, Part II," Vol 28—Summer 1950
Meserve, John Bartlett, "Chief Coleman Cole," Vol. 14, No. 1, March 1936; "Chief Allen Wright," Vol. 19—December 1941;"The McCurtains," Vol. 13, No.2; "Chief Benjamin Smallwood and Chief Jefferson Gardner," Vol. 19, No. 3; "The Plea of Crazy Snake," Vol. 11, No. 3; "Chief George Hudson and Chief Samuel Garland," Vol. 20—1942;"Chief Gilbert Wesley Dukes," Vol. 18—March 1940; "Chief Wilson Nathaniel Jones," Vol. 14—December 1936
Morrison, W. B., "A Visit to Old Fort Washita," Vol. 7—June 1929; "Colbert Ferry on Red River, Chickaswa Nation, Indian Territory," Vol. 16—September 1938; "Fort Towson." Vol. 8—March 1930; "The Saga of Skullyville," Vol. 16—June 1938
Nesbitt, Paul, "J. J. McAlester," Vol.11, No. 2—June 1933
Nieberding, Velma, "St. Agnes School of the Choctaws." Vol. 33—Summer 1955
Perry, Dan W., "Twenty-seven Years a State," Vol. 12, No. 4
Perry, Mrs. A. E., "Colonel Forbis Le Flore, Pioneer and Statesman," Vol. 6—March 1928
Shirk, George H., "Mail Call at Fort Washita," Vol. 33—Spring 1955
Underhill, Lonnie E. and Daniel F. Littlefield, "Wild Turkeys in Oklahoma," Vol. 48—Winter 1970-71
Ward, Mary Jane, "Now The Wolf Has Come: The Civilian Civil War in the Indian Territory," Vol. 71—Spring 1993
Wright, Allen, "Wheelock Seminary," Vol. 1—October 1921
Wright, Muriel H., "A Brief Review of the Life of Doctor Eliphalet Nott Wright, 1852-1932," Vol. 10—June 1932; "American Corn Dishes," Vol. 36—Summer 1958; "Early River Navigation in Oklahoma," Vol. 8—March 1930; "Historic Places on the Stage Line from Fort Smith to Red River," Vol. 11—June 1933; "Old

Boggy Depot," Vol. 5—March 1927; "The Great Seal of the Choctaw Nation," Vol. 33—Winter 1955

Wright, Muriel H. and George H. Shirk, "The Journal of Lieutenant A. W. Whipple," Vol. 28—Autumn, 1950

Personal Interviews

Black, Kay Brown, personal interviews, numerous, 2004

Broyles, Betty J., personal interviews, March 20, April 6, May 10, July 13, 2004

Bray, Francine Locke, personal interviews, numerous, 2003-2004

Day, Jo Anne, personal interviews, July 12, September 24, 2004

Edmonds, Myrtle, personal interviews, March 23, June 20, 2004

Haag, Marcia, personal interviews, July 19, August 14, 2004

Milligan, Dr. James C., personal interviews, August 1 and 19, 2004

West, Dorothy Arnote, personal interview, June 20, 2004

West, Mary Ann, July 6, 2004

Willis, Henry, personal interviews, July 8, September 24, 2004